THE GOSPEL PROJECT

How Far Does God's Good News Really Reach?

i

THE GOSPEL PROJECT

How Far Does God's Good News Really Reach?

by

Roger Hooper

The Gospel Project – How Far Does God's Good News Really Reach?

ISBN: 978-0-6484648-1-5

Ebook ISBN: 978-0-6484648-0-8

Special thanks to so many friends who volunteered so many perspectives. These gave me a starting point for the writing of this book. I really value our various perspectives and friendship.

Many thanks also to Jane, who was my primary encouragement to pursue this task, and in the demands of family life, always found acceptance for the need to write.

In memory of my good friend Chris Brumm.

I miss you so much, even if we were lucky to catch up face to face only once each decade. Your passing was way too soon.

I value your contributions to this book, and look forward to seeing you again and appreciate how for so many questions we shared you now have the answers.

Rest in peace dear friend. I have no doubt you do.

For I am not ashamed of the gospel, because it is the power of God that brings salvation to everyone who believes: first to the Jew, then to the Gentile.

For in the gospel the righteousness of God is revealed – a righteousness that is by faith from first to last, just as it is written: "The righteous will live by faith".

Romans 1:16-17 (NIV)

Contents

Foreword

Ebola!

Hottest summer on record!

The Barrier Reef is dying!

Worst Flu season ever!

Typical headlines of any recent year we could care to remember, and once again it is the end of the world, several times over.

If we haven't become numb from the incessant proclamation of bad news, we probably believe it really is the end of the world. It is too easy to forget the previous time we thought it was the end, was just the year before. And so the media wants us to believe. Bad news does sell rather well after all.

This year isn't really any different from the past 50 years I can remember. The end of the world was nigh back in the 70's when I was at high school.

If there is any comfort to be had from any of this, it has to be the "end-of-the-world" set have always been wrong. Predicting the future is not a major strength of the "expert" community. My cynical side will suggest the loudest "experts" are perhaps the most likely to be wrong.

Still, there is much to rightly concern us. Death stalks the land in many countries, and always has. Power is too often abused, and good news is hard to come by. Dare I say the positive has often been a rare commodity for much of humanity in much of human history?

Nearly 2000 years ago a man rose to the fore talking about good news. At first he gathered quite a following. It would surprise no one if the record of history is true.

He not only carried a message of good news; he also healed many sick and broken people of their diseases and emotional infirmities.

Eventually politics got in the way of his good news message. News like this was a threat to the power structures of the day, not to mention the man himself might be a threat.

Someone close to this messenger was bought out. "Useful idiots" were even coaxed to raise false accusations, and the man with good news who also healed the sick was put to death.

It seemed like all hope was lost for the tiny band of men and women who followed this man to his apparent premature end. The message of good news was lost in the grief of a tragic betrayal and execution.

It couldn't get any darker, when good news was suddenly proven right, if the record of history once again is to be believed.

This same man who healed others came back from the dead.

As hard as this may be to believe, many of his most faithful followers willingly gave their own lives in support of such a testimony. Would one really give one's life for something if it was only a con?

The name of this man with the good news message was Jesus of Nazareth.

With this in mind, I was sitting with some friends, when Matt, a local Brisbane pastor, made an interesting comment. He said if we were to ask any follower of Jesus what the Gospel is, we would get all manner of different answers.

I sat there thinking how important it was to me I am able to answer such a question. It might also be appropriate I not spend time in research thinking about it.

Surely after more than 40 years as a Christian, I should be able to answer such a question without hesitation or deep reflection.

As another friend would say, it made sense I always have my "elevator pitch" on the Gospel ready for any time I needed it.

This is not to say many people we meet are likely to ask us such a question. But what if someone did?

Matt continued his point by saying how much he liked the basic answer: "Jesus".

I don't mind this answer myself. Still, when I think about the post-modern world we live in, "Jesus" is sadly more of a swear word than anything else.

For this reason, I didn't think it was the best answer for me to come up with in a post-modern world.

To be fair to Matt's answer, I understand it might lead to further discussion on the subject. He might find opportunity to expand on what Jesus did and represents for mankind today. Matt is a gifted evangelist after all. His church is proof of that.

But what would I say?

Without too much thought (hopefully), my Gospel elevator pitch was:

"The Gospel is the good news of what Jesus has done and is doing to make everything right between mankind and his creator - God."

Okay, so I did have something to say if ever I was asked. That would normally have been sufficient to satisfy my curiosity. I could then move on to other things.

It was not to be. For the rest of the week, my mind was stuck on this Gospel question. I couldn't help but notice my "inner writer" was engaged too. It was urging me to start writing about it, but I didn't know what to write or why.

I'd never in my life thought of writing on the subject of the "The Gospel". It seemed like the ground work had well and truly been done on the subject. There was nothing more to say.

Plenty of other authors had already covered the subject in painstaking detail. Surely The Church didn't need me to add to the mountain of Church literature already in the book stores.

Regardless of my protests, I couldn't help but notice I was forming a book in my head without any serious intention on my part. Questions were beginning to form. Was the Holy Spirit showing me something? I hope so.

The lead of the Holy Spirit is such a subjective business. In fact, it can be so subjective; many Christians won't ever go there. Nevertheless, I still had to ask the question:

"Was this a lead from the Holy Spirit?"

I could find only one answer to that question. It was filling my mind in place of all the other book topics on my burgeoning book idea list. Sometimes we have to just step out on the water and find out.

Will I have a clear answer to this question once feedback comes in?

This book began with a fairly open question of:

"What is the Gospel?"

From the feedback of so many friends on this same question has emerged an examination of the deeper questions begging from this simple beginning.

No one disputes the meaning of "Gospel" as "good news". This was the simple part. The much harder question to answer was how far such good news could reach, and the impact on those never reached.

If we could not answer those questions effectively, we are then left wondering if the Gospel is only good news in a limited sense.

The reach of this good news became the central focus of this book. Hence my subtitle of:

"How far does God's good news really reach?"

With this in mind I've unpacked a number of common views which act as pillars in the central thinking of so many churches today.

If they don't really serve a message of "good news", I've done my best to explain why, and how we can better understand the intent of Bible verses used to establish these pillars of thinking formed many hundreds of years before.

So for whom am I writing this?

I'm glad you asked. It is an important question. I'm a thinking man (trapped in a male body?) so this is definitely for thinking people. I'm also a Christian, and have been for well over 40 years now. I'd love to think non-Christians will find this book interesting and compelling, as much as I write for the same outcome for Christian readers.

I'm also someone who is not scared of asking questions. I recall how in my engineering studies at university many of my class mates would ask me to ask the burning questions of the lecturer whenever we could not make sense or understand what he was saying. I'm not sure what it was about me to earn this reputation, but it served me well nevertheless. I did graduate and I was not the only one to do so.

So yes, I write for those with questions; those who understand there is always something more to learn in life and our walk with God.

After asking questions for over 40 years now, I'm constantly amazed at how much my views and dogmas have changed with time. I'm not saying I now think the Bible is somehow wrong when once I thought otherwise. Rather, my understanding of scripture has deepened, and at times I've had to face the simple fact I really didn't understand aspects of the Bible, and therefore change course completely with so much of my understanding.

My respect for the Bible has never stopped growing, perhaps in proportion to how I learn how much I can be in error and need to change course in my thinking.

Dare I suggest I'm also writing for those who think they have arrived at final understanding of all there is to know about God and understanding of the Bible?

I know you won't be easy to reach or impress. I was just like you in so many ways myself in former days gone by. It can be a safe and cosy place when we have all the answers and nothing more to learn in our doctrines and Church teachings.

Perhaps I could ask you to read for the sake of showing me how once again I've been mistaken. Please do then take this book to heart, unpack my thinking, and set me straight. You'll be so glad you did, and I will be forever grateful.

I'm open to the suggestion I've been a fool. To be so would place me in good company.

To quote Alfred Lord Tennyson (Tennyson): "Forward the Light Brigade!"

1. So What?

Into the Valley of Death...

I don't mean to sound too dramatic here, but after ending the Forward with a statement from Lord Tennyson's poem "The Charge Of The Light Brigade", I thought I may as well carry the theme a little further.

Let's face it; daring to write on any topic in a Christian setting can open one up to all manner of assault. To quote from one modern day thinker, Jordan Peterson:

"In order to be able to think, you have to risk being offensive." (J. B. Peterson)

I don't mean this as a specific criticism levelled at Christians. The Church is made up of people, and people at their core are essentially the same, no matter what label they may come under. That is my view anyway.

No matter what group one is in, some will love what you think, some will hate it, and some will be indifferent. Such is life.

Within a week of the idea first entering my head, I was at my computer sorting the outline of a book. It had been forming in my head all week. I may have had an outline, but I somehow struggled with how to start.

What was I really trying to prove?

I didn't know yet. Still, I began to see if this whole idea had begun with the question of "What is the Gospel?" answers would vary from Christian to Christian. If so, why not ask the same question?

Fortunately I live in a modern age, with technology at my fingertips, if not in my pocket in the form of my smart phone. How good is social media!

In no time I posed the question to over 40 Christian friends of various theological persuasions, and held my breath.

Would anyone reply?

Would they wonder if I'm only looking for an argument, and so not reply?

Would they be too embarrassed to reply, scared of what I might do with their reply, or expose their ignorance?

Fortunately my well-formed paranoia from too many social media engagements with theology was not to be satisfied.

Within 2 days I had 24 replies, and with my friend Matt in mind, with "Jesus" as his answer, I had a good 25 responses. They were all different responses too.

I began to see how blessed I was to have friends I could approach from so many different perspectives of the Christian faith - Protestant, Catholic, Reformed, Arminian, Pentecostal, Baptist, Calvinist, Seventh Day, and all manner of in-betweens.

I even learnt a new word. I'd never seen "adumbration" before, but there it was, as an answer to the simple question - what is the Gospel?

This particular friend knew how to be brief in his response, as well as intriguing. Trust a PhD to have me pull out my dictionary. He was right too. Thank you Chris Brumm!

I could well understand why he would say the Gospel was an adumbration, even if in a sense he was joking.

Many who replied pointed out there was far more to the Gospel than what their brief answer would allow. I couldn't agree more.

If there was a common thread in most of the replies, I could see universally, everyone had a positive view of the Gospel. It was something positive - really positive.

Such is the nature of Good News, and this is what many of us grew up understanding. This understanding is the word Gospel, as translated from the Greek, means "good message", or more commonly understood as "good news".

I was actually quite impressed with the variations in how everyone expressed their answers. I loved the way too everyone was essentially on the same page, even if drawn from all manner of different denominations.

At its core, I could still see there was unity in the fundamental Christian message. This was encouraging!

Still, what was I to do with this growing list of replies? What was it all for?

As much as I could see on the surface a unity in expression, I knew too well there was underlying divergence. The Gospel was good news. Everyone could agree on this. The question I didn't ask was one I didn't need to.

How far does it reach? Is it good news for only a small part of the human race, and therefore predominantly bad news?

I knew without asking. In this question, one would discover all manner of differences. I knew this from over 40 years as a Christian. I knew this from sitting in hundreds, if not thousands, of church meetings where the message given was not necessarily good news at all. It might have been good news for some, but definitely not good news for everyone.

Is the Gospel message only for a minority?

It became apparent I needed to revisit what I'd been hearing for over 40 years. I needed to unpack and examine those messages (in a general sense). I needed to explore if the negative outlook I'd been hearing for over 40 years in the overall "good news" context, really was warranted.

This was therefore where I knew I had to point my sharpened pen. It was easy to see everyone agreed the Gospel was good news for those "qualified" to receive it. It was not so easy to see how many would qualify, and how they would qualify.

The necessary focus for this book became obvious. I had to tackle the difficult questions surrounding the reach of the Gospel. Just how far was this Good News intended to reach? Was it for a minority, or a majority?

It was obvious there were all manner of opinions on this topic of the reach of the Gospel message. Why was this so? Why would perhaps the most important message in all of human history be surrounded by so many questions? This book intends to answer at least some of these important questions.

Before I proceed, I do need to lay some ground work.

Let Them Be Cursed!

I'm getting used to the dramatic sub-chapter headings. I can't promise I'll manage to find one for every sub-chapter, but for now I'll run with it as far as I can.

In so many ways I'd like this subject to be fresh and uplifting, rather than heavy and full of foreboding. At the end of the day, "good news" has got to be more about the former than the latter. I hope it is anyway!

When I used to tutor engineering students at university the central question I'd always hit them with in every assignment was "so what?" It is only right I apply the same measure to myself.

Is there a "so what?" when it comes to the Gospel? Is it a topic of importance, or is it really just a take it or leave it subject?

If I can't answer a question like this in the affirmative, then I'm really presuming to waste anyone's time who would be so kind as to consider reading this. There has to be some serious value in the subject. Otherwise I may as well go back to the other topics on my book idea list.

There had to be a reason why the topic stayed in my head all week long after my friend Matt raised the topic. Consider these simple words from the Apostle Paul in Galations:

> But even if we or an angel from heaven should preach a gospel other than the one we preached to you, let them be under God's curse! **Galations 1:8** (NIV)

I can't help but notice there is some fairly heavy language used here by Paul. I don't think he was joking either. In his mind it really does look like the Gospel was an important topic. It was so important; he basically felt it appropriate to curse someone who preached a message different to what he preached.

Ultimately the Gospel was a message he died for, and so did many others who carried the same message. This fact, with Paul's comment above, is sufficient for me to consider this topic is important. There must be something to the Gospel for so many to die for it.

In the mind of Paul there was no take-it-or-leave-it where the Gospel was concerned. If one looks at the statements of Paul after verse 8 above, he even repeats the point about a curse. Could he be saying there is a double curse on someone who stuffs up his message? I certainly wouldn't want to be on the receiving end of such an outcome.

Okay, I'm satisfied. There really is something of significance in the subject of the Gospel. It is worth pursuing, and taking our understanding further. For such an important topic, would it not make sense we are blessed if we grow in our understanding?

Before I do, there is one thing on which I really want to caution every Christian. As far as it was appropriate for Paul to pronounce curses on people who preached a false Gospel (some may want to dispute that, but I'm not going to bother), I would not want to rush in 2000 years later with a big head and do the same.

There is no shortage of "big heads" in the realm of mankind. I've noticed the same can be found in church circles too. It is all part of the basic folly of mankind. What is common to man in general is common in the church too. It is hard to escape this if one is in a church setting long enough to really notice. It's all part and parcel of how God works with us.

I propose if one thinks they have the final word on the Gospel message, in its purest form (naturally!), then please tend to be grateful rather than judgmental towards someone who one thinks doesn't really understand it.

If we really do have a perfect vision of the Gospel message, then I would suggest this is a gift from God and something never to be used to big-note oneself.

Wisdom would also demand, in my opinion anyway, we always walk circumspectly, and ever cautious. It is always best to consider we may not know it all. Time has a way of proving we don't.

There is something I've learned over more than 40 years as a Christian now: whenever we think we have the final word on a topic we tend to be obnoxious. We also tend to stand tall on the honour roll of fools. Let's face it, who really wants to hear good news from an obnoxious religious fool?

This is not the time to be throwing curses at one another because we have differences of opinion, understanding, and perspective. We are looking at scripture penned nearly 2000 years ago, where context, nuance, and translation, can be veiled in ways we may not ever imagine.

There is no end of scholarship, and much of it is laudable. I'm personally grateful for it. Still, like anyone who has seriously undertaken research knows, the more we learn, the more we realise there is much more to learn. There just isn't any space for thinking we have the final word.

Curses are serious business. Let's take Paul's statement as a personal warning to take the subject seriously and walk circumspectly. To use it as an excuse to throw barbs at one another would reveal far more about the state of our hearts in a negative sense, than it would about anything we think we know.

Rather than curse anyone, we need to seriously desire to bless and see people of all persuasions deepen their understanding and appreciation for the Gospel. If our focus is on blessing, then surely in time we will all be better off.

No More Religion.

When I said the Gospel is the good news about what Jesus did and is doing to make things right between mankind and God, it really is. The reason why I state this may not be immediately obvious.

All the other gods I'm aware of have set up religious structures detailing the requirements on mankind for making things right with that particular god. They are all about what we as people have to do to get right with them as gods.

Jesus is nothing like that. His message - the Gospel, is all about what he has done and is doing. This makes the gulf between Christianity and the worship of other gods insurmountable. There is no religion on earth like Christianity. By extension, there is no other god like Jesus.

Frankly, I really like Jesus, and everything he represents. He doesn't dump religion on me. All the other gods would. In so many ways, Christianity represents the end of religion. To me, Christianity is not another religion at all. I personally think it is fair to state Christianity is the end of religion.

I am using a certain measure of poetic license here in my use of the word "religion". By definition, it is a word used to describe the worship of any god. I'm well aware of this.

What I see throughout history, in the worship of gods, is so much effort and ritual man has to undertake in his practice of any particular religion. In essence, religion represents to me all the hoops one has to jump through to make a god happy and accepting of the person. Christianity doesn't have this. Such is my current understanding.

I've lived with plenty of religion as a Christian. Over time I've learnt it was baggage of human design. I realised I could safely discard it without offending God. In fact, I think God is actually happy to see me lose so much religion over the years. I even think he has been teaching me to discard religion!

The human tendency is to add religion to Christianity by whatever means it can. This is what I've observed anyway. As much as Jesus said his burden is easy and his yoke is light, I've known plenty of Christians, and include myself, who carried huge burdens and religious obligations.

To be a Christian can be a huge weight to carry if we take on board all the religion people over the ages have hitched on to it. It's no wonder so many look on Christianity as just another religion. Without understanding Christianity itself, onlookers have seen so many Christians labouring under religion. It's no wonder it has earned a bad name in certain respects.

Religion needlessly added to Christianity can take various forms. They usually all come under the term of "obligations" which if not satisfied, mean God is really unhappy with us, or we won't be saved, blessed, or qualified any more.

One example is centred on money. This type of religion, which can latch on to a Christian is all about chasing cash from the worshippers. Strict guidelines are given on how much and how often one is to give.

The victims are usually encouraged by alleged Biblical promises on what they can expect from God as a result of all their sacrifices. Naturally, some will have testimonies to support these notions. Where it doesn't work and God has not delivered, the fault is naturally with the suffering church member, and never the teaching.

In essence, it is no different from the pagan religions of ancient times, where sacrifice was employed to try to bend gods to the will of the worshipper, or simply to appease the gods who were basically nasty at the best of times.

The ones who pedal this type of religion can hide behind all manner of scriptures in the Bible. They do this without realising their arguments are built on Old Testament contexts, not compatible with the New

10

Testament which represents the core of Christian understanding.

Mention of the abuse of teachings on money is not to say all forms of giving in a church context, and teaching on the subject, are wrong. Giving offerings in church and teaching on the subject can be sound and healthy. Where it represents a form of bondage and religious coercion, I do advise one to beware.

It isn't my intention to digress too far into this topic of how religion can spoil the essence of Christianity. This is a subject worthy of many books in itself, and fortunately some authors have taken on the task, and done an admirable job with those books. One author in particular who comes to mind is Andrew Farley, who wrote an excellent book called God Without Religion (Farley).

2. But Is There A God?

Is There?

There are still a couple of points that need consideration before I look more closely at the replies to my Gospel survey.

I've no idea who will end up interested in the topic of this writing. It may even be someone who is not yet a Christian may be curious and wonder what it all means. Christians may appear to be quite foreign and strange to someone who doesn't know God. "Does God exist?" may still be a question on one's mind. It is certainly a common topic of discussion in some circles on social media.

If I've learnt anything from my time on social media, it is how no one can be persuaded about anything against their will. There can be all manner of reasons why someone won't or doesn't want to believe in God. I have no problem with this. I can seriously empathise with so many of those unanswered questions and points of offence some have towards the Christian God, and other gods too.

I have a number of frustrations and unanswered questions too, as a believer. I can also relate to the offence so many feel towards the historical practises of so many under the Christian banner.

Many are unsure as so much doesn't make sense to them. They often sense there has to be something, as the order and intricacy of the universe can't be an accident. Still, they don't really have any personal experience with God. Without that, God is merely an intellectual discussion.

If I know anything about becoming a Christian, it's impossible to give one's life to a good argument.

If "there ain't no God", then really this whole topic of "good news" is a waste of time. I can't persuade anyone to believe in him, but can at least explain why I don't have a problem believing in him myself, even if he does sometimes leave me feeling let down and perplexed at times.

The Science of God.

Early in my time in high school, I remember going up to my Chemistry teacher and asking him how radioactive materials were still radioactive.

It wasn't a dumb question. It is a well understood scientific fact radioactive material is constantly breaking down to become the metal we know of as lead. Lead is the end point for radioactive decay. If these radioactive metals had always existed, why were they not all lead?

The response of my Chemistry teacher was simple. It was also without hesitation:

"It had to be created."

I nodded, told him I thought so too, and went back to my desk.

The person who wants to argue there is no God, has to argue there was no creation. If there was no creation, there would be no radioactive material.

An atheist can try to argue for origins without a creator. Great! He or she can have a lot of fun with such a theory. At the end of the day, all they will have is a theory, and one that can never be tested, measured, or repeated in a science lab.

To me it requires far more faith to believe there is no God who created everything, than it does to believe there is a God. Who's more religious - the atheist or the believer? I suspect the more dedicated man of faith is the atheist.

Moving on from Chemistry to Physics, I like to consider the Law of Entropy. This is a law, and not a theory. A theory is something which hasn't been proven. It doesn't mean it won't be proven but it is probably safe to say in the vast world of theories, many never will be proven.

Entropy is well and truly proven. It can be demonstrated everywhere we look, if we look hard enough, and are prepared to be patient. It can also be demonstrated in a scientific lab, time and time again.

The Law of Entropy states everything moves from a state of order to disorder. Just look at any sand castle one can build on a beach. A sand castle serves as a case study requiring less time to demonstrate entropy in action. This would contrast for example, with a house left empty over a 10 year period, or the many decayed stone castles littering the landscapes of Europe. The latter require more time to demonstrate entropy.

Entropy requires we provide intelligent maintenance to so many things we build, just to keep it close to the original state in which it was made, or at least in a useful state.

Entropy also requires a creator of the original state of order. Only when we have original order is it possible to decay into disorder. For me at least, it isn't hard to understand God is at the foundation of all we see and know of in our universe. He is the origin of all things, before entropy began.

Taking this concept a little further, as an engineer, I know too well the effort, deep thought, and sometimes even angst, it takes to create something which not only looks like the original plan - it also works and functions according to the plan.

It is never by accident anything is built, but this is the necessary concept required if we wish to believe the universe really does not have a God who created it. As an engineer I know nothing I've sought to achieve has ever happened by accident.

Digging a little further inside the realms of engineering, I'd like to point out the software programming required for any engineering process system can never happen by accident.

Writing code can take incredible effort, and errors are common. What is not common is a complex code written with never an error before its final approved handover.

One of my highly intelligent atheist friends comes equipped with a PhD. He is no dummy. I've had a number of exchanges with him in social media about proving God exists or doesn't exist.

He was able to dismiss the concept of basic engineering, and how it can never happen by accident. He didn't dismiss it with a clever counter argument. He didn't have one. Still, my point was not able to leave him with a sense of obvious discomfort sufficient to shift his thinking. He had never designed and constructed in the manner of my own life and career experience.

Fortunately I was able to strike closer to home by talking about computer programming, with which he is very familiar. When I spoke about how functioning code could never happen by accident, he did actually pause and confess he had no answer for that one.

Naturally, he has not changed his mind. As I said before, it is impossible to change someone's mind against their will. He reasons the mechanism will be discovered eventually which will explain creation without a creator. He is indeed a man of great faith, as am I. We have much in common.

I personally believe some people may not want to believe in God. To believe in God would create discomfort in their current state of mind, so they avoid it if at all possible. Sometimes I wish I could avoid such discomfort myself. Knowing God can be challenging at times.

Knowing God.

I began this discussion on the existence of God by looking at it from a purely intellectual level. My background is engineering. This makes me an "applied scientist". This is why I have a personal liking for such aspects of the question. Many of course won't really care about the science behind the argument of God's existence. I'm fine with that. Not everyone has a leaning towards science.

Few if any, I suspect, have a relationship with God born out of science. I know I don't. My relationship with God is born out of personal experience with God, just as my relationship with my wife began and continues through personal experience.

I've made the points of how science points us to God partly for the sake of those who have no personal experience with God. Without this personal experience, there is nothing left but science and what we observe to declare the wonders of God.

I also make the point about science and God because there are some rather vocal scientists out there who think God does not exist. They also happen to be rather determined to prove this too. With this in mind, I personally want to present the case on behalf of the many scientists who do believe God exists. I don't ever want to allow the notion somehow only atheists hold a corner on the market of science. I don't want anyone to think they are the only credible voices when it comes to speaking on the existence of God.

There is a value in knowing the science, even if it doesn't change too much in the thinking of someone who disagrees. At least they can know from listening to my reasoning how my Christian decision is born out of something greater than "mere" faith.

So what is this "knowing God"? Everyone I'm sure who knows what I'm talking about will have different experiences they could share.

For myself, I became very aware of God from a very young age. I really needed to, growing up as a latch key kid in a broken family. For many years my sister and I basically ran the house. She was just 2 years older than me.

We rarely saw our mother as she would come home late at night from work at around 2 in the morning. Without going into too much detail here, our mother was basically slave labour at a restaurant in Sydney. She worked 7 days a week.

I'm certainly not trying to earn points for having it tough as a kid. It just serves to paint the picture of a young kid carrying a lot on his shoulders, and needing a heavenly father.

To add to the tensions at home, there was something very spiritually dark about the house in which we grew up. Demonic spirits would harass me at night periodically to make the point obvious.

With such impactful experiences from the spirit realm, clearly of an evil nature, it wasn't hard for me to realise there had to be a God. The spirit world was very real, and I knew it without any doubt.

I did attend Sunday School at my local Anglican church for a number of years before I was 12, but the reality of God came to me in those dark nights, petrified in bed. There were times when somehow I had the presence of mind to ask God to comfort me, and he would. I'd feel his warmth flow over me and chase the fears away.

I had a Bible from Sunday School. I remember reading it even before I was 10. The stories about Jesus were very real to me. In my understanding, believing is a gift from God, and I was given such a gift at a very young age.

A cynic can easily dismiss my earliest experiences as the delusions of a young child. I'd expect this from a cynic. Nevertheless, over 40 years on, my experiences with God are still very real, sometimes supernatural, and very personal.

Sometimes he says things to me which blow my mind. His words have a power and logic, which to me as an Engineer leave me in awe at those rare times when I do hear his direct voice.

As I've said before, one cannot dedicate their life to serving a good argument. Every transformation of a human being to becoming a Christian (conversion) has to have that personal touch or encounter with God. Without it, there is no relationship, and no conversion. When it happens, there is no mistaking it.

For those looking on, without this personal encounter, they can only be left wondering what we are talking about. I only wish it was otherwise.

Some of my friends who are not Christians are a little perplexed I'm talking about something they don't experience themselves. It can make God seem capricious to the point of being a respecter of persons.

I know he isn't. What I don't know is why he chooses to reveal himself to some, but not others, at any particular period of time. I can theorise in a general sense it all fits into a bigger picture. That I can accept. I just don't know the finer details where it concerns so many of my friends.

I'm confident a day will come when he reveals himself to everyone. Until then I have to be patient. In the meantime, I remain confident of how hard it is to prove someone I know personally doesn't exist.

Those who think he doesn't exist do so as they have not yet met him. Many have never met my wife. She is still very real, regardless of whether someone thinks she is not.   Perhaps more sagely, one could posit no woman would be fool enough to marry someone like me?

My own personal walk with God is not primarily the subject of this book, so I won't say too much more on it here.   It does still serve to illustrate some basic introductory points on the subject of the Gospel - the good news Jesus brought for and to all mankind some 2000 years ago.

3. A Brief Case For A Christian Gospel

There is one final point of introduction. I see it as necessary before I unpack in more detail the responses I received to my question on the Gospel. It is worth talking briefly about why I'm a Christian, and not a follower of another god.

Which God?

As much as people may debate on the existence of God, another common debate I've encountered is why I should be so certain about my Christian God, Jesus, and no other.

The question is very fair and reasonable. I grew up in a nation which at the time in the 1960's could have been considered a Christian nation. I'm not so sure I would call Australia one now. It makes sense someone would conclude I'm only a Christian because I grew up in a Christian nation.

Many millions are born into nations which hold to a different spiritual path. It is natural they adopt the religion of their parents and nation. Some examples include Islam, Buddhism, and Hinduism. Is there really a good reason to worship a Christian God, or are they all just the same?

Maybe we are all worshipping the same God, under different names?

Many, after all, do think the same god inhabits all the different expressions of faith in the world today. On the surface it looks like a fair proposition. It is certainly PC (Politically Correct), if nothing else.

Firstly, for me, my personal encounter with God was with Jesus. I did not have a personal encounter with Krishna, Allah, or Buddha.

Yes, it is true I was under Christian influences as a child, and I'm really glad I was. In saying this, I do have to add the example of Christianity from my parents was nothing spectacular. I certainly don't intend any disrespect towards my parents. They did the best they could with what they understood, as most Christians tend to do.

Some who know my family I'm sure would say I had every reason not to be a Christian. Of this I have no doubt. I won't go into the details here of why. That story may warrant another book in addition to the one already written by another author.

As stated before, I did go to Sunday school. Many years later it is clear only some are now Christians who were with me in Sunday school then. Only some of us ultimately could claim to have had personal encounters with Jesus. Without such personal encounters it would be impossible to continue with anything but a superficial faith in Christ. Sunday school is not the determining factor in what makes one a Christian.　It might help, but on its own, it determines nothing.

Some eight years after Sunday school, I went to a Bible college to get a theology degree.　Now 30 plus years later, thanks to the internet and social media, I'm in contact with many of my fellow students and friends from those days.　Catching up with one another through the recent advent of social media has been amazing.

I'm making the following comments from a purely objective stand point, with no interest in making value judgements or assuming a high moral ground concerning anyone and their current place in life. Some of my friends from Bible College have been through incredible hardship.　Naturally their views on God and faith have been shaped in all manner of different ways, and I would dare to suggest my views on God and faith might be in far worse shape than theirs if the same had happened to me.

Many having grown up in a Christian environment, got the theology degree, and now no longer profess Christianity.　Maybe they never were.　I don't know.　Some are now atheists.　Some are agnostic.　Some are Wiccan pagans.　Some are still Christians.　In spite of the changes in our thinking, we are still on the whole good friends.　It is quite special really, given the proclivity for people to tend to feel uncomfortable with those who leave a particular group or community.

It may be true to say for some who are now not Christian, they never had a personal relationship with Jesus.　Still, this may not be true at all for some.　How would I know?　From learning of their various life journeys, extreme hardship and personal suffering has left a burden of too many unanswered questions.　I've already stated if I'd been in their shoes, I could not have expected a different outcome in my own thinking. All I understand is how it is not for me to bear malice, assume a high moral ground, or project condemnation towards any of my friends, no matter what path they choose to follow.

In a broad sense, with no one in particular in mind, I would dare to suggest a small number who might sit in any church may be Christian by name, but still have no personal experience with God. They may be Christian by culture only. It may also be true some are very much saved by faith in Jesus, yet still waiting to have their first personal encounter with Jesus. We all have different stories.

I'm not making value judgements here. I'm just speaking hypothetically. I'm personally not into trying to work out if someone who says they are a Christian really is. I just know it is possible for it to not be so, regardless of the badge or label one may carry.

Anything is possible with people. Having a personal relationship with Jesus is not a function of how good a person is. It has nothing to do with being better or worse than someone else. It is all in the hands of God how and when he deals with each of us. No one can force the hand of God.

Having made these points, I wish to summarise I am not a Christian because of my parents, national culture, Sunday school attendance, or a theology degree. I am only a Christian because of my personal experiences with Jesus.

4. The Survey

Summary.

By the time I got this far in my writing, I'd received 33 replies to my Gospel survey on how so many individuals would describe the Gospel. Naturally, they expressed their thoughts in all manner of different ways.

Some were quite long, and some were quite short. I was impressed to receive 3 one word answers - all different. I don't mind simplicity. Each of those who gave the 3 one word answers knew their simple answers would require explaining.

If one really was to ask us in the street what the Gospel was, a simple answer would certainly sort out if the person was genuinely interested and worth more of our time. If they were serious, more questions would follow, and lead to expansion of the topic.

As I looked at each answer, I could see most tended to dwell on a particular aspect of the Gospel, which naturally would have been what was foremost in the mind of my friend at that time. This drew me to search for a key word in each reply to try to capture the essence of what they were saying.

The key words I identified were as follows:

- Salvation
- Testimony
- Freedom
- Truth
- New creation
- God speaks
- Kingdom
- Redemption
- Communion with God
- Life
- Hope
- Love
- Jesus
- Reconciliation
- Grace
- Adumbration

I've included "adumbration" out of respect for my friend's sense of humour. My son Joseph even told me he had heard a new word is added to English every 15 minutes. I've no idea how true this is, but adumbration is in my dictionary, and has been around for a while. It must be time I learnt how to use it!

Long lists are not always helpful, even if they are accurate. I could see in the list above some points had a certain synergy with others. In my attempt to narrow the list to capture the essence within the essence, I chose the following:

- Jesus
- Freedom
- Truth
- Kingdom
- Grace
- Reconciliation

- Life
- Hope
- Love

It would have been really cool to have only 7 items in the list to satisfy those fascinated with numerology.

I do apologise to anyone who really wanted 7 points. I tried putting grace in with reconciliation, but to do so would not really be accurate. Grace and reconciliation are not the same thing, even if they are related. This would have left me with eight points, and no way I could justify leaving any other word out. We are stuck with my nine.

I loved the way each of the replies to my question had a focus on one or two of the above elements. The various ups and downs of life can bring into focus certain aspects of the Gospel which will hold particular significance at different times. I could even say the Gospel is good news for all seasons.

There was one word left out. No one mentioned it. I'm sure if I had asked more people, it would have come out eventually. Which word is that?

Forgiveness!

No one had to explicitly mention forgiveness. It is part of the process making every other key word of the Gospel possible. I've no doubt everyone who has a sense of the Gospel's meaning understands their sins are forgiven.

Three cheers for good news!

Various Foci.

The loss of a loved one would bring into focus the message of life in the Gospel. Hope would also be in play too, knowing we can look forward to seeing again those who we loved and lost.

At different times we can feel strangled by the demands of our current world systems we live under. Freedom and the kingdom aspects of the Gospel shine for us at such moments.

Truth is known to be the first casualty of war. At certain times more than others, we may be confronted with a strong sense things are not always as we are told. Delusions and indoctrinations surround us at all times. No matter where we live, the flow of information from the media is controlled by someone. It will be so good to be free of this one day.

Central to our walk through all the mess of life is the assurance God loves us. Sometimes we won't be sure he really does. I've experienced those doubts myself. Still, embedded in the Gospel, at the very core, is the greatest act of love ever granted - our very creator, God, died for us.

It takes time to really grasp this - God really loves us! The message is always there, no matter what life in this present age may throw at us.

Knowing God loves us can open the way to loving ourselves. It can be easy to denigrate people and say we are all selfish. This may be true. Still, there is a way to love ourselves that is not selfishness. We can learn this love from Jesus, and this love enables us to love others.

Jesus made some interesting comments about love of self in Matthew 22:

> *"Teacher, which is the greatest commandment in the Law?"*
> *Jesus replied: "'Love the Lord your God with all your heart and with all your soul and with all your mind.' This is the first and greatest commandment. And the second is like it: 'Love your neighbor as yourself.' All the Law and the Prophets hang on these two commandments."* **Matt 22:36-40** (NIV)

Loving oneself may seem strange to some. It can be misunderstood as selfishness. I don't see selfishness as the best expression of the second greatest commandment. Self- absorbed, selfish people don't tend to be happy. Still, Jesus refers to love of oneself.

Self-love could end up being another one of those huge topics. Huge topics which I won't go into here will come up more than once I'm sure.

I won't pretend to have a perfect definition for it here. An example of Godly self-love would be looking after one's health. Another would be working hard. On a counter point, another would be getting sufficient rest. Avoiding sin is very much an expression of loving oneself. Sin, after all, never ends well for the sinner. Sin leads to pain and hardship.

I can think of many who don't love themselves very well. I hardly do a perfect job of it myself. Knowing God loves me, via the Gospel, does help me love myself. I expect it can open the same door for others. I call that good news!

Our lowest moments can sometimes be defined by when we fail to live up to expectations. Missing the mark may not only rest in what Jesus would want of us. Many of us carry responsibilities of what others would want from us.

Such demands are not always wrong. Our kids make huge demands of us. They can't help it. They are helpless without us. Our employers make demands all the time, and they are not necessarily unreasonable.

Sometimes the one making the greatest demands is oneself. Failing oneself is not uncommon. Some never seem able to ever forgive themselves. Whoever we may let down, our greatest comfort is in knowing at least through the Gospel we are reconciled with God. Knowing this can sometimes lead to reconciliation with others. It may even lead to reconciliation with ourselves.

Grace is related to reconciliation. It is a critical function of the whole outworking of the Gospel. Without grace we have nothing. In some ways the subject of grace is like a hot potato. It challenges our religious thinking like nothing else does. I love that!

If one would like to know more on the subject, I know no better works than What's So Amazing About Grace, by Philip Yancey (Yancey), and Unmerited Favor, by Joseph Prince (Prince).

How Far Does It Go?

As good as the good news is for me, I have to say it represents a life time of learning. In my 40 plus years of walking with God, I've been getting to know him better. As I do, I keep learning more about his Gospel and the message behind it. I'm nowhere near the end of this road. Every Christian is at various stages on this same journey, just like me.

Some may not understand what I mean by a journey in learning about the Gospel. I suspect they will one day, just like I did. It takes time to realise we don't know as much as we once thought we did.

If I was to pick just one aspect of the Gospel - love, it may make more sense. It does take time to really grasp God loves us. If any of us is a rare exception, be grateful. Please don't be too hard on the rest of us now.

Knowing his love for us has a profound impact on our lives. How we face life reveals much on how well we know his love.

Many never had truly loving parents. If so, it can be hard to think of a Father in heaven loving us. This can be particularly so if we think of heaven as far away.

For me, another major journey aspect of the Gospel has been realising the reach of the Gospel may be greater than I thought possible. Just how far does this good news go?

Is it good news for everyone today?

Is it good news for everyone who has ever lived?

Is it good news for those who reject it?

Is it bad news for some?

If so, how so?

As I stated in the first chapter titled "So What?", these are questions this book seeks to answer. If I can come up with some decent answers, we may be surprised to learn Good News can indeed be good.

5. The Good, The Bad, & The Ugly?

Mixed Messages.

I've sat in a number of different churches across the years. I've heard all sorts of different messages. Many messages are really positive. It isn't hard then to see the Gospel shining through.

Some messages are downright bad news. They seemed to be bad news to me anyway. It usually takes the form of how many people are lost. They don't know God. I understand that. Further, there was no hope at all for them unless we could somehow reach them to tell them the good news.

God himself was apparently helpless in the face of such a conundrum. I've heard this indirectly every time I've visited one particular church here in Brisbane. For whatever reason, God needed us to get to these lost people so they could be saved. God would not save them unless we tried to save them first!

That's a scary thought. The salvation of thousands rests in the hands of a congregation. Now that can't be good news.

Is this burden of salvation depending on us really true?

Is the Gospel as much about bad news as it is good?

Does salvation of the world really depend on us?

Bad News Background.

I grew up with a very basic view of God's plan of salvation. There were two possible destinations - heaven, or hell. Bad guys went to hell, and good guys went to heaven. No one was really good, so we needed Jesus to die for us so we wouldn't have to go to hell.

In Sunday School we would give money to fund missionaries in places where people didn't know Jesus. Apparently, if missionaries didn't get to people before they died, those who died not knowing Jesus were stuck with hell as their only destination.

No one discussed the awkward questions that might come forward if we were older. The depth of my questions as a pre-teen was on more simple matters like whether our pets went to heaven. I remember asking this question in scripture class in Primary School. Mrs Lygo told me no one knew. I had to be a teenager before I would begin to entertain any of the tougher questions.

Did it make sense God would put salvation in the hands of a missionary?

What if his car broke down?

By failing to make it to a particular village, all these people were doomed to an eternity in hell. The popular view too was of a hell full of fires. These fires somehow burned the wicked, unreached, and unfortunate, for eternity.

All this suffering because a missionary was having a bad day. What if he had no translator?

Perhaps no one thought about such questions hundreds of years ago as the life of a missionary was too often extremely perilous, and can still be to this day. It took serious courage and faith to journey into uncharted lands, facing potentially violent people groups.

Given the high death toll of missionaries in places like Africa, the Americas, and the Pacific Islands, it may have seemed like fair justice for anyone not reached to go to hell.

There really was no guarantee the missionary was going to save anyone even if he was able to reach them. The native peoples may have had memories of Christian soldiers shooting their people in a previous generation.

There can be all manner of reasons why someone may not like a missionary. It's not just about the message. What if he was French and insisted they had to speak French too?

I certainly don't want to rubbish the work of missionaries. Particularly so in this day, missionaries are well aware of the mistakes of previous generations. Today they are usually well skilled in cultural sensitivity.

The work so many of them do is heartfelt, selfless, and life changing for so many in the communities they serve. Nevertheless, I certainly would not want to carry the thought the salvation of thousands depended on me and my skills and presence as a missionary.

How could I be worthy of salvation if by my own failings so many were consigned to an eternity of suffering in hell?

This isn't a pleasant thought. Maybe I should try harder to save those around me? Plenty of Christians are trying that.

I never thought I needed to be a missionary to reach people who didn't know Jesus. Maybe I did? So many I meet seem to know Jesus already. They so often speak of him. It could be argued they are really speaking to him, but closer examination of the circumstances often reveals his name is a common swear word, with no thought whatsoever for all he represents or who he is.

For people who don't believe in him, some certainly refer to him quite often. In some ways I see the way people swear using the name of Jesus, as a sign he is the real deal. I've never heard anyone swear using the name of any other god.

It seems to me, in complete ignorance, many are speaking out his name as a swear word in defiance one could only direct to the one true God. I don't really know. I can only wonder.

I'm speculating with this last point. It doesn't stand as an absolute proof of anything. It does stand as a point of significance for me as a believer.

All around me as a kid it was obvious many didn't believe in Jesus. Somehow he didn't mean anything to them, the way he did to me. I wasn't the only Christian who knew this either.

Quite a few friends expressed fear for those in their families who might die not knowing Jesus. It seemed their non-Christian family members often refused to believe in him. They refused no matter how hard their Christian relative tried to reach them with the Gospel.

How happy could we be with all this good news? It was one thing to be saved. It was another to live with the thought of so many we knew and loved not saved. Their fate was the stuff of nightmares.

Here I am now, some 40 years on and I can see clearly such thinking is not reserved for 12 year olds. Plenty of Christians today live with the same paradigms. I can understand why too.

Simple reading of the Bible can bring forth all manner of scriptures which might support their position:

> *If your hand causes you to stumble, cut it off. It is better for you to enter life maimed than with two hands to go into hell, where the fire never goes out.* **Mark 9:43** (NIV)

The above verse seems quite straightforward. We certainly have a place referred to called "hell", and there is a reference to a fire which never goes out. It doesn't say one will be burned forever in such a fire. Neither does it say one will have to stay in such a place forever.

For all we know from this single verse, hell could be a place where one is thrown to be killed by fire, rather than actually living forever in a fire. What would happen after one is killed is anyone's guess.

At this point I've not looked at issues of translation or context. Neither have I looked into who this particular fate is reserved for. It may not be for people who have never heard the name of Jesus. It might be for others who have, but rejected him.

But I tell you that anyone who is angry with a brother or sister will be subject to judgment. Again, anyone who says to a brother or sister, "Raca", is answerable to the court. And anyone who says, "You fool!" will be in danger of the fire of hell. **Matthew 5:22** (NIV)

I chose the above verse from Matthew to indicate it wasn't just one Gospel writer who referred to hell as a particular fate. This particular verse from the Gospel of Matthew also mentions the fire aspect of hell.

I won't labour the point here by giving other Gospel mentions of the word "hell". Jesus did use the term quite often. There clearly is a case to be made for the idea people can, or at least could, end up in a place called hell. Who exactly, and for what particular end is still to be determined.

It is probably worth pointing out hell is a destination for bad guys in a number of different streams of religious thought. It is no wonder so many Christians interpret references to hell in the Bible in a similar light. It could be argued hell is part of the thinking of our culture, and of many others, given the global religious support for the idea.

It remains to be seen if a deeper examination of the issue would still allow for such thinking. Christianity just might represent a whole new perspective. It might be radical.

From my own study of ecclesiastical history, the impression I've had is the concept of the fate of sinners burning forever in hell was a mainstay of the more common belief system of Christians from medieval times until the 20th Century.

Truly, if longevity of an idea was the sole criterion for truth, then burning forever in hell would win hands down.

Saying this, it might be worth pointing out much of this period was represented by a time when the common man was without access to scripture for personal reading in his own tongue. He or she was also not allowed to read scripture for themselves. Such privileges were reserved for the clergy.

Still, maybe the priests were right. Who am I to say they weren't? I'm just left with lots of questions. I'm also left wondering how well they really knew God.

Surely the foundation for understanding scripture is to know God? This is just my opinion, but I think it bears mention, for reasons I'll point out later.

Bad News Consequences.

I've presented the picture of a certain message from some Christians. It has a rather bleak outcome. But is this just my opinion? What have I seen in Christian circles as a result of this hell fire paradigm?

Is anyone familiar with the questions a Christian can have after a non-Christian relative has died? I know I am. The biggest fear I've seen in so many Christians I know is someone has died unsaved. It is such a huge fear because the reality in their mind is the person who died is now in hell, suffering torment – torment that will endure forever.

It's a horrible thought. Sometimes a Christian with this mindset is left wondering if they tried hard enough to get this person to believe in Jesus. Not too many dwell on the thought for too long as it is rather overwhelming to consider the full impact of failing to save someone from hell.

I remember a Bible study with some friends. We were talking about Christians carrying the burden of feeling they have to get out and save people. This is driven by a need to keep as many as possible out of the fires of hell. I was impressed how a number of us denied many Christians carry such burdens.

The full impact of the denials hit me later, driving home. I realised 2 of the pastors in this group who denied many carry such a burden, were both part of a church I like to visit, where I hear of this same burden every time I visit. Truly our hearing is indeed selective. If not, our memory of what we hear is.

Every time I visit their church, an elderly gentleman, fired with tears and intense fervour, gets up in front of the congregation, and is given the microphone. He then tells everyone how short time is, and how we have to save the unsaved from eternal damnation.

Maybe the repetition, which I only hear on infrequent visits, makes them deaf to the weekly message of this particular elderly gentleman. I know it isn't good news I'm hearing from this guy. The fate of sinners is depending on the actions of the people in this particular congregation. It isn't a burden I'd be happy to bear.

Clearly, plenty are not being saved. If they were, I'm sure this herald of doom would be telling us things were getting better. He hasn't so far. I probably need to keep visiting to keep up with the latest on this salvation dilemma.

I look at the fruit of this hell fire belief system, and I see a combination of torment for the living (thinking of the dead), as well as torment for the dead. I also see a huge burden hanging over the church to get out there and evangelise to save as many as possible from such a horrible end.

If I was fully engaged in such thinking, desperation would be my daily bread. The task of saving so many is truly enormous, and the stakes are so high.

Is there even time to think of good news in such a dilemma? I don't think one could afford the luxury. There is too much work to do, and so little time. It's a constant refrain.

With what type of message would I hit the unsaved? Do I tell them good news? That's been done for 2000 years, and only a few seem to hear it. Maybe bad news is more motivating? Should I frighten them into church? It seemed to work in the Middle Ages.

Still, does frightening people save them? I can't think of a single scripture speaking of salvation by fright. I understand salvation by faith, but not dread.

If I was to step back and consider so many I know carrying this burden, I would have to say what I observe is resigned defeat on the faces of most - the work is too hard, and the demands are too big. Very few are actually engaged in trying to save the lost. Their enthusiasm for such a task died out long before under the weight of such an impossible burden.

This is the standard thinking I grew up with in a typical local church congregation in the 1960's. For many today, is the thinking still the same?

6. A Solution For Bad News

Intro to Calvinism.

About 500 years ago a major shift in Christian thinking as expressed by the Catholic Church, emerged in Europe. This period of great change in Christian thinking is known as The Reformation. Martin Luther (1483-1546) is perhaps the most famous of those who led this movement. A reformation leader who emerged contemporary to Luther was John Calvin (1509-1564).

John Calvin is best known as the founder of Calvinism or Reformed Theology. The ideas he presented did not begin with him. He became famous as the one who was best at articulating and systemising the theology, so hence it bears his name. These same ideas can be traced back as far as the theologian known as Augustine (354-430) and it is also worth noting Martin Luther held similar views (Walls and Dongell 8-9). At its core is the primary idea God decides who will be saved and who will not be saved.

By saying God determines who will not be saved, we have to conclude God plans for some to be born with the ultimate end in mind for them of eternal damnation. I can't speak for all on what one imagines such a damnation to look like. I will assume it varies from burning forever in hell fire to some form of eternal conscious separation from God.

Most people I know today would find such an idea to be abhorrent. We can't help but view how this portrays the character of God as downright cruel. It doesn't make sense in the thinking of so many Christians today. We understand love as the primary characteristic of our God. Unfortunately, it was not such a strange idea 500 years ago.

The refinement of Christian thought has continued from the tumultuous years of The Reformation to this day. I can only assume the predestination of many to damnation by God did not seem as strange in the time of Calvin and Luther as it does today. Many contemporary Calvinists do qualify their views to be less extreme from those of John Calvin. Most of my Calvinist friends admit to this, and I can understand why.

I can only wonder how John Calvin processed such thinking. Perhaps he could see so many people were just so evil, they easily deserved what was coming to them. It isn't an easy thing to reconcile today. Some of us realise many people they know who are not Christians are nicer people than we are.

We know we are saved by grace. Still, accepting so many people better than us are just evil cows and deserve to be tortured in a fiery pit forever is a bit rich. Many Christians fortunately just can't settle for that. It doesn't make sense.

Anyone who has been out street preaching, or who knows someone who has, knows getting people to give their lives to Jesus just doesn't come from having a good argument. Still, very few people get saved at any one time by hitting them with a message of what Jesus did for them.

The answer for some, or how to make sense of this, is to settle for the concept of divine election and predestination as defined by John Calvin.

One could get a good summary of this theology by looking it up on Google. Wikipedia also has plenty of material one can read if one wants to look into the details.

Calvinism presents some solutions to the questions I've raised coming from my traditional background of Heaven or Hell teaching. In some ways, I think his teaching suits the modern day far better than the 1500's. Back in Calvin's day, most people grew up with a Christian world view in Western Europe. The culture of Western Europe was "Christian" in form, so it was expected one would naturally be "Christian".

Today we don't live in the same Christian culture. Our culture is still based on Christian principles, but many in society today seem to be really keen to remove those influences. I'm not so sure such endeavours will end well, but this is another subject entirely.

By my observation only, I'd say the majority of people who surround me in my suburb, or anywhere in Brisbane, where I live, are not Christian.

Calvinism has a good explanation for this. It presents the concept to be a Christian you have to be selected by God. The majority of people are not selected by God, and never will be. Therefore it won't matter what you say or do to try to encourage them to be Christians. They never will be.

Under Calvinism there is still a requirement to preach the Gospel, as this is one way those selected by God will be reached and saved. Don't expect to convert or reach too many of them. We'll only end up disappointed if we do. The proof is in the pudding. Most people just aren't interested, and don't like pudding, no matter how clever the argument may be to accept Jesus as saviour. We don't have to lean towards Calvinism to know this.

What Jesus did for us at the cross is the greatest expression of love the world has ever seen or heard of. Yet, even if we are able to perfectly convey this message of God's love, most people are not interested. Calvinism would seem to understand why.

The fires of hell or eternal separation are still the final stop for all these people not chosen by God. The good thing about it is, if one can find anything "good" in such a thought, at least we don't need to worry or blame ourselves if we can't save them. They were doomed from the moment they were born, so there really isn't any point in worrying about it. God decided it, and we need only be grateful to be among the few who God predetermined to save.

Scriptures for Calvinism.

The scriptural support for the Calvinistic position is apparently quite abundant, strange as it may seem. It all comes down to interpretation. Perhaps one of the most powerful sections in scripture to give apparent support for this position is found in Romans 9:

What then shall we say? Is God unjust? Not at all! For he says to Moses:

"I will have mercy on whom I have mercy, and I will have compassion on whom I have compassion."

It does not, therefore, depend on human desire or effort, but on God's mercy. For scripture says to Pharaoh: "I raised you up for this very purpose, that I might display my power in you and that my name might be proclaimed in all the earth." Therefore God has mercy on whom he wants to have mercy, and he hardens whom he wants to harden.

One of you will say to me: "Then why does God still blame us? For who is able to resist his will?" But who are you, a human being, to talk back to God? "Shall what is formed say to the one who formed it, 'Why did you make me like this?' Does not the potter have the right to make out of the same lump of clay some pottery for special purposes and some for common use?

What if God, although choosing to show his wrath and make his power known, bore with great patience the objects of his wrath - prepared for destruction? What if he did this to make the riches of his glory known to the objects of his mercy, whom he prepared in advance for glory - even us, whom he also called, not only from the Jews but also from the Gentiles? **Romans 9:14-24** (NIV)

The message is quite powerful in these verses. We are obviously the clay in the hands of God, the potter. He can do what he wants with us, and I have noticed he does. I personally have no problem understanding this. Yet still, I'm not a Calvinist.

The reference to Pharaoh is from the book of Exodus in the Old Testament. God hardened the heart of Pharaoh so he, Pharaoh, was incapable of letting the Israelites leave Egypt until all the punishments of God had been experienced in Egypt.

Was God unfair? Probably. Is there any rule that states God has to be fair? Not in my mind, but I'm sure others would dispute this. Life isn't fair, so somehow expecting God to be fair when everything I observe in the natural order is not fair is a bit childish in my mind. This is particularly so in the short term, meaning less than any person's lifespan.

Paul shows in these verses from Romans 9 God was tough on Egypt for a purpose primarily for the benefit of Israel. Too bad if you were born an Egyptian. This can be hard for a non-Christian to understand. It can make God seem harsh, cruel, and insensitive. I get that.

It also gives one with a Calvinistic background justification for thinking God really does only save a few. By extension the vast majority of people are headed for an eternity of torture in hellfire. I'm not sure what place "good news" has in all this, but there is comfort knowing there is good news for at least some (really?).

Fortunately I know many with Calvinist leanings have been thinking, and their thinking has forced them to moderate the conclusions they draw on the possible outcomes for those unsaved. As I've said before, some of my Calvinist friends will say they are only partially Calvinist in their thinking.

Likewise every Christian is probably partially Calvinist in different ways. This can be without even knowing it.

A friend I made on Facebook was able to convince me my thinking was more Calvinist than I ever could have imagined. I won't go into how here. That is another topic. I'm sure I could be convinced too I am partially Catholic and partially protestant in my thinking. We all share similar aspects of our respective expressions of Christian faith.

Referring briefly back to Romans 9, I should point out the reference to those prepared for destruction does not mean the destruction is eternal in nature.

Some will assume it does, but this is just an assumption. There is nothing in these verses specifically indicating the "objects of wrath" are automatically headed for an eternity in hellfire.

It may well be they were only chosen as objects of wrath for a particular time and purpose. Their ultimate end may not be as extreme as Calvinism would propose.

Thinking of other verses to support the Calvinist theology of salvation, Matthew 7:14 comes to mind:

But small is the gate and narrow the road that leads to life, and only a few find it. **Matthew 7:14** (NIV)

This verse certainly seems to support a position of only a few people will ever be saved. It certainly matches what we see. For those with the view I grew up with, it can make the effort of trying to save people seem like a losing battle. Nevertheless, because we care, we do what we can to save just a few more by hopefully convincing them onto the narrow road leading to life.

I have to admit, I struggle to see if "good news" can be understood in this reference to the narrow road. I'd love to find this statement was really a reference to the spiritual state of the Jews in the time of Jesus, to which he was bringing good news. If this was the case, then the idea of a Gospel can begin to make sense.

Could it be the once narrow road is now wide, all because of Jesus?

Those with an Arminian way of thinking (to be explained later) might argue the gate is now large, and the road wide, but still few travel on it. Perhaps more will later, if they don't now? Would that be good news?

Back to Calvinism, it is not my intention to provide an exhaustive list of scripture references which lend apparent support to the Calvinist theory of salvation. I do still wish to refer to John 6:44 as it reveals another aspect of Calvinist thinking:

No one can come to me unless the Father who sent me draws them, and I will raise them up at the last day. **John 6:44** (NIV)

The point made in this verse is simple. It is outside the power of a person to decide to follow Jesus, and receive eternal life. Free choice or will does not have a place in the process described in this verse. We don't choose to follow Jesus. God chooses us, and then we follow Jesus.

Naturally, language has a certain elastic quality about it, so it can be possible to argue God is now drawing everyone, but he wasn't when Jesus made his statement in John 6. Some will contend free choice to decide was given to all men after Jesus was crucified. It is a fair hypothesis to put forward. Do scriptures after the Gospels support this view? What about our observations? Does what we see in everyday life support this view?

If this is true, my observation is the drawing of God on every person does not appear to be particularly strong. So few respond to this drawing, if indeed it does exist. I also have to wonder what exactly they have to respond to if a Christian doesn't reach them with a "lifesaving" message. Does everyone lie awake in bed at night hearing: "Choose Jesus!" regardless of whether a Christian preaches to them or not?

I've never heard anyone preaching the Gospel message is going out "on air" into the minds of all people, whether a Christian reaches them or not. If I may be so blunt, it really does look like the idea God is universally drawing all men and women simultaneously at every point in time and place since the death of Jesus is a theory with precious little to support it.

If such a process is in force now, and actively so, why are so many preaching of a desperate need to reach the unsaved?

Jesus was clear the drawing of God was necessary and selective in order for anyone to follow Jesus before his crucifixion. Very few were drawn in comparison to the much larger number of those not drawn. If this is still true today, free choice is quite a whimsical notion. It deserves a chapter all on its own. I'll need to say more on the subject later.

A Historical Context.

I really hope anyone reading this can see Calvinism itself begged many questions. It is effective in removing the burden of responsibility for getting people saved. Saving people is clearly up to God. We might play a role in the process through getting the word out there. With Calvinism the buck doesn't stop with us when it comes to convincing someone. We can know we didn't need to just try harder if someone rejected the message.

Strangely enough, back in the 1500's and the centuries before, I don't know if people in general had much thought for the unsaved. The "heathen" in far off lands were definitely lost, but very few had any capacity to do anything about it. Reaching the world with the Gospel was probably more of a corporate church concern having no relevance for the common man who was a slave in so many ways.

My observation of the modern day dilemmas I've mentioned was probably only in the minds of the few who had access to scripture, if it was in their minds at all. In a culture where most if not all were born into the church, maybe the biggest challenge was staying saved, rather than saving others. Calvinism aided the staying saved question too. If one was chosen, they would always be saved. Salvation was not something one could lose in Calvinist thinking.

There was a lot of comfort in knowing one could not lose their salvation. Still, the nagging question was always there:

"Am I really saved?"

If one would like to explore some of the deeper aspects of Calvinism, I would recommend an excellent book by Robert Peterson and Michael Williams called Why I Am Not An Arminian (Peterson and Williams).

7: A Solution For The Solution?

The Answer To Calvin's Answer.

People at the time of John Calvin were probably not concerned with the questions raised by Calvinism today. I may be incorrect with this opinion. I hold it as life was too hard back then for most to really care about the subtleties of theology and reason. Still, back then, did Calvinism make total sense? A guy called Jacobus Arminius didn't think so. He was originally a Calvinist, but questions arose. They would not go away.

I won't in any way claim to be an expert on Arminianism or Calvinism. The topics do interest me as they seem to define two basic sets of Christian thinking. Whatever denomination one may belong to, the denomination is usually either Arminian or Calvinist in outlook.

For myself, I don't see myself as belonging to either camp. I just want to be a Christian, and nothing else. I can only hope that such a claim is possible. Now back to the topic on hand...

There could be many reasons why Jacobus Arminius began to question Calvinism. Predestination was certainly one core issue. I won't make an in-depth study into his thinking as I believe I can approach the topic based on what is obvious to me from what I see in the contemporary world.

He So Loved.

An immediate and obvious cause for concern to me comes from one of the most famous scriptures in the Gospels:

> *For God so loved the world that he gave his one and only Son, that whoever believes in him shall not perish but have eternal life.* **John 3:16** (NIV)

This verse is so well known, I didn't even need a concordance to look it up. I just know this verse is John 3:16. It has been drilled into my consciousness from my earliest days at Sunday School, before I even turned ten.

The beginning of this verse says so much - God so loved! It means to me his love for mankind was great. It was huge! Really? OK, really huge!

Yet John Calvin would have us think a God with such great love would bring people into existence who were predestined to eternal torment for their sins. Why not just skip creating them? They don't need to be created if their only hope is eternal torture. Do they?

I see redemption as a defining feature of all Jesus stands for. To give birth to a whole set of people for whom there is no redemption possible is just plain weird. Is it even weirder if we want to claim God still loves them?

I'm really sorry if what I'm saying is offensive to my Calvinist friends. I really don't want to offend anyone, and neither do I think badly of anyone for holding to these doctrines. I really want to be objective as best as I can, rather than judgemental. Is it too much to hope for the same towards me? I hope not.

The tragedy I see in Calvinism is how it is basically saying God is akin to some of the worst figures in history one can think of. So many non-Calvinists looking in on these concepts can see it as plain as day, while those in it just can't see it, or are trying desperately to justify it and somehow explain it.

I am so grateful so many Calvinists I know don't hold to the view one hundred percent. It shows they are thinking. There is always room for thinking in church. There is in my ideal picture of church anyway. We just need to think in a civil manner towards one another, and not be offended if someone disagrees with us.

A New Way Of Thinking?

So Jacobus Arminius, in the face of perceived problems with Calvinist thinking, brought forth an alternative way of thinking. Today we call it Arminianism.

Some may wish to claim it was a return to former thinking before Augustinian or John Calvin. They'd say it wasn't new. I'm sure for some people it would be a true statement, while for others it would not be true. It doesn't really matter here.

If I could find two words to define Arminian thinking, back in the late 1500's, they would have to be "free will" (or "free choice", if one so desires).

To Arminius, there was no predetermined decision of God for someone to receive damnation or salvation. It was all about everyone being free to choose for themselves.

All the church had to do was preach the Gospel. Those reached with the Gospel message could then make up their own mind. The person hearing the Gospel took full responsibility for their response to it.

If they ended up in hell, it was their fault entirely. They chose the destination because they refused to repent and give their lives to Jesus. What could be fairer than that?

Naturally, there must be verses in scripture to support this position. One would hope so, given so many denominations I'm aware of are Arminian in the foundation of their theology.

Let's begin in the first book of the New Testament:

> *"What do you think? If a man owns a hundred sheep, and one of them wanders away, will he not leave the ninety-nine on the hills and go to look for the one that wandered off? And if he finds it, truly I tell you, he is happier about that one sheep than about the ninety-nine that did not wander off. In the same way your Father in heaven is not willing that any of these little ones should perish.* **Matthew 18:12-14** (NIV)

The illustration here is of a flock of sheep where one wanders off, and the shepherd (God), drops everything to find that one lost sheep. The closing statement claims God doesn't want anyone to perish. This point is made in the context of a child who Jesus is bringing to the attention of his disciples.

Does the will of God for saving everyone only extend to children? We could argue this if we really want to be picky.

How old then must one be when God is no longer interested in you? It gets a bit silly if we start thinking God is not interested in saving everyone. Maybe Jesus didn't die for everyone? What does this verse from the first letter of Paul to Timothy say?:

> *That is why we labor and strive, because we have put our hope in the living God, who is the Savior of all people, and especially of those who believe.* **1 Timothy 4:10** (NIV)

As this verse says, Jesus is the saviour of everybody. He died to save everybody, and by extension, not just those predestined for salvation, and not just little children.

There is a condition for this salvation. The condition is belief. The person must believe.

Arminian thinking has that everyone is free to believe. Hence we are also free to reject the Gospel. By such thinking, if we believe, it is because we have chosen to believe.

To add further to the scriptural support for Arminianism, the following verse from the Gospel of John is important:

He came as a witness to testify concerning that
light, so that through him all might believe. **John 1:7** (NIV)

By this verse we can think it is possible for everyone to believe. The word "might" is important. All "might" believe. Still, some might not. I say this as free will allows for either possibility.

As with Calvinism, I won't give an exhaustive list of scriptures to support the position of Arminianism. There are more, and I leave it to the reader to seek them out if they so wish.

The important point to make here is it is possible to put together an argument from scripture to support the Arminian position. By saying this, I don't mean to impute scripture contradicts itself.

Calvinists and Arminians can both put together scriptural arguments to support their respective positions. Scripture does seem to be written this way. It gives us a lot of room to move. It gives us all the space we need to express huge errors in thinking and interpretation, if we are so inclined to do so.

As I've said before, this does not demand we think less of scripture. It may be more important and accurate if we think less of ourselves. If we are able to come up with flawed ideas from what we all believe is flawless scripture, does that tell us something about ourselves?

How lazy are we if we hold to theological positions, knowing so many scriptures are not in harmony with our view? How intellectually honest are we if we push the conclusions interpreted from one set of scriptures, while wilfully ignoring so many other scriptures?

To be fair, we may well have a different interpretation of verses others use to support views contrary to our own. We may not be lazy or intellectually dishonest at all. We just need to try to be objective with ourselves and what we are really doing and expressing. This objectivity is not always easy. To really know oneself may require a lifetime.

8: What Was Jesus Doing?

What was the example of Jesus?

I've begun to point out certain elements of Christian thinking beg a number of questions. This is particularly so in regards to what happens after we die. The conclusions we draw from this have a major impact on how we view the Gospel, or good news.

What can we glean from what Jesus was doing and teaching? I'd like to go to the beginning to find out:

> *After John was put in prison, Jesus went into Galilee, proclaiming the good news of God. ¹⁵"The time has come,"* *he said. "The kingdom of God has come near. Repent and believe the good news!"* **Mark 1:14-15** (NIV)

The above verses from Mark serve as a good opening statement for the beginning of Jesus' ministry. Many events happened before his official ministry began, but there was a definite point in time when after much preparation, it was time for Jesus to hit the road so to speak. When he did, there was reference to "good news".

This opening statement for this ministry period uses "good news" as its defining term. There was good news in his message. He wanted at least some of us to believe it too.

Saying that, is it really good news we believe, or maybe not-so-good news?

My friends in my gospel survey certainly had a grasp of good news, but I still have a question. Did they believe other things too? By "other things", I'm referring to ideas which can have an impact on how we walk with that good news.

I was almost frightened to ask. I was beginning to realise I had to. I eventually did, and I'll look at the responses to my extra question a bit later.

Back to what Jesus was doing, it makes sense to me any reference to "good news" has to be in a context of bad news. If there was no general setting of bad news, then good news would hardly be a message, let alone anything to respond to.

It would also make sense Jesus would, as part of his teaching, juxtapose his good news against the prevailing bad news. Not too many messages would be complete without some reference to context.

With this in mind, I have to wonder if the real good news message Jesus was sharing was standing in stark contrast to the prevailing bad news context he was probably referring to more than we realise.

Is it possible much of the Christian worldview is or was shaped mistakenly around the bad news context of Jesus message? There are certainly plenty of different perspectives out there on the message of

Jesus. Many directly oppose each other. They can't all be right.

Is it then possible the impact of Jesus' good news was a necessary change to the then prevailing bad news context? If the good news was that good, then it just might have meant a serious change was coming.

With the benefit of hindsight, we know there was a serious change that did come on the thinking of the times back then. We have to keep this in mind so we understand both the bad news and the good news present in the message of Jesus.

One Bad News Context.

Matthew 19:16-26 provides an interesting illustration of how Jesus set the scene for his Gospel message. It is also an excellent example of how I've seen Christians misinterpret conclusions from Jesus' "bad news context". In doing so it leads to a distortion of the overall Gospel message:

> Just then a man came up to Jesus and asked, "Teacher, what good thing must I do to get eternal life?"
>
> "Why do you ask me about what is good?" Jesus replied. "There is only One who is good. If you want to enter life, keep the commandments."
>
> "Which ones?" he inquired.
>
> Jesus replied, "'You shall not murder, you shall not commit adultery, you shall not steal, you shall not give false testimony, honor your father and mother,' and 'love your neighbor as yourself.'"
>
> "All these I have kept," the young man said. "What do I still lack?"

Jesus answered, "If you want to be perfect, go, sell your possessions and give to the poor, and you will have treasure in heaven. Then come, follow me."

When the young man heard this, he went away sad, because he had great wealth.

Then Jesus said to his disciples, "Truly I tell you, it is hard for someone who is rich to enter the kingdom of heaven. Again I tell you, it is easier for a camel to go through the eye of a needle than for someone who is rich to enter the kingdom of God."

When the disciples heard this, they were greatly astonished and asked, "Who then can be saved?"

Jesus looked at them and said, "With man this is impossible, but with God all things are possible." **Matthew 19:16-26** (NIV)

It may not be immediately obvious, but I can see how Jesus set the context of this passage quite powerfully in his opening response to the question from the man at the beginning of the passage. There is a great deal in the opening statement from Jesus. He explains there is no one who is good.

In that day, good was defined very clearly to the people of Judea who Jesus was reaching with his message. Good was defined by the law as outlined by the Torah, or first five books of the Old Testament in the Bible. There were hundreds of regulations prescribed, and many were ceremonial in nature.

The essence of the laws and statutes given in the Torah was wrapped up in the Ten Commandments. This was essentially the response Jesus gave to the man for what needed to be done to be saved - keep the Ten Commandments.

If we understand the laws were originally given through Moses around 1400 BC (some may want to argue around 1200 BC), then we have roughly 1200 to 1400 years of people trying (maybe not always) to be good. How did it go for them?

If Jesus' opening statement is anything to go by, not too well – no one was good. No one, after at least 1200 years! That isn't a good track record, but maybe it served to make an important point – no one was going to save themselves, even if given the formula to do so.

I've drawn some pretty heavy conclusions from Jesus' simple statement of "There is only one who is good." It may seem a bit rich to draw so much from so few words. I'm normally very careful to not read too much into just one verse of scripture, particularly if it really is the only one speaking of a particular detail.

In reality, I've drawn my perspectives from much of the Bible, but I don't have space or time to cover every detail here. Please do forgive me being brief. Be assured I do understand any concerns or questions that may come from what might look like a superficial sweep of the panorama of scripture. Hopefully I'll support the points I'm making further as the bigger picture unfolds.

Back to Matthew 19, we see Jesus introducing an end to keeping the 10 Commandments as the means to being right before God. This end was never in the original script. I say this as when the 10 Commandments were originally given to the people of Israel, via Moses at Mount Sinai, there was no mention of eternal life.

The original incentive for the commandments was the blessing of God for the nation and the individual in the here and now. As far as I can gather, there was nothing in the Old Covenant made between

God and Israel having anything to do with eternal life. If I am wrong here, I'd love someone to point out where in scripture it says otherwise.

If I am correct, then it would seem this man who posed the question to Jesus was doing so because he had heard Jesus speaking of eternal life in his public preaching. I really can't be one hundred percent certain, but I suspect this is a fair assumption.

In case there was any doubt as to which commandments Jesus was saying needed to be kept to qualify for eternal life, he gave some examples so there was no mistaking the particular list to which one needed to look.

The man must have felt pretty good about it all. In his own mind, he had been doing an awesome job of obeying the law. Still, in case there was any other minor detail to add to the mix, it was worth asking Jesus if there was anything else needed. I suspect he felt he had it all in the bag. I even wonder if he was only asking the question as he wanted Jesus to acknowledge how good he was. He would not be the first to walk this earth deluded by his perception of his own goodness. Nor would he be the last.

Oops! Jesus wasn't going to play along with his delusions. At this stage in the history of Israel, Jesus didn't want anyone to kid themselves into thinking they were able to qualify themselves as righteous. It was time to make things plain.

This guy had told Jesus he was good. In his own mind he was probably thinking he was really good. What Jesus had just said about no one being good was likely missed. It was a classic proof of how we often hear only what we want to hear.

Jesus telling the guy to sell his possessions was not a prescription for every person who wants to follow Jesus. That would end up being just another form of mindless religion. Jesus did know the context of this particular fellow.

Telling him to sell his possessions would cut to the core of an issue for this particular man. It was not about the idea having stuff or being wealthy was wrong.

The issue for this man was having another god before God - his wealth. He couldn't give it up if God required it of him. This man was not self-qualified as righteous after all. Jesus certainly knew how to burst his bubble.

Jesus follows up in verse 23 by saying how hard it is for the rich to enter his Kingdom of Heaven. This Kingdom of Heaven is another way of describing eternal life. If we misunderstand what Jesus was saying, there is a whole new way of religious thinking ready to emerge from his statement – salvation through poverty, and beating up on the rich. Many have fallen into this trap, as history shows.

Think about it. Step forward for a minute. This next question is for those of us who really grasp salvation comes through Jesus, and nothing or no one else.

Is the message of salvation really all about being poor?

Let's unpack this further. Can we really get right with God, as a rule, by deliberately being poor?

Hell no!

Poverty is not the way forward with God. Only Jesus is.

I've seen and heard so many leap to absurd conclusions about wealth from these verses in Matthew 19. It is only if we can correctly unpack such thinking we can truly unravel the mistaken conclusions I've heard so many draw.

But wait (!), someone may say. Did not Jesus drive the point home even further by saying it is harder for a rich man to enter the kingdom than for a camel to go through the eye of a needle?

Surely it must mean it is much easier for a poor man to enter?

Really?

Is it easy, in contrast, for a poor person to enter the kingdom of heaven?

Yes?

How poor does one have to be for it to be easy?

How is it measured?

What is the scale of righteousness we can find in scripture showing us how poor we need to be to automatically qualify for eternal life?

It isn't there!

Am I saying Jesus was lying?

Am I saying Jesus didn't know what he was talking about?

No!

Everything Jesus said was spot on. It really is hard for a rich man to qualify for eternal life. It really is! I'm sure we can understand this.

Can we then also understand it is also really hard for a poor man to qualify for eternal life?

In this context, "really hard" means impossible!

The details behind why may differ between rich and poor, but the fundamental fact is the same for both - nobody can qualify themselves.

Still, some people will naturally run around in religious thinking patterns. Some will end up thinking somehow poor people are better than wealthy people. In reality both are the same before God. Both need saving.

This is an illustration of just one example of how we can run off into wrong conclusions about what Jesus is saying to us in scripture today. The bad news Jesus was highlighting was no one is good.

I don't know for sure, but I have to wonder if in those days, a lot of religious types tended to be fairly wealthy, thinking of the Pharisees as just one example. Some may have even thought their being well off was a sign of God's personal favour towards them. I'm sure some think this way today. Such is human nature when it gets religion.

No wonder the disciples were quick to despair when Jesus said it was hard for the rich to enter God's Kingdom. All the super spiritual types they could think of as being close to God happened to be wealthy. That is what I suspect.

Did the Pharisees use their wealth as a delusional mark of God's favour? It would not be the first time someone has done so if they did.

Was Jesus picking on the rich in this particular example to make a point about the prevailing religious thinking of the day?

I've no doubt if Jesus wanted to illustrate a counter point with the poor, he could have easily done so. A poor person can have just as much reason to want to hang on to something as a rich person. It is not only the rich who have gods before God.

I've heard many over the years expound from Matthew 19 about how wealth can keep us from God. It is always done with no mention of how wealth really has nothing to do with salvation. Every time they do, I'm hearing they don't really understand the role of Jesus in salvation.

Jesus summed up the message quite well in verse 26 above. With man, eternal life was not going to happen. It would only come from God. The disciples seemed to get the message. They somehow knew it was no better for a poor person. Truly neither a poor man nor a rich man can earn their way into God's Kingdom.

From our view 2000 years later, it would seem to many Jesus was making the main point about wealthy people. The disciples knew he was referring to both rich and poor. Have a close look at verse 25 above if there is any doubt.

I can clearly see the bad news context of Matthew 19. No one was able to save themselves. All the laws Israel had from the Old Covenant hadn't saved anyone. The message from Jesus was so plain the disciples were quite disheartened.

Fortunately Jesus gave them a glimmer of light, and the beginnings of a message of hope in a hopeless situation.

Yes indeed! There is hope. There is hope even for the wealthy.

Eternal Worms.

Nobody likes the idea of having worms. This is particularly so in our sanitised Western world where dead bodies of any kind of animal, let alone humans, are rarely seen.

This was not the case in the time of Jesus. Public execution by the Romans was indeed public to serve as a warning. Life was tough in the time of Jesus, like most if not all of history. Back then is much like it is today in many parts of the world.

In any battlefield of Jesus' day, it would not take too much time for flies to get to work on both those wounded and the dead. The same was true for any animal which died of natural or unnatural causes. It was particularly so if the cadaver was left in the open for any length of time.

I expect few would have had trouble picturing the imagery employed in a statement made by Jesus in the book of Mark:

> And if your foot causes you to stumble, cut it off. It is better for you to enter life crippled than to have two feet and be thrown into hell. And if your eye causes you to stumble, pluck it out. It is better for you to enter the kingdom of God with one eye than to have two eyes and be thrown into hell, where
> "'the worms that eat them do not die, and the fire is not quenched.'
> Everyone will be salted with fire.
> "Salt is good, but if it loses its saltiness, how can you make it salty again? Have salt among yourselves, and be at peace with each other." **Mark 9:45-50** (NIV)

There may be a number of ways to understand what Jesus is saying above. In one sense, I can see him driving home the tough point of how the Old Covenant was merciless.

The opportunities for breaking the laws of the Old Covenant were numerous. If there were places you could go that would lead you astray, cut off your foot so you don't go there. The same was said of one's eye, as we can too easily look on things that might lead us to sin.

The way to the Kingdom of God, via the law-based Old Covenant, was not easy. In fact, as Jesus already pointed out in Matthew 19, it was impossible.

Jesus knew those he was talking to were not going to reach for the knives to cut off their feet or blind themselves. I suspect Jesus was making this point for the same reason as I discussed earlier about Matthew 19. He wanted the bad news context to be clear - really clear! In this way his good news message would be seen clearly for the good it represented.

Still, there is this sticky mention of hell again. It is illustrated further with references to what seem to be eternal worms or maggots in the midst of a fire no one can put out. Is this form of punishment only relevant to the Old Testament?

Maybe not, if the worms and fires are eternal in this place called "hell".

But what is this place called hell?

If we don't answer this question soundly, we can end up stuck in dogma and traditional thinking that may have no basis of fact, unless we do.

According to Thayer, in his Greek-English Lexicon (Thayer 111), the word translated as "hell" comes from the Greek word "Gehenna". Thayer describes this as The Valley of Topheth, or Gehenna, just outside Jerusalem. The significance of the place goes back many hundreds of years as child sacrifices to a pagan god called Moloch took place there for many years.

Josiah, the 16th monarch of Judah, abolished the practice, but the site was so defiled and abhorred, it became the rubbish dump of the city, and in particular, a place where dead bodies of animals and criminals were dumped and burned. The fires had to be constant to contain the smell.

I can see a context beginning to form here. Before I unpack this further, I should digress and mention the reference of Jesus in Mark 9 to the worms and fire come from Isaiah 66:24 stated as follows:

"From one New Moon to another and from one Sabbath to another, all mankind will come and bow down before me," says the LORD. "And they will go out and look on the dead bodies of those who rebelled against me; the worms that eat them will not die, the fire that burns them will not be quenched, and they will be loathsome to all mankind." **Isaiah 66:24** (NIV)

The prophet Isaiah was speaking in the time of King Hezekiah, who was the 13th monarch of Judah. Another reference in Isaiah specifically refers to Tophet in Isaiah 30:33.

Topheth has long been prepared; it has been made ready for the king. Its fire pit has been made deep and wide, with an abundance of fire and wood; the breath of the LORD, like a stream of burning sulfur, sets it ablaze. **Isaiah 30:33** (NIV)

I do find a significant link between these three verses. Jesus makes specific reference to the place called Tophet. The two verses from Isaiah in chapters 30 and 66 do the same. Both Jesus and Isaiah also refer to worms that don't die. They also refer to fire.

Jeremiah refers to the same place again in his 7th chapter:

> "*The people of Judah have done evil in my eyes, declares the LORD. They have set up their detestable idols in the house that bears my Name and have defiled it. They have built the high places of Topheth in the Valley of Ben Hinnom to burn their sons and daughters in the fire-- something I did not command, nor did it enter my mind. So beware, the days are coming, declares the LORD, when people will no longer call it Topheth or the Valley of Ben Hinnom, but the Valley of Slaughter, for they will bury the dead in Topheth until there is no more room. Then the carcasses of this people will become food for the birds and the wild animals, and there will be no one to frighten them away. I will bring an end to the sounds of joy and gladness and to the voices of bride and bridegroom in the towns of Judah and the streets of Jerusalem, for the land will become desolate.*" **Jeremiah 7:30-34** (NIV)

This is a fairly grim pronouncement Jeremiah is making about the people of Jerusalem. This place where the people would sacrifice their own children would become the dumping ground for their own bodies after the Babylonians had destroyed the city.

Much of the work of Jeremiah was a final warning to the people of Judah. This was just before the Babylonians did indeed come and destroy Jerusalem. I can only wonder if the people of Judah had gone back to child sacrifices after Josiah abolished them. Nothing would surprise me.

When I put all these references together, I can see a bigger picture emerging. Were these worms or maggots that did not die really immortal?

I suspect not. It makes sense to me it was figurative language to drive the point home this was a catastrophic outcome of huge proportions. Hyperbole is in play with the language used in these verses.

Do the worms not die because there are so many bodies to feast upon?

Maybe. I wasn't around 2000 years ago to understand all the nuances in the colloquial language of the time.

Were the fires unquenchable because there was so much fuel to burn in the total destruction of the city?

Were the fires also unquenchable because there were countless bodies to burn, in figurative terms (hyperbole)?

It strikes me as a fair point to make.

If we really want to be specific can we start wondering how a dead body can burn forever?

It can't, and neither is there a need for it to do so. If we really want a literal rather than figurative interpretation, should we also be asking how worms can be eternal in a "consuming" fire?

A fire of the "consuming" kind is a term commonly used in Biblical language. Just before the warning of Isaiah above about Tophet, there is mention of it in chapter 30, verse 30:

The Lord will cause people to hear his majestic voice and will make them see his arm coming down with raging anger and consuming fire, with cloudburst, thunderstorm and hail. **Isaiah 30:30**. (NIV)

A reference to a consuming fire impresses far more than just a fire, and far more than a fire which somehow does not consume. Much does depend on translation, but I hope we have the picture here. Consuming can be translated as "raging" in some translations. It doesn't really matter. What does matter is the need to understand hyperbole perhaps far more than a need to take everything literally.

Maybe I'm wrong. Perhaps God needs the bodies of wicked people to burn forever, in a consuming fire which does not consume, even if the spirit of that person has long since departed. I don't think he does, but maybe that is something he hasn't shown me yet about himself. Perhaps I need to be aware of anger issues here yet to be resolved?

One thing I am certain of is the funeral pyres from the slaughter taking place when Jerusalem was destroyed by the Babylonians do not burn today. Neither do those bodies exist today.

The time of their destruction has long since gone. The fact of their destruction, for disobedience to God, is with us to this day.

Jesus understood the context of the point he was making in regard to worms and fires in Tophet. It is possible many listening to him back then understood too. I'm not so certain those listening to Jesus today understand the context as clearly as they did back then.

Something only Jesus knew at the time, that the listeners did not know, was how a similar fate was about to befall Jerusalem once more. Some 40 years later, the Romans destroyed Jerusalem. Jesus knew full well what was coming for the city.

Was the warning of Jesus about worms and fire in Tophet more for the listeners of his day, than for us today? Few if any of us have seen, let alone visited the Valley of Tophet. It is a location far from the majority of those who read the Bible in the 21st Century.

If context means anything, I can see a strong link between what Jesus was saying about "hell", and what he knew was coming for the city of Jerusalem. "Hell" may mean nothing more than that.

Does anyone still need convincing?

Let's take a look at these verses from Matthew. They cover one of Jesus' final public statements before his arrest. He is speaking to a crowd, about the Scribes and Pharisees, and no doubt there were Scribes and Pharisees in that crowd to hear these words:

> *"You snakes! You brood of vipers! How will you escape being condemned to hell? Therefore I am sending you prophets and sages and teachers. Some of them you will kill and crucify; others you will flog in your synagogues and pursue from town to town. And so upon you will come all the righteous blood that has been shed on earth, from the blood of righteous Abel to the blood of Zechariah son of Berekiah, whom you murdered between the temple and the altar. Truly I tell you, all this will come on this generation.*
> **Matthew 23:33-36** (NIV)

Jesus was fairly blunt. He was telling these same religious leaders they were headed for hell –

Gehenna hell. I'm sure they knew what he was talking about. They knew the texts from the prophets Isaiah and Jeremiah. They well understood what Gehenna represented.

Jesus also told them why they were destined for Gehenna. They were no different from those who had preceded them. They were all killers of God's prophets. The days to follow would be final proof of that. They were soon to murder Jesus.

The blood of all the murdered prophets of God would fall on this generation. Gehenna was slated to burn one more time, and it did, when Jerusalem was destroyed, along with the nation, in AD70.

If this is not context, I don't know what is.

Still, if one really wants to stretch things further and say Jesus was speaking about the fate of all sinners from every point in time and geography, they are welcome to it. I can't change anyone's mind. It just seems like a stretch of the imagination if they really do so.

So if we go back to the point I was making of Jesus setting a bad news context for his good news, it does make sense to me Jesus is doing this again with his reference to worms that don't die and fires that won't be put out.

Jesus was not going to stop the destruction of Jerusalem. Fortunately, that destruction was not the end of the story. Just maybe, in that context good news would have its place.

Lazarus and the Rich Man - Setting the Scene

I don't think any exploration of the topic on the fate of sinners is complete without looking at the story of Lazarus and the Rich Man. So many Christians I know think of this story in scripture and use it as a reference for how they think on the subject of life after death.

Before I do, I will make a point about parables. It may surprise some readers.

When I was in Sunday school, and even on into high school scripture classes, I was taught Jesus spoke in parables so people could understand better what he was saying.

We were taught parables were a way of speaking in the language of the common man. It was a bit like speaking down to his or her level so they could easily make the connections and get the real point of the message.

I was very surprised then to read this in Matthew 13:

> *The disciples came to him and asked, "Why do you speak to the people in parables?"*
> *He replied, "Because the knowledge of the secrets of the kingdom of heaven has been given to you, but not to them. Whoever has will be given more, and they will have an abundance. Whoever does not have, even what they have will be taken from them. This is why I speak to them in parables:*
> *"Though seeing, they do not see; though hearing, they do not hear or understand."* **Matthew 13:10-13** (NIV)

A similar point is made in Mark 4:

> When he was alone, the Twelve and the others around him asked him about the parables. He told them, "The secret of the kingdom of God has been given to you. But to those on the outside everything is said in parables so that,
>
> "'they may be ever seeing but never perceiving, and ever hearing but never understanding; otherwise they might turn and be forgiven!' **Mark 4:10-12** (NIV)

And again, the same point is made in Luke 8:9-10

> His disciples asked him what this parable meant. He said, "The knowledge of the secrets of the kingdom of God has been given to you, but to others I speak in parables, so that,
>
> "'though seeing, they may not see; though hearing, they may not understand.' **Luke 8:9-10** (NIV)

Sorry to labour the point here by giving 3 references. I've done so to point out how 3 separate authors make the same point. I'm not just talking about one obscure verse that might have several meanings.

Maybe I shouldn't say there are no other ways of reading these verses. Perhaps there are. Anyway, I've not said anything yet about what they are saying. I'll start with a question. Do they agree with what I was taught in Sunday school?

Personally, I don't think they do. I also have to wonder if "the secrets of the Kingdom of Heaven" were also hidden from my Sunday School teachers!

That is a horrible thought really. I hope it isn't the case, and it probably wasn't. If anything, it does serve to show how misled we can be in our reading of scripture. I guess it also shows how we can be bound up by traditional thinking, even when it seems to very clearly contradict scripture.

I referred to this point as an introduction to the parable on Lazarus and the Rich Man. Given how it appears likely parables were given to obscure meaning, rather than enlighten, is it possible the parable of Lazarus and the Rich Man can be misunderstood?

I think prudence would demand we at least admit we should be careful thinking we understand parables 100%. That is my viewpoint anyway. So, on with the show, from Luke chapter 16:

> "There was a rich man who was dressed in purple and fine linen and lived in luxury every day. At his gate was laid a beggar named Lazarus, covered with sores and longing to eat what fell from the rich man's table. Even the dogs came and licked his sores.
>
> "The time came when the beggar died and the angels carried him to Abraham's side. The rich man also died and was buried. In Hades, where he was in torment, he looked up and saw Abraham far away, with Lazarus by his side. So he called to him, 'Father Abraham, have pity on me and send Lazarus to dip the tip of his finger in water and cool my tongue, because I am in agony in this fire.'
>
> "But Abraham replied, 'Son, remember that in your lifetime you received your good things, while Lazarus received bad things, but now he is comforted here and you are in agony. And besides all this, between us and you a great chasm has been set in place, so that those who want to go from here to you cannot, nor can anyone cross over from there to us.'

"He answered, 'Then I beg you, father, send Lazarus to my family, for I have five brothers. Let him warn them, so that they will not also come to this place of torment.'

"Abraham replied, 'They have Moses and the Prophets; let them listen to them.'

"'No, father Abraham,' he said, 'but if someone from the dead goes to them, they will repent.'

"He said to him, 'If they do not listen to Moses and the Prophets, they will not be convinced even if someone rises from the dead.'" **Luke 16:19-31**. (NIV)

If this does not serve as proof for sinners going to flaming hell fires after they die, I don't know what does. If it doesn't serve as proof, we better start asking if anything does. So, does this parable serve as proof?

Can we start with considering one angle of context? Why not? We need to start somewhere. Here we go: this story is not referred to as a parable.

Okay, but many parables are not introduced in the text as parables. Hence I'm not so sure we can draw anything from this particular angle.

If one is to look at the subject under Wikipedia, one will find there is all manner of dispute as to whether it is a parable or not. Fortunately, I don't think such disputes are needed in this discussion.

What I do find interesting is the Lazarus parable (or story) follows on from a lecture from Jesus to the Pharisees who had just tried to insult him in verse 14 of Luke 16. The point made about the Pharisees is how they were covetous, or fond of money.

In the same chapter, in earlier verses before those referring to Lazarus, Jesus has commented on a diverse range of topics. These topics include divorce laws; how God values things differently from men; and the enduring nature of the law (verses 15-18). They serve as an unusual mix of subjects before launching into the story of Lazarus and the Rich Man.

As unusual as this list may be, does it bear significance to the story or parable to follow about Lazarus and hell fire?

Lazarus and the Rich Man - The Substance.

An initial message one could draw from this story is how a poor person qualifies to go to heaven, while the rich go to hell.

I doubt this really is the point. I suspect the context is more about the problem of the Pharisees with their covetous love of money. This would explain the apparent rich versus poor aspect of the story. Jesus is most likely directing the warning in the message specifically to the Pharisees.

If then we accept the message in this parable is directed to the Pharisees, I would not be surprised if one method employed by Jesus to make his point was to use the belief system of the Pharisees to make his point.

The beliefs of the Pharisees make a topic worthy of a rather large volume all by itself. I don't wish to get lost in such a digression. The one reference I will make to Pharisaic belief is one made by Josephus, a Jewish historian, who was himself a Pharisee.

Josephus lived in the time just after Jesus, and wrote extensively, in the employ of the Romans, on the fall of Jerusalem. He also wrote on other subjects relating to his people. According to Josephus, the Pharisees believed the souls of bad men were subject to eternal punishment (Josephus 478).

Has anyone heard of Frodo Baggins? He's a character from a popular modern day story called The Lord of the Rings. The story in The Lord of the Rings is so powerful and well known; some sermons have been given referring to the story to illustrate certain spiritual points made in the Bible.

Does one listening to a sermon containing reference to The Lord of the Rings decide from such a message elves, orcs, and ring wraiths exist?

Does someone listening to such a message necessarily walk out of the church in disgust thinking the minister is promulgating false teachings about elves and orcs? I hope not. Still, nothing would surprise me of people. We can be needlessly silly at times.

My Expositors Bible Commentary states the parable may have originated in Egyptian folklore (Liefeld 992) If this really is the case, it may have been a story well known in the time of Jesus, just as is The Lord of the Rings today.

It would have provided a fitting background for making Jesus' point to the Pharisees. Was Jesus turning their particular belief in eternal punishment back at them? It would make sense if he was. The references then to hell fire would not be proof of their nature and the fate of the dead at all.

Maybe Jesus did teach extensively to his disciples the wicked would be punished in an eternal fire for eternity. Maybe he didn't too. If he did, it cannot be proven from the story of Lazarus and the

Rich Man. We will need to find resounding proof from other parts of scripture if such really is the case.

Think about if Jesus didn't teach on such an outcome of eternal suffering in fires of hell. Would Luke have been thinking Jesus was spreading contradictory teaching by discordantly referring to the parable of Lazarus and the Rich Man in his discourse to the Pharisees?

Somehow I doubt it. If Luke always had in the back of his mind Jesus never believed in eternal suffering in fires of Hell, the use of the story about Lazarus by Jesus would in no way demand serious question marks in the mind of Luke. Luke I'm sure was used to Jesus' style of not teaching so all would understand him.

Any internet search will show us there is much speculation on what Jesus was really saying in the parable of Lazarus and the Rich Man. We can't even be sure if it is a parable or not!

Should we be surprised?

Not if we understand Jesus was not always teaching in a manner to make things clear to everyone who would hear him.

I hope such uncertainty is not too disturbing for the reader. For me, such uncertainty is what helps to lend life and vibrancy to the Christian walk. Maybe I should write on this further. It too is a subject deserving of a volume all by itself.

To cover this point briefly, I will say I am intrigued by the subjective nature of scripture. I'm intrigued because it serves to tell us much about ourselves and how we view God.

If we believe Lazarus and the Rich Man supports the view of eternal suffering for the wicked, it says something about how we view God. It also says something about us, for better or for worse.

If we really want to believe our God does reserve the wicked for eternal conscious punishment, the parable of Lazarus and the Rich Man assists with such a purpose well. It assists, but it does not prove.

If we don't, the same parable need not throw uncertainty at such a position. My current understanding is this story or parable in no way compels me to believe in eternal suffering in hell fire. It holds no compelling proof for the reasons I have already outlined. As a closing statement, whatever we want to believe, I do wish us all well with our various perspectives.

9: The Second Survey

I wasn't so certain I would follow up my initial survey question. My gut feeling held I was dealing with a sensitive topic if I followed up with what I had in mind.

There was nothing like stepping out to find out. I really wanted to know what my friends were thinking. If they told me, fine. If they didn't, that in itself might also say something.

My question was quite simple:

"To whom is the Gospel intended, and what is the end for anyone who rejects it?"

Within 2 weeks I had 19 replies from my 40 original subjects who all received my second question. This compared with 32 responses to my original question.

Does the difference prove anything in itself? As an engineer I have to say no. One set of data proves nothing. All I can say is it didn't surprise me.

Why so?

Out Of Africa.

Some weeks after I sent out the second survey to my 40 targeted Facebook friends, I was on Skype talking with a couple in Africa. It made sense to hit them with the set of questions while we were online.

They gave me the standard replies for the definition of the Gospel. So far so good. There was nothing out of the ordinary. It was the same again with the first part of my second question - who is the Gospel for?

When it came to talking about the fate of those who rejected the Gospel, it was really hard to get an answer. This was coming from pastors too I might add.

I wasn't satisfied to be told they missed out on eternal life. I needed to know what it meant for such a person. Would they burn in hell forever, or what?

The struggle to answer my question was obvious for the husband of the couple. His wife had given the simple answer of "separation from God".

In order to help my friend out, I was happy enough to ask him after some awkward pauses if he would settle for separation from God, similar to what his wife had said. I wasn't going to create any more tension by insisting on further details, lest the tension develop into tension between us.

Why the concern tension might arise over such a topic?

Bringing It Home.

I've always found the subject of the ultimate fate of the unsaved to be a really uncomfortable topic in Christian circles. It is hardly the topic of choice at a dinner party. Given what so many of us have grown up with, I'm not surprised.

I'll never forget some years ago in a home group I was a part of talking about how there may be an alternative view to burning forever in hell fire. Some in this group erupted like volcanoes. They expressed extreme outrage for thinking such a thing was possible.

I was staggered! Why get so aggressive about such a question? The violence in their opposition was really disturbing. Was it possible to have a rational discussion on such a topic? I thought it would have been until then.

The response to my broaching the topic was irrational. It left me wondering if there was spiritual resistance from the dark side to my suggestion. Was the end for those never-to-be-redeemed really less severe than what so many were raised to believe, including myself?

If we think God will burn sinners forever in the fires of Hell, does this make it easier or harder to tell people about a God of love?

I know a little bit about how secular people think. I hear about it every day. I learn from my work colleagues, friends, and the media.

In so many ways, I feel like the high moral ground in today's world has been taken from the Christians. It is now clutched tightly by the secular. They won't let go of it easily.

91

I wouldn't blame anyone for thinking it is not the best subject to raise with the secular. Who really wants to tell someone burning forever in Hell is a consequence for unrepentant sin, and all from a God who really loves them?

I know the simple answer is if it is true, you had better tell them or else! The problem is many people out there have kids of their own. They understand it is psychotic to torture someone you love.

The last thing I want to do is ditch the truth to be accepted by the secular. On the other hand, disapproval from the secular does not serve as a marker of truth.

The Replies - First Part.

At this point I'll make more direct reference to the second survey question and the responses.

The first half of my second question was simple to answer. I didn't expect too much diversity in the replies. The vast majority thought the Gospel was for all mankind. Just one respondent considered it was for mankind and angels as well - all created beings.

If the Gospel is for all mankind, it does beg a question:

If we don't hear the Gospel before we die, where or when will we?

Other questions then by necessity follow:

- Is the Church failing mankind by not reaching them?

- Is the Church failing God by not reaching those he wants to save?
- Are these questions really called for?

The Replies - Second Part.

The second part of my second question offered a more diverse range of replies. What is the end for those who reject the Gospel?

Some replies were clear, and some were not. As with my first survey, I tried to break the replies down into a few key words:

- Eternal separation from God.
- Death without existence or suffering.
- Unsure.
- It won't be rejected.
- God is more love than the lake of fire would imply.
- Inability to enjoy the same heaven in which we all coexist.
- They choose Hell - the place where everyone does what they want, in company with the demons.

Clearly, I didn't do too well finding one or two word summaries for the variety of replies I received. Some of the perspectives were so intriguing I didn't want to take away from their uniqueness.

There was one particular standout I noticed: no one simply stated those who reject the Gospel would burn forever in Hell. Fire still was not without mention. It was used more in the context of a place of final death, but not with an eternity of consciousness in that death.

The Bible does speak of such a fire, near the end of the story, in the book of Revelation:

"Anyone whose name was not found written in the book of life was thrown into the lake of fire." **Revelation 20:15** (NIV)

Yes, it doesn't say anything about eternal suffering in such a fire. Neither does it say the fire will burn forever. There is another verse in Revelation. It might shed some light on such a topic. It is given earlier in the same chapter of Revelation:

"And the devil, who deceived them, was thrown into the lake of burning sulfur, where the beast and the false prophet had been thrown. They will be tormented day and night for ever and ever." **Revelation 20:10** (NIV)

This verse certainly speaks of eternal suffering. It seems to anyway. It looks like the devil will be tormented forever, and it could even be understood the beings referred to as "the beast" and "the false prophet" will share with similar eternal suffering.

If anyone needed support for a position sinners go to hell for a life of eternal suffering (death?), then on the face of it, these verses would support such a view. It does make sense here why so many do believe this. Nevertheless, why didn't anyone mention this?

Eternal Separation.

Eternal separation from God is one response I was definitely expecting. I think I must have first heard of the concept back as a teenager in the 1970's. I was beginning to think and ask questions back then.

I don't know why, but the concept was devoid of fire with most of those from whom I heard it. It was more about just living apart from God. It resembled a void of nothing, in which one was conscious.

I've no idea where the idea first came about. Looking back, it does reflect to me it was the beginning of Christians thinking about the fate of sinners. Were they finding what they'd grown up with did not match with the God they knew?

One particular verse comes to mind as support for the position, in Matthew:

> *I say to you that many will come from the east and the west, and will take their places at the feast with Abraham, Isaac and Jacob in the kingdom of heaven. [12]But the subjects of the kingdom will be thrown outside, into the darkness, where there will be weeping and gnashing of teeth."* **Matthew 8:11-12** (NIV)

In this verse from Matthew we have a place of darkness. Fire tends to create light, so I have to conclude this does mean the place of darkness is without fires. It has some resemblance to a verse from a parable in Matthew 22:

> *"Then the king told the attendants, 'Tie him hand and foot, and throw him outside, into the darkness, where*

there will be weeping and gnashing of teeth.' **Matthew 22:13** (NIV)

I note definite consistency between these 2 extracts from the Gospel of Matthew with the repeated reference to weeping and grinding teeth. I also note both references come from a parable. With this in mind, one has to be careful about firm conclusions drawn from the details found in parables. Still, we have 2 references to a place of punishment with darkness rather than fire.

Matthew 25:30 has a similar reference in a different parable. Clearly, the concept of punishment in a place of darkness is not without scriptures to support the theory.

Just to make things interesting, I thought I should point out one of a number of verses in the Gospel accounts, which put the weeping and teeth grinding in a different light (no pun intended):

As the weeds are pulled up and burned in the fire, so it will be at the end of the age. The Son of Man will send out his angels, and they will weed out of his kingdom everything that causes sin and all who do evil. They will throw them into the blazing furnace, where there will be weeping and gnashing of teeth. **Matthew 13:40-42** (NIV)
This is how it will be at the end of the age. The angels will come and separate the wicked from the righteous and throw them into the blazing furnace, where there will be weeping and gnashing of teeth. **Matthew 13:49-50** (NIV)

Both of these references come from the conclusions of two different parables. In these cases we have the weeping and teeth grinding in the context of fire. Maybe one has to pass through the fire to make it to the darkness beyond? Who knows?

Another thought is the punishment by fire is uniquely specific to Jerusalem in AD 70. The punishment by separation and darkness may be a separate event of a more eternal nature. Once again - who knows?

I hope I would never pretend to be an expert on Hebrew thought 2000 years ago. I'm certainly not raising these apparent discrepancies to try and make out the Bible is inconsistent. I don't think it is at all. What I see as another possibility is how the nature of a punishment is not to be taken as literally as the fact of the punishment.

Something specific does stand out to me. It is how the time context of these events is based around the end of an age. They don't seem to fit with any random time, where individuals are dying and facing punishment day after day, year after year, like people die now.

Just maybe, as mentioned above, these verses really do all refer to an event distinct from the standard "your fate is eternal hell fire", with which I grew up.

I've already made the point about parables being given to keep us from understanding. If anything fits with this, these verses just might do so perfectly. It would then make sense to me we should err on the side of caution and avoid drawing hasty conclusions from these verses.

Still, there is justification for those who lean towards a perspective of separation from God, without the focus on fire and eternal torture.

Uncertainty.

Only 2 of my survey replies came back with a statement of uncertainty. I knew they both knew their Bibles well enough to be aware of the concept of eternal hell fire, or verses that at least alluded to such ideas.

Still, in spite of what they were well aware of in scripture, I think it is very fair to say they knew enough also to consider things just may not be as cut and dry in scripture as some may think.

As with all the replies I received, I don't want to cast aspersions against anyone and their perspectives. Naturally, with those who plead uncertainty, I cannot find direct scriptural support, unless I juxtapose a number of scriptures like those I've mentioned, which paint different pictures. Jesus never ended his teaching with "who knows?" like I can. Then again, I would dare to quote the Apostle Paul from the first epistle to the Corinthians:

> *For now we see only a reflection as in a mirror; then we shall see face to face. Now I know in part; then I shall know fully, even as I am fully known.* **1 Corinthians 13:12** (NIV)

Perhaps those who plead uncertainty are closer to the truth than any of us. I actually have a great deal of respect for those who can say they don't know.

Sometimes one can know a great deal, sufficient to realise one knows very little. Such humility deserves honourable mention on many topics.

As much as I could claim I have an out to quit this writing right now, I do have more to say. Only time will tell if I've proved the saying it is better to say nothing (or little?) and be considered a fool, than open my mouth (say more?) and remove all doubt.

Can't Reject It.

I don't feel it would be right to include a certain specific reply in with the sundries, which is still to follow. The reply of how the Gospel won't specifically be rejected came from 2 respondents.

I may be wrong, but I have the impression neither knows each other to have formed the opinion together. One lives in the USA, and the other here in Australia. Both would seem to have drawn the same conclusion independently of each other.

Neither respondent appealed directly to particular scriptures in making their replies. It wasn't called for in my original question. I was interested in brevity. Both though did state their reply from the perspective of knowing God.

"I don't see how our puny brain could resist and reject the power of the Holy Spirit, Jesus the Christ, and God the Father, once they are fully revealed and once the brain is fully healed from faulty ungodly reasonings."[1]

The second was as follows:

---

[1] Name withheld. Friend in California, USA. Correspondence with author. April 2015.

"The Gospel is for those God is ready to move in their hearts, and if it is Spirit led, it won't be rejected for long - not in his timing!"[2]

I'm not ready at this point in the discussion to bring forth a list of scriptures to either support or refute such a perspective. All I will say here is I find the argument to be one worth coming back to.

Sundry Replies

The sundry replies I received were so original I had to make mention of each as they really do add spice and flavour to this study.

The first was as follows:

"I believe God is more secure in the face of billions of "unconverted" than most Christians think. I also believe he is more love than the lake of fire theory implies." [3]

The mention of a God with no insecurities is an interesting one. For myself, with a strong sense of a God who is all-powerful and infallible, I like the idea.

Is it fair to expect God is perfectly secure within himself?

---

[2] Name withheld. Friend in Queensland, Australia. Correspondence with author. April 2015.
[3] Name withheld. Friend in Western Australia. Correspondence with author. April 2015.

I would say he is. He has always shown himself to be totally secure in his dealings with me, over more than 40 years now.

The followers of some gods I know would seem to reflect a god who needs his or her honour defended. It is never really sound in my view to judge any god by their followers. I cringe at times when I see how some Christians behave. I cringe at myself. I don't want anyone to judge my God by me. It is inevitable some will. I've learnt to live with that.

Perhaps I should ask my friend for more info. Does he mean God is ultimately happy to have an eternity with unbelievers and believers?

Without asking him, I think he doesn't mean that. I suspect he is thinking God will work out the conversion of most if not all. This would then be similar to my friends who suggested the Gospel won't be ultimately rejected.

The "lake of fire theory" my friend is referring to is the same lake of fire I mentioned earlier in Revelation 20. Most would assume the fire is for one of three possible outcomes.

One possible use for the fire is the eternal torment of those "deserving" of such an end. An alternative view is for their annihilation. With the latter, they would face death once and for all, with no eternal suffering thereafter. A third view is the fire is purely for refinement, similar to how silver is refined in fire.

My friend is either suggesting the fire is more for purification and redemption, or figurative of something else that isn't necessarily terminal for the recipient.

The bottom line is my friend is basing his conclusion on how he knows God personally, rather than academically, via reading about him in the Bible. I don't know if he thinks his view can be supported by scripture or not. I'll leave such questions hanging for now.

The second sundry reply was as follows:

"In terms of salvation, in my mind, we are all saved by the gospel, so that isn't even a question. Any other idea seems, to me, to require explanations of the infinite exceptions: people who have not heard; what about little children; what about extenuating circumstances of life experience?

So, I go to the scene in The Last Battle (C.S Lewis). Everyone is in heaven at the end...well, with the exception of those who didn't enter the tent.

C. Baxter Kruger wrote a book called The Great Dance which influenced me greatly. We are all present at the party, but we aren't all dancing. This image holds much meaning for me with experiences at college dances.

In terms of rejection, how do you react when your children reject you? I know that I grow frustrated, but my child never ceases to be my child.

And children have no choice in adoption, so if God chooses to adopt us how can we reject that? We can run away, perhaps. But he is always on the porch waiting for us to come home."[4]

Once again we have a response which is a challenge to orthodox thinking. Is that such a bad thing?

---

[4] Name withheld. Friend in Texas, USA. Personal correspondence. April 2015.

Knowing some church history, I know for some this view would be extremely offensive. The world we live in today is sadly not short of those ready to burn heretics. Such extremes are fortunately no longer a part of our culture. The State no longer sanctions the burnings, but such thinking is still out there.

The "infinite exceptions" I can well relate to also. I began to think of them as a teenager. The topic is huge, so I will come back to this particular detail later.

It is well over 35 years since I read the final book in the Narnia series (The Last Battle). I don't recall the tent at the end. From the comment about all being at the dance, I suspect it ties in with the idea of being able to access heaven, but for whatever reason, staying out through personal choice.

I've not read the dance book, referred to by my friend. I have to wonder if it refers to a Kingdom of God theology placing the Kingdom of God in the very here and now for all of us. This "here and now" of the Kingdom is made possible because we have the Holy Spirit.

The presence of God within us in the here and now means the Kingdom is here and now. If we struggle with this concept, is it only because we haven't learnt to dance?

I know I struggle with such a concept. I have no firm conclusion, but I understand the logic. It is compelling. For all I know, thinking of the reference to a tent above, it may be only a tent flap separating me from a much greater reality.

To be fair, I probably do need to learn to dance better. I may be enrolled in those lessons now, without knowing it. I'm sure God is working on me all the time, and in ways I'm not aware of.

The reference to the rejection of a child could link well with a response from those who think the Gospel cannot be rejected. Can a child really reject us when healed of all the wrong thinking causing such rejection?

The point of adoption I understand. I do see adoption as a condition occurring after one has received and accepted the Gospel. We are focusing here more on the context of coming to accept the Gospel, before we are saved, or whether it is possible to reject such an invitation to be saved.

In summary, I think my friend is saying heaven will be open to everyone at the very end, but some may refuse to enter. They think they can't dance, using the analogy again to which he referred.

Before we decide such a concept cannot hope to have Biblical support, consider the following scripture from the Book of Revelation:

"Blessed are those who wash their robes, that they may have the right to the tree of life and may go through the gates into the city. Outside are the dogs, those who practice magic arts, the sexually immoral, the murderers, the idolaters and everyone who loves and practices falsehood. **Revelation 22:14-15** (NIV)

Those verses above from Revelation chapter 22 have the potential to throw a huge curve ball at many theologies out there. The reason I say this is simple. These verses occur right before the closing comments in the very last chapter, in the last book of the Bible.

In theory, this takes place after the new heavens and new earth is established. This is the time when

God is reigning finally on earth in the New Jerusalem, which was brought down from heaven.

In such a setting, there are still evil doers, right at the end of the story. They would seem to exist outside the New Jerusalem.

Such verses could beg many questions. Many questions, yes - not necessarily firm conclusions!

The linear thinking we employ while reading scripture can make us assume the timing in scripture. Such timing may not have been in the inspired mind of the writer, whose thinking may not have been so linear. Still, I cannot escape the reference to the city right at the end of the Bible, which I assume is the New Jerusalem.

Is the space outside the city a lake of fire? I don't know. Maybe the expectation is all those outside the city will eventually wash their robes and enter. Who knows?

I do know such verses create a tension between what some of us may think we understand, and the ultimate reality. This tension can only be good for all of us. I suspect none of us have a clear picture and perfect theology.

In the meantime, my friend's unintentional advice to get out and start dancing is playing very much on my mind....

The third and final sundry reply was as follows:

Sadly, human propagation of the gospel has often had more of a flavor of conquest than invitation but from the beginning it has been an invitation to be accepted or rejected. Those who accept it and are transformed into the divine nature of love, always sacrificing self for other as demonstrated on the Cross, inherit Heaven. Those who reject it, who wish to do what they want to do rather than subject themselves to the needs of others, choose Hell.

That wording is important. Although there is an undeniable punitive element to what the scriptures say about Hell, we often do a Satan act and turn around to blame it on God - as if He has cast us there because we broke His arbitrary rules. I believe it was in a dialogue with Saint Faustina that God said He never sends anyone to Hell; all who go there choose it. The best description I have for Hell is the place where everyone does what they want to do. God offers Heaven to those who are willing to live its lifestyle of sacrificial love. Those who choose not to, go to the place which is not Heaven, the place where people do not self-sacrifice but do what they want. That separation from God is the second death and the place is Hell.

The thought is frightening. A place where everyone does what they want. They can inflict any pain, any sexual desire, take anything, say anything, do anything. Power to the powerful who destroy their own selves by their oppression and in a place where humans are no longer the top of the food chain - where demons can do what they want as they destroy their own selves, too. And in this horror, death cannot be an escape because we are already dead and there is no hope of it ever getting better as it is an eternal judgment. What a horrifying thought!

So God offers Heaven to all through the Gospel even if only at the hour of death. All are free to accept that gospel and choose a life of love in the abode of Heaven or they can reject it and go to the place where everyone does what they want.[5]

---

[5] Name withheld. Friend in Maine, USA. Personal correspondence. April 2015

I've thought at length on whether I should have condensed the above reply. In the end I thought it would be selfish to keep it all to myself. What he shares is detailed and well thought out. He offers a great deal to think about.

He makes no mention of hell fire, which is fine by me. Few seemed to want to refer to it. I can imagine he views the concept of hell fire as an allegory, more than something to be taken literally. He may not too. That is perfectly fair and reasonable in my mind.

We have imagery from Jesus speaking of both fires of hell, and also "outer darkness". It would make sense to draw the conclusion that some form of allegorical interpretation is appropriate.

The concept of hell as a place where people do what they want is a good description of many of the worst places on earth today. One could argue the Kingdom of God, and Heaven, is available now, as is Hell.

Many people create sadly their own private hell through substance abuse, as just one example. I'm not so sure they are all totally responsible for their choices. Neither am I convinced they are all "free" to do otherwise. Free choice may exist in the framework and boundaries defined by ones slavery to personal stupidity. Does free choice exist beyond such boundaries for the addicted? I'm not so sure it does.

An earlier reply referred to being healed of our ungodly dysfunction that would have us reject God. I do certainly see much of mankind under this form of bondage. It reminds me of comments made by the Apostle Paul:

For the creation was subjected to frustration, not by its own choice, but by the will of the one who subjected it, in hope that the creation itself will be liberated from its bondage to decay and brought into the freedom and glory of the children of God. **Romans 8:20-21** (NIV)

Paul is talking about the whole created realm, and not just mankind, in his comments above. Still, mankind does come under the same banner of "creation" in my view. I recognise human dysfunction as part of the above "frustration".

Perhaps I have the advantage of knowing a number of alcoholics and other substance abusers? I might have free choice, but I've known many with harmful addictions who don't. I'm not making excuses for them. I'm just speaking from the painful experience of some I've known.

Part of the Gospel is we can and will be freed from such bondage. Until we are set free, this verse from Romans 8 seems to be implying our bondage to dysfunction was ordained by God from the time of Adam. We had no choice in the matter.

So, my friend above, who thinks of Hell as a place of choice, may find healing may be available for those who might make such a choice. Is the choice for hell then something that can be reversed? I hope so. I know my friend would be thrilled to learn if such was to be the case. We are both free to differ in our conclusions, and still hold each other in great respect.

His thinking is influenced very much by philosophy surrounding free choice. As I stated earlier, free choice is a topic I still need to come back to.

Regardless of who is right or wrong, the current reality is many today are choosing to live in various forms of "hell" in the here and now. This is regardless of how free or not free they are to choose otherwise.

There is another point I want to raise from the meaty discourse above. This is the reference to people not having death as an option of escape as they are already dead.

"You cannot die, as you are already dead!"

It almost seems contradictory, but if we think of a person as composed of spirit, body, and soul, then it is perhaps not so strange. The argument would be the body and soul can die, but the spirit of a man will live on.

Those who believe in eternal torment as a punishment will subscribe to this theory or something similar. Those who believe in death as a punishment, but with no consciousness beyond that death, will not hold to such a theory.

I'm sure there are scriptures which can lend apparent support to either approach. The distinction will be made then based on our philosophical leanings and how we know God.

As a closing comment to this section, I want to stress again how I in no way mean to denigrate anyone and their perspectives.

The scriptures have been given to us to interpret and unpack for nearly 2000 years now. That is if we look at the New Testament. The Old Testament has been with us for much longer.

In my view, some of the greatest crimes committed in church history stem from those who thought they had the final word on a subject and were the ultimate authority on truth.

I don't wish to join the ranks of those so self-assured by their own scholarship; they would persecute those who saw things differently.

10: What The Hell?

Now is probably as good a time as any to unpack the subject of hell in a little more detail.

I pulled up every reference to "hell" in the King James Version on my e-Sword software (Meyers). I narrowed my initial search to the New Testament. In the book of Matthew, I found 9 mentions of "hell". All but 2 came from the Greek word "Gehenna" which I've already referred to as relating to the Valley of Tophet. The other two uses of the word came from the Greek word "Hades".

All up there are twenty three uses made of the word "hell" in the King James Version. Fifteen are in Matthew, Mark, and Luke. No mention is made in the Gospel of John. The book of Acts, and the Epistles have four mentions, and the book of Revelation also has four.

Of the twenty three occurrences, twelve are from the Greek word "Gehenna". Eleven of these specific "Gehenna" references are in the Gospels, and the one outlier is in the epistle of James. It does seem that Jesus had more to say about Gehenna than anyone else.

Hades

All together, "Hades" - the Greek word translated as hell, occurs 10 times in the New Testament. As with Gehenna, this word needs some explaining. Vine (Vine 527-528) states it is sometimes translated as "the grave" in place of the word "hell". He describes Hades as:

"...the region of departed spirits of the lost (but including the blessed dead in periods preceding the Ascension of Christ)." (Vine 527)

Vine believes the word never denotes "the grave". He also believes it is not a place of permanent abode for the dead. Rather, in his view it is a temporary place before the judgement fire of Gehenna (Vine 528). He doesn't explain why he has a problem with translating Hades as "the grave". It may be a translation as "grave" can diminish the impact of the message he perceives Jesus giving. "Hell" has more punch, if one views hell from a traditional standpoint. His own personal theology may be evident here.

He also has a problem with the translation of "Hades" as "grave" in 1 Cor 15:55 (Vine 528):

O death, where is thy sting? O grave, where is thy victory? **1 Corinthians 15:55** (KJV)

"Grave" can be simply a place where a body is buried, with no significance to punishment, or consciousness in that punishment. I understand some Christians view death as a state of unconsciousness.

112

I suspect Vine views death as a state of consciousness, away from the body. This view is essential for the doctrine of burning forever in hell. If he is passionate about such an idea, then it may explain why he does not approve of a translation which does not lend support for his personal perspective.

The temporary nature of Hades in the view of Vine gives an explanation of the opposing perspectives of fire versus darkness. The place of darkness referred to by Jesus could be Hades, prior to the place of fire, which is Gehenna.

Is it possible the conclusions of Vine are shaped by the doctrines he grew up believing? Only further research could prove or support such a concept.

I understand we can carry the bias of our upbringing into all manner of scholarship. The emphatic nature of Vine's writing in no way serves to prove he is right. He may be, but also, he may not be.

The Unseen Place

I never would have carried this thought deeper if I hadn't recently had a good talk with a friend, Barry Tattersall, who is now a retired Pastor in Geelong, Victoria.

He kept referring to "hell" as "the unseen place". His reference to such a term made me remember how I'd seen that word "unseen" in my Strong's Concordance (Strong) under the reference to "Hades".

By my understanding of what Strong is saying in his concordance, the word Hades comes from another word with a negative meaning of "unseen". Strong simply explains Hades then as:

"properly unseen, that is, "Hades" or the place (state) of departed souls:- grave, hell" (Strong G86).

From this I can see how Barry simply would translate it as "the unseen place". Anything buried in a grave is hidden, or unseen.

In my previous reference to Vine and his perspective, Vine wanted to make "hell" or "hades" a very specific reference to a place where departed souls dwell. Most likely Vine would have those souls conscious in this place called Hades. Such a place is very distinct, as opposed to any old hole in the ground which was used as a grave to hide or bury a body.

My friend Barry was keen to not allow any added meanings to the word Hades which would come from the perceived doctrines or theologies out there. He wanted to stick with the original simplest meaning of the word, rather than embellish it with theology.

This is subjective. If the correct translation really was just "the unseen place", it really would not take away from any particular theology. It just would not support it.

Barry I know says he cannot be totally certain but he leans towards the view souls in Hades after death are not conscious. As with all of us, his view of a translation is shaped by his underlying beliefs. He would be happy to admit this. I'm not so certain others would.

This is one of the reasons why I respect Barry and his perspectives so much. He understands he doesn't have the final word.

Barry supports his perspective on the meaning of Hades by explaining in his blog (Tattersall) how the English word Hell comes from the Saxon word "helan", which means "to cover" or "to hide". We see similar derivatives of this Saxon word in the English word "helmet". A helmet covers or hides the head.

What I draw from all this is Hades or Hell can be a place that really does refer to a grave or hole in the ground where something has been buried. Saying that, It can also be a place where conscious dead people dwell, if such really is how God has designed the afterlife.

Take your pick. Many already have. We will lean one way or the other depending on what we believe.

We may not even lean. We may simply be happy to say we just don't know. This makes perfect sense to me.

Tartarus.

There is one final Greek word often translated as "hell". I've not mentioned this one yet. This word is "Tartaroo". Vine says it is neither Hades, Hell, or Sheol. Rather, it is a place of incarceration for demonic spirits. They are waiting there for judgment.

For if God did not spare angels when they sinned, but sent them to hell, putting them in chains of darkness to be held for judgment; **2 Peter 2:4** (NIV)

This Greek word "Tartaroo" is usually translated as "Tartarus" in English. In many translations of the Bible it is still translated as "hell".

I've heard a number of people give testimonies on their after-death experiences. Such experiences come about from various events. Some die on an operating table, and then later come back to life, as just one example. Not everyone has spiritual encounters. Some people simply say they experienced nothing at all while they were dead. Those who did certainly have a story to share.

Some tell stories about how they got to visit hell. None of the stories I've heard have referred to seeing the classic eternal fire type of hell. If a visit to hell was on the itinerary, it was always the hell of darkness. Usually they got to speak to some of the beings there.

I used the term "beings" as I don't know if those they encountered were really dead people, or demons. Everyone who experienced this visit to hell always interpreted it from their understanding of what hell represents. They always assumed anyone they spoke to there had to be departed people, and not simply demons.

I don't know who or what they were talking to in hell. I do understand it is possible they were speaking to demons incarcerated in Tartarus. They were not aware of this possibility as their traditional heaven/hell theology did not include Tartarus as an option. It did not exist in their understanding, so they interpreted their experience through a lens of more limited understanding.

The important point I'm making here is if we want to use these after death experiences to shape our view of life after death, it would help to include

Tartarus as part of the bigger picture. Some assume these experiences do serve as proof of eternal conscious suffering for people after death. I would suggest an understanding of the existence of Tartarus should render such "proof" as questionable.

We can find further scriptural support for the concept of this place of incarceration for fallen angels in the Epistle of Jude:

> *And the angels who did not keep their positions of authority but abandoned their proper dwelling--these he has kept in darkness, bound with everlasting chains for judgment on the great Day.* **Jude 6** (NIV)

This in my mind does support the view Tartarus is a place of incarceration for demons.

Sheol.

One may recall the brief mention of "Sheol" under the topic of Tartarus. Vine made mention of the term when he said Tartarus was not to be confused with Hades, hell, or Sheol (Vine 553). In some ways, this word represents the elephant in the room.

Sheol is the Hebrew word in the Old Testament translated as Hades when a Greek translation was made of the Old Testament. This happened before the time of Jesus. This Greek translation of the Old Testament is known as the Septuagint.

The King James Version of the Bible translates Sheol as "hell" thirty one times in the Old Testament. Maybe it isn't really an elephant in the room, if the New

Testament refers to hell twenty three times in a much smaller volume.

Still, the Old Testament covers a time span of perhaps 4000 years, in comparison with the seventy to ninety year span of the New Testament (depending on when one wants to date the writing of Revelation).

Sometimes it was translated as "the grave" in the Old Testament. I did a rough count and came up with thirty one instances. The last thing I want to do is get bogged down in word studies when the main subject is The Good News.

Let it suffice to say one will view Sheol as a term equating perfectly with a classical heaven/hell theology if one really wants to. If one doesn't, it can be viewed as a hole in the ground dug to receive bodies of the dead. My friend Barry gave me some insights on this, as explained previously.

The word is used poetically a number of times in the Old Testament. In my view, trying to get it to have a rigid specific meaning is a pointless exercise. There is no sound academic support for such rigidity.

Some may disagree, but I really think we are too far removed from the original writing of the Old Testament to really know with any honest certainty. We can kid ourselves we know, but are we intellectually honest if we do?

I really like the Old Testament words of Job:

If only you would hide me in the grave and conceal me till your anger has passed! If only you would set me a time and then remember me! **Job 14:13** (NIV)

The Hebrew word translated as "grave" in the above verse is "sheol". Job doesn't seem to have any concern for such a place as one of punishment. He does refer to it as a place of concealment and hiding. I won't say this is a final proof of anything, but it does give food for thought.

Somehow, I think the Good News will manage to stand apart from any petty arguments over the meanings of certain specific words. I think I'm happy to stand on this statement as an act of faith. Surely Jesus, the inspiration of the Bible, is much bigger than our petty wrangling.

How cool if we found out he was?

11: Do We Need Good News?

I've examined some foundational issues surrounding the story of the Gospel. I'm ready to return to the core subject at hand. This subject is "good news", but do we all need it?

Are there some who don't need it?

Is good news only relevant to a few of us?

The Crutch Of The Matter.

I've heard people refer to Christianity and faith in God as a crutch. In their minds it is no different from dependency on something like alcohol. If we cope with life through our relationship with Jesus, we are no different from one who copes with life through a bottle. Or so goes the thinking.

Jesus made an interesting statement in regards to this:

While Jesus was having dinner at Matthew's house, many tax collectors and sinners came and ate with him and his disciples. When the Pharisees saw this, they asked his disciples, "Why does your teacher eat with tax collectors and sinners?"

On hearing this, Jesus said, "It is not the healthy who need a doctor, but the sick. But go and learn what this means: 'I desire mercy, not sacrifice.' For I have not come to call the righteous, but sinners." **Matthew 9:10-13** (NIV)

Jesus said he came for the sick – those who needed him. He was being figurative in referring to himself as a doctor. Did it mean others didn't need him? Probably not.

He said he came to call sinners – not the righteous. No one really was righteous. All were sinners in Jesus' day, just like today. Some however thought they were pretty good. They were righteous in their own eyes, and for some, particularly so. A religious group called the Pharisees certainly did think this way, and it was to them Jesus was specifically directing his point.

The Pharisees had fallen into the trap of thinking by their religion they could achieve goodness, or righteousness. Another way to put it is by their own efforts they thought they could be good – good enough to please God.

They weren't. They failed just like anyone else who mistakenly thinks religion and self-effort can impress God.

I'll extend this to the modern day. We live in a very secular society. I do in Australia, anyway. Most don't think about God, let alone think they need him. Most have found they can do quite well without any need for God. This isn't a criticism. It is just an observation.

If Jesus came today, I suspect the majority of those he would reach and minister to would be those who were not so self-confident in their day-to-day living.

In essence, Jesus has come today. He's come in the shape of the Church, or the people of God - Christians - those who know him as Lord. As with those he reached 2000 years ago, Jesus is still reaching those who know they need God. They only know as he has revealed to them their need.

Do the vast majority today, who don't know Jesus as their Lord and saviour, really have no need for God?

Certainly many think they don't. They will likely be very honest about the fact life does present challenges to them, as with everybody. I dare say most would look back on their lives and see how they have managed with former challenges, without God's help. Once again, this is not a criticism.

Why think we won't get by without him next time? This question does make perfect sense to me.

I could argue God allows everyone enough reason to not seek him, unless he has decided it is their time for being called. The imperfections in the Church throughout history have sometimes served this purpose well. Who would want to be like those Christians?

One doesn't need knowledge of Church history to come up with a reason to not want to be a Christian. There is at times enough scandal amongst those who call themselves Christians to provide every excuse, as with any group of people of any persuasion. I have no objective reason to exclusively mention the Church in this respect.

Still, at any point in time, some will be in the process of learning they do need God. Jesus would be in the process of calling them. He would be waking them up to their need.

Over time, they would become Christians. This process has been in constant play since the time when Jesus died for us, some 2000 years ago.

Neither Church history, nor contemporary church scandal will matter to those who are waking up to their need. They will know they need a God who is way above, and the answer, for their human failings on this earth.

They may even be aware their own shortcomings are every reason to not judge others for their particular shortcomings. And so the church which Jesus founded some 2000 years ago will continue to grow. Human foibles will never stand in the way of God's purpose.

So is Christianity a crutch?

Sure!

I've no qualms saying it is. So is water and food, if I think about it. My family is also, and my friends. I don't want to live without them. Life is so much better this way. There's nothing I need to prove.

Least Resistance.

When Jesus said he came for the sick and sinners, it wasn't because he doesn't love those who are "well". He does. Neither was it because there are those who are not sinners, who somehow God doesn't like as much as he likes sinners. Every one begins this life as a sinner, and God loves us all.

I could argue at this time God is taking the line of least resistance. Could one say he is reaching for the low hanging fruit? Maybe.

This would not be as God finds it hard to call anyone and convert their thinking. The conversion of Saul of Tarsus, in the book of Acts, is a classic case in point.

Saul was a Pharisee (one of a particular religious sect), and extremely zealous for his cause. He hated Christians with a passion. He saw them as a serious threat to his religion. Saul loved his religion, and he didn't want to lose it.

His zeal for his religion and the god who he thought he served was so great; he presided over the death of any Christian on whom he could lay his hands

Two issues were in play with Saul. The first was his passion for his religion. The second was the zeal with which he persecuted Christians. Both points would present serious resistance to an effort to convert him, or change his thinking.

It isn't easy for anyone to admit they are wrong. It would have to be so much harder for Saul to admit he was wrong about his religion and God. The blood of so many Christians was on his hands. Still, nothing is too hard for God. This was good news for Saul.

Jesus met Saul on the road to Damascus. The presence of God was so great, Saul could not even put up a token resistance. He caved totally. The rest is history.

Jesus even changed his name from Saul to Paul. The most ardent enemy of Jesus became his most vocal advocate. Paul became responsible for more of the New Testament than any other writer. The impact of this man is with us to this day. God has been using Paul for nearly 2000 years now.

So, I rest my case, knowing one example doesn't make for ultimate proof of anything. For those already called by Jesus, I think they understand the point I'm making. I've not yet met any Christian who can think of anyone who Jesus could not convert. The idea would be silly.

Still, we read in Paul's first letter to the Corinthians:

> *For the foolishness of God is wiser than human wisdom, and the weakness of God is stronger than human strength.*
> *Brothers and sisters, think of what you were when you were called. Not many of you were wise by human standards; not many were influential; not many were of noble birth. But God chose the foolish things of the world to shame the wise; God chose the weak things of the world to shame the strong.* **1 Corinthians 1:25-27.** (NIV)

Does this sound like low hanging fruit? It does to me. It really does appear in this present age of the Church, God is primarily choosing to call those who are easier to call – the weak of the world. They are those more likely to understand they need God, particularly with his prompting.

Why would he do this? Why discriminate? Surely every cancer scare proves we all need God in the end?

Perhaps what God is doing is allowing our fallen nature, without God, plenty of room to prove itself.

126

Prove what?

Well, maybe what it proves is ultimately the best mankind can come up with, without God, really isn't so great. It does seem God has desired to make this point throughout the past 2000 years of church history. God doesn't have to prove it to us. We prove it ourselves.

We have two stories taking place in parallel throughout time since Jesus came and died for us.

One story is of mankind without God. It's a story of hell on earth for most participants, by my way of thinking. It was the only story before Jesus came.

The second story is one of the Church – the followers of Jesus. They weren't perfect. Indeed, many claiming they were Christians may not have been at all. Whatever their weaknesses, as Paul referred to above, they changed the world for the better. I illustrated this briefly earlier in this work, when I referred to the impact of Christianity on human history.

The wise of this world

So here we are in this current age, with two stories unfolding. It's obvious to me many people have little control over their lives. This is particularly so for those without God.

Some of our greatest economic minds are at this very moment working on a strategy for managing a global debt problem. Their solution is to solve the problem with more debt. Go figure! We even pay them six figure salaries to preside over such brilliance.

Our greatest minds are thinking the best way to solve an addiction to credit is to feed it more. Mankind has really come a long way, haven't we?

Publicly, they maintain a facade of being in control. They have to, as so many look to them for guidance or reassurance our pension plans are intact and will be when we retire.

They are not really in control. How could a small group of financial sages hope to be in control of animal spirits which can drive financial markets into nightmare scenarios?

2008 and the heat of the Global Financial Crisis proved this, yet do they want to hear the good news about Jesus from me? How about from someone else? Dare I suggest we know the answer to this question?

Do they need the good news? I'd say they do as much as the worst of us. Odds are they just don't realise how great their need is. Often we don't.

I sometimes think of the "greats" of this world in history. They don't have to be good people - just "great". They'd be the people of power and influence.

Maybe "great" is not the best word to describe them. Could they be referred to as the "wise"? It depends how we measure wisdom. Maybe "those with huge egos" is the best descriptor? The "Elite" may be the simplest term.

If I consider a man called Hermann Goring, I have a good example. He was a decorated German fighter pilot in World War 1. Somehow he had enough political skill to land a plum job in Hitler's Nazi Germany. He was clever enough to get right up close to Adolf Hitler – a despot who was for a short time the most powerful man in Europe.

Goring had a huge ego. He loved to dress the part. A smart uniform, with lots of medals, and shiny boots was how he liked to be seen. He witnessed the loss of everything the Nazi war machine achieved (?) in Europe in the 1940's. Did he learn anything from it?

From what I read of his circus act at the Nuremburg Trials after World War Two, there was no contrition in the man. His dealings with prison guards reflected a man who still had a huge ego. He was proud to his very end.

There was no pride left in his dead body. He left us with his body hanging on a rope in his prison cell.

If one is known by his entrance and exit, the exit of Goering was a clear statement. It's how I will always remember him – pathetic in his own self-delusion.

Many, for at least a short time may have considered him to be a great man. Was he so great after all? Was he so great at the end of his story?

I have to wonder if his story is any different from any of the world's "greats" in history. Joseph Stalin was likely responsible for the deaths of well over twenty million of his own people. It takes a lot of influence to drum up a morbid tally like that.

How well did he present for his end? All I know of his passing is how he finished in the same state as those he had murdered.

We don't have to think of tyrants to illustrate my point. Steve Jobs created the largest company this world has ever known – Apple. By the time this book is published it may no longer be so. Nothing is forever.

Steve was probably a contemporary great man in the minds of many of us today. Only time will tell how long his legacy will last. Like most, it won't endure forever.

If we'd been with Steve in his last hours, I don't think any of us would have wanted to trade places with him. At that point, his wealth didn't matter. Neither did his influence, which at one time was huge.

Steve was in serious need of everything the Gospel of Jesus Christ represents for all mankind.

No matter how the world views any of us, we cannot escape the truth we were all born to die. As with Steve Jobs, any of us could succumb to a debilitating disease.

My own father was a doctor. His greatest fear was he would contract Parkinson's Disease. I'm so glad he didn't. He knew too well how humiliating an experience it is for anyone who suffers from it.

There is minimal greatness to perceive in anyone with Parkinson's Disease. They might look back on what they thought they achieved as great. Maybe their former glory would be written in history. Nevertheless, the disease would be foremost in their mind now – nothing to shout about. A disease like Parkinson's is a great leveller.

Death itself is the ultimate leveller. So far, no great or wise person has ever escaped it. I know plenty have wanted to. Imagine if they did! How long would it be, before the man-made hell of any age contemporary to them woke them up to thinking maybe they'd rather take the escape death might offer? I can only wonder.

The average seventy years of mankind seems way too short for most of us. Would an extra hundred years tacked on make us see things a little differently?

Maybe not for the few with power, money, and influence. What about the rest of us?

Would most of us be crying out for good news from somewhere?

12: What Choice Do We Have?

Remember that you were slaves in Egypt and that the Lord your God brought you out of there with a mighty hand and an outstretched arm. **Deuteronomy 5:15** (NIV)

So you are no longer a slave, but God's child; and since you are his child, God has made you also an heir. Formerly, when you did not know God, you were slaves to those who by nature are not gods. **Galatians 4:7-8** (NIV)

"But the less aware we are of our philosophical assumptions, the more they control our thinking." (Walls and Dongell 19)

Dinner For Six.

Some years ago Jane and I had a tradition of catching up with 2 other couples with which we were friends. It was an annual catch-up to which we always looked forward.

In keeping with tradition, everyone at the table had a turn to talk about the previous year. I can't recall exactly, but I do remember I was one of the last to open up. Other details followed; details Jane and I would never forget.

The night had been going really well. It always does with close friends. The food, wine, and company were excellent. Why would it be different this time?

I was always known to be a thinker. Up till then I'd never had reason to believe it was a problem for any of us. They certainly knew I was harmless. Didn't they?

Well... how do I put this?

Thinking can present problems... even amongst friends, it would seem.

I happened to mention I had been thinking about what happened in the Garden of Eden. I said how it was interesting the Tree of the Knowledge of Good and Evil was positioned smack bang in the middle of the garden. Adam and Eve could not miss it. It was always under their nose. If God really didn't want them to take of this tree, why put it right under their noses? Why not off somewhere on the perimeter?

I'm sure these were not the exact words I used. It was some years ago now after all. If anyone reading this now is feeling triggered, please do let me know as it could mean my memory still serves me at least somewhat well.

The reaction from 3 of the 4 friends with whom Jane and I were sharing the meal was something I won't forget. It was explosive, to put it mildly.

Apparently, what I'd said threatened the whole fabric of "Free Choice Doctrine". I never knew till then there was such a doctrine. Clearly there was, and I had somehow stumbled upon it. I'd talked my way onto holy ground, with no idea I had no business to be there, let alone ask questions about it.

I'm sure I wasn't wearing stilettos. I'm not that kind of guy. There was a look of rage however, evident in the eyes of my 3 deeply-offended friends. One could be forgiven for thinking a stiletto had stabbed right in the middle of this up-until-then unknown (for me) "holy" doctrine.

It was clearly painful. The stiletto was not only sharp, it was also long. It sliced oh-so deep. I didn't mean to cause so much pain. I was only thinking out loud with some friends.

The look in my eyes was surely one of shock. I was caught totally off guard. Nevertheless I did my best to mount a rear-guard defence of the point I was making and why it was actually a fair and even rational question to be asking. My friends did not want to know for some reason. Questions on this topic were verboten, or at least had to be vetted before they could be tabled.

The only thing missing in their protest was the outstretched arms with appended crucifixes. I should count myself lucky. Had I been spat on by a Roman?

So the night went off with a bang. To this day I still wonder why. I think it was something about a doctrine I'd never heard of, let alone read about in my Bible. This is not to say it isn't in there. I just hadn't seen it or been taught on it. Needless to say it was the last time; sadly, we ever saw that small group of friends. Religion does at times impact us in ways both tragic and unexpected.

Clearly I needed to know about "free choice". Until I did, for me not even the fires of Hell were of sufficient heat for my ill-considered thinking!

The Disclaimer

And so we have as good a time as any to consider the thorny issue of free choice. I did say I would come back to it earlier in the book. I now understand it as a vital part of any discussion on the Gospel of Jesus Christ. I know I didn't some years ago, as the previous story illustrates. I had much to learn. I only hope in doing so I don't learn there is never a good time to consider this subject.

For some, "free choice" or "free will" is central to the Gospel message of Jesus. If it is, why on earth is such a topic so thorny? I'm almost scared to offer suggestions. I'm only grateful it doesn't make me trigger like it does some.

Before I go any further, I do have to state I in no way think free choice is something which does not exist. I'm sure it does. I just don't know why someone has created a doctrine around it. I can understand doctrines surrounding subjects like salvation, love, grace, sanctification, faith, baptism and all manner of subjects one can find clearly stated in scripture. These are important topics, and the Bible clearly refers to these topics by name.

Incredible as it may seem, the Bible does not mention free choice or free will by name anywhere. This is not in itself a proof of a subject's insignificance. It really isn't. Still, I'd been reading the Bible for some 30 years before I'd ever heard of a doctrine of free choice. I never knew anyone needed one, and had always done fine without one.

My background was certainly not Calvinist. It's important I mention this as Calvinism is known for a non-free-choice focus. If my friends had not triggered, apparently I would have never known I'd even entered such a minefield. I could have walked on out of the minefield and never known I'd been there.

To this day, I've never heard a sermon on the topic of free choice. This I find interesting as I've been sitting in churches for some years now where I am aware the ministers do think about it and view free choice as significant to their Christian world view. Given the interest at least some of my Christian friends (and ex-friends?) have on the subject, why doesn't anyone make it the central topic in a message in church? I'm sure someone has somewhere. I only wish I'd been there when they did.

If it is central to the Gospel message, why have I never heard a message in Church about it?

What Is Free Choice?

With my disclaimer behind me, I'd best dive into the nitty gritty of the topic.

Now I've started looking at it, I've learned free choice, or free will, is one of the deepest rabbit holes I know of in Christian thinking. Perhaps it reaches beyond Christian thinking too. Before I go much deeper, I need to put forward a definition. I think the one put forward by Peterson and Williams is pretty good:

"The ability to choose the contrary or its equivalent." (Peterson and Williams 117)

They further refer to an author by the name of William Hasker who stated free choice was having the power to perform an action or refrain from an action. (Peterson and Williams 117)

Hasker's definition is really just another way of saying what Peterson and Williams said.

I wish to put my own words to this, to give some further clarity in a Christian context. I'm not saying Hasker, Peterson, or Williams don't give their definitions in a Christian context. I just wish to zoom in somewhat.

How about these:

- "Free choice is the ability or power to do something or its direct opposite."
- "Free choice is the ability or power to do either right, or wrong."
- "Free choice is the ability or power to sin or not sin."

Of itself, such a definition seems fine to me, and many years ago I would have simply said "so what?" if someone tried to explain to me what it was. It had no bearing on critical aspects of my thinking as a Christian. If someone had told me I needed to have a doctrine on the subject I would have needed a good reason why. After all, what did free choice have to do with the good news of the Gospel?

This is where it starts to get interesting. Only in the last 15 years or so have I learned some Christians think free choice is a central issue in the subject of the Gospel. It is central by the perspective free choice is part of what God has given mankind as part of his expression of love for mankind. Some believe having free will is critical to us being able to have a meaningful relationship with God. It is an interesting concept. The counter claim is often made how without free choice we are nothing but robots! Maybe it's true!

If it is true free choice is critical for a meaningful relationship with God, we need to look more closely at what it is. To look more closely, there in nothing better than concrete examples to make sure I'm clear with the definition. If free choice is essentially the ability to do either right or wrong, how does it look if we consider the following:

- "Free choice is the ability or power to steal or not steal."
- "Free choice is the ability or power to curse God or not curse God."
- "Free choice is the ability or power to lie or not lie."
- "Free choice is the ability or power to do drugs or not do drugs."
- "Free choice is the ability or power to be an alcoholic, or not be an alcoholic."
- "Free choice is the ability or power to be depressed, or not be depressed."
- "Free choice is the ability or power to be a paedophile or not be a paedophile."
- "Free choice is the ability or power to murder or not murder."

My apologies for referring to the darker aspects of human nature as my list progressed. I'm trying to thoroughly test the definition here. If this is free choice, is this really something critical to a sound relationship with God? One could even ask if it is critical to a meaningful relationship with anyone. If so, is it really a subject to defend from questioning and rational thought at the cost of friendships?

I can understand I want the ability or power to not murder, to not be a paedophile, and to not do drugs. But do I really want the opposite ability or power to do those things?

Would it not be better to just have the power to refrain from evil? Why would anyone of sound mind want empowerment to engage in evil? Does lacking this make me a robot? Does having self-control by which I don't engage in such behaviour, really mean I am nothing but a robot?

Does an ability to act in an evil manner really bring sound meaning to our relationship with God, or anyone else?

Maybe those who hold dearly to a doctrine of free choice are really just like me? They don't want the empowerment to engage in evil, equal to the empowerment to refrain. It almost seems strange to raise such a point, but I do because some I know hold free choice up on a pedestal. They tell me free choice is something special God has given us.

I'm not saying free choice is something I don't think exists. To be alive after all does mean we have a certain degree of free agency and creative ability. I'm just not certain it is something we should look upon as a gift from God like faith, grace, or eternal life.

Maybe the theologians with their particular definition of free choice or free will are at odds with the laity?

If I'm trying to nail down a clear and simple definition for free choice, I do need to make sure I've not just adopted a definition from theologians the common man would never consider.

Maybe when non-theological-type Christians think of free choice, they think of something other than what the theologians say it is. Perhaps the laity only think of the positive side of free choice, much like me, and see no need for the negative?

If I only have ability to refrain from evil, does this mean I don't have free choice?

Even worse, does this mean I am a robot?

If this is so, is this so bad? Rather than an ability to sin, I really want an ability to just not sin – to never sin. Why would I want it otherwise? Is not this the same as having self-control and sound character?

When I think of my friends at the dinner for six, they must have been thinking about the choice Adam and Eve made to eat the fruit from The Tree of the Knowledge of Good and Evil. Choice was between eating, in defiance of God, or not eating, in obedience to God.

From this, a laity view of free choice is one can either obey or disobey God. I can't be certain this is how everyone thinks when free choice is mentioned in sermons or whatever. A concern I have is many Christians wouldn't be able to say what it is if they were ever asked, even if they are ready to claim it is somehow important and sacred to them in their walk with God.

To make sure, I simply messaged a number of friends who I knew did not have a theology degree. I wanted to find out what they could say was their definition of free choice.

They all came back to me with answers basically in line with the theological view. To double check I asked if they agreed the theological definition I had was acceptable to them, after they gave me their initial definition. Everyone agreed free choice was the power or ability to do something or its direct opposite.

I won't say I have conclusive proof most people in churches will understand free choice in the terms I've been exploring here. I do suspect 99% would probably still agree with the definition I gave to my friends above. I can't think of a reason why anyone wouldn't.

Whatever the definition, we still need to determine if free choice merits a place on the mantelpiece of Gospel thinking. We will unpack this further in this chapter. For some it is clearly important.

I'll now move on from the basics of defining the term and wander deeper into the rabbit hole. Who knows what I might find?

Do I hear "Robots!"?

Why So Curious?

The topic of free choice or free will is a curiosity for me as I've ministered to so many who don't have free choice in so many critical areas of their lives. Alcohol addiction is one area as an example and also things like anger and plain simple demonisation. These people suffer with conditions whereby they need outside intervention to break free. They are not free to free themselves without help.

This fits well with points made in Romans 8 about being controlled by the flesh. I see it everywhere, and particularly in my volunteer and paid work with troubled youth. As soon as they are told to just exercise their free will they come under more condemnation as they know how messed up they are.

On the flip side of the coin, looking at one example of human weakness, I am fortunate to not suffer from alcoholism. I am free of this problem. In fact, I am so free; I find it hard to understand how I could have free will to be an alcoholic. It is something; fortunately, I can't bring myself to do. This lines up with Romans 8 where it speaks of being controlled by the Spirit of God.

Please don't get me wrong. Just because I can proclaim I am not an alcoholic, it does not mean I'm somehow free of all human vices. I'm not, and no one I know is. Such is the nature of mankind, even if one is born again and thereby a Christian. By the grace of God I don't have this problem, and I'm grateful I don't.

Maybe I have free choice in other areas of my life?

If I think about anger as just one example of areas where I know I am not perfect, I can see a certain halfway point between letting loose with anger, and holding it back.

Only certain things will make me angry. Just ask my family. There is no certainty either as to whether I will let loose at any given trigger, or hold it back and master the impulse. It depends on the day and circumstances. If I'm really tired for example, I know I have less restraint. I'm sure anyone reading this will understand what I'm saying.

Free choice is the ability to go one way or the other, according to the theology books it would seem. In this example, it is the ability to get angry, or hold it back. I have to say with anger, I have free choice. Sometimes I get angry, and sometimes I don't.

It makes sense with some things, where I have a reasonable measure of good character, I have no free choice. To choose the negative behaviour is never an option. The only option is the right choice. If this means I'm a robot, is this a bad thing?

Where I struggle with a serious ingrained bad habit, I also have no free choice. In such situations, the wrong choice is the one I'd most likely choose. Just ask anyone with a substance addiction. Just ask anyone with worry, anxiety or depression. They all know they are trapped in their negative thinking and behaviours.

Those who have studied the human brain understand how certain reactions, habits, and behaviours are hard wired into our neural connections. This is painfully obvious in the trauma kids I've worked with in the school system.

It would seem free choice or free will only exists in the realm of unformed character. Even then, depending on the behaviour or condition, the choice may not be a straight 50/50 probability. I would like to think the longer I am a Christian, as God forms his character in me, the probabilities skew more and more towards the right choice rather than the wrong choice.

So here I am with an observation free choice is something certainly not universal to every condition in our personalities and character. It really is something I ultimately don't want as I want to reach the point where my character is perfect so I have no freedom to choice a wrong option.

This is how I see it. Free choice or free will is something I wish to move away from, towards the perfection reflected in the character of Jesus Christ. In the matter of good character, I really want to be a robot! How terrible of me!

This makes perfect sense to me. Nevertheless, I hear many speak of it in church as if it is the ultimate objective of our Christian lives. Some I've heard speak of free choice as what Jesus came to give us. They say Jesus came to give us freedom as expressed by free choice. He came to give us the ability to do both right and wrong.

Really?

Weird as it may seem, I actually believed for most if not all of my 40+ years as a Christian Jesus came to set us free from not only bad character and habits, but also free choice. I didn't originally know what it was. I understand this now, only in looking back.

He didn't come to keep us in the no-mans-land of only so good or 50/50 character. He actually came to take us to a place of perfect character where there is no freedom to sin, miss the mark, or make poor choices with our behaviour and character.

It is true no one ever attains perfect character in all areas of life as a Christian before we die. I'm sure God has a really good reason for this too. It is also true in some aspects of our character we do and can attain perfection before we die. God does after all know what he is doing when it comes to perfecting us in this current life.

But here I am, surrounded by many Christians who think free choice or free will is the ultimate gift of God. Some even refer to "the power of free choice"! How good is that?

It is somehow powerful to be trapped in the middle between bad and good character. I really don't get this, but don't dare ask how this can be so as the reactions are sometimes violent. I know this because I have asked these questions.

Theologies can sometimes present ideas as if they are always black and white. For example, I'll try to encapsulate so much I've heard:

"Free choice is what we all have no matter the circumstance, because that is what Jesus came to give us."

Once again... really?

Some points of theology are black and white to me. Jesus died for our sins is one example of a plain simple fact in my Christian theology. Free choice is not in this simple realm of black and white for me. Sometimes we have it. Sometimes we don't. The troubled kids I've worked with over the years are proof of this. Does anyone really have an argument against this?

I can see failing to understand free choice can lead to much confusion in our Christian lives and this is why I seek to understand it better and if possible, deconstruct some of the errors in our thinking on this important subject.

I say the subject is important as I've been waking up to how many are under its spell, and the fruit of such thinking is not good. Losing friends over this subject, as I've already described, is just one aspect of bad fruit.

Why are some so fierce in their defence of this idea?

For the purposes of this particular book, I'm only going to gloss over the subject of free will or choice. The more I have unpacked this subject, the more I realised it was too important to do it justice in just one chapter. It really needs a book all to itself. At this point, given how much thought I've had to put into it, I can see it as the next book to write on my list.

With this in mind, I'm happy to leave some questions unanswered on the topic.

Slaves In Egypt.

Why did I place references to Deuteronomy 5:15 and Galatians 4:7-8 at the beginning of this chapter?

> *Remember that you were slaves in Egypt and that the Lord your God brought you out of there with a mighty hand and an outstretched arm.* **Deuteronomy 5:15** (NIV)

The key point the Deuteronomy verse above makes is Israel was in slavery in Egypt, and God set them free. They were not free to leave their bondage in Egypt without the powerful intervention of God. We should also note God chose to liberate Israel at a specific time in history. Israel had no say in it. They had no free choice to simply leave Egypt. This is much like those I know with all manner of difficulties in their lives, whether alcoholism, anger, or depression.

The details of this liberation from slavery in Egypt can be read in Exodus chapters 1 to 15. Please note it was the power of God which set the Israelites free. They were at no point free to just leave of their own accord. The Egyptians had invested too much in the Israelites. You don't let your slaves go without some resistance. William Wilberforce faced similar resistance when he fought for the abolition of slavery in the British Parliament back in the early 1800's.

So you are no longer a slave, but God's child; and since you are his child, God has made you also an heir. Formerly, when you did not know God, you were slaves to those who by nature are not gods. **Galatians 4:7-8** (NIV)

The reference from the Epistle of Paul to the Galatians is given to show how slavery can be a term to explain the condition of the unconverted as part of New Testament understanding. Before we knew God we were in many respects slaves to the ways and thinking of the world. If we were slaves, we were not free. I hope this point is obvious. A slave does not have free choice or free will in many aspects of their lives.

It is important to ensure this thinking is consistent with conditions outside of the Old Testament. If we don't, we might have to question if somehow all non-Christian people are no longer slaves to Satan simply because Jesus has now died for us. There is plenty in the New Testament, and life in general, to show people are as much in bondage since Jesus died and rose again, as they were before he died.

Many regard the quitting of Israel from Egypt as a type of how a Christian is delivered from the slavery of sin. It is also viewed as a type or analogy of the salvation process, and hence a type of the Gospel.

When we embrace the Gospel and give our lives to Jesus, we are set free from the terminal consequence of sin – death. We are no longer slaves to sin and its ultimate consequence, as we were before we knew Jesus. We receive the gift of eternal life.

The point God wanted Israel to remember in Deuteronomy above was how Israel was in slavery, and it was God who set them free. They did not set themselves free. Their slavery in Egypt, and coming out, was not a matter of their free choice to stay or leave. God had to do it for them.

> *But thanks be to God that, though you used to be slaves to sin, you have come to obey from your heart the pattern of teaching that has now claimed your allegiance. You have been set free from sin and have become slaves to righteousness.* **Romans 6:17-18** (NIV)

The same point is true in regards to our slavery to sin, referenced above from Romans chapter 6. As slaves to sin we had no free choice to just quit sin and its lifestyles. If this was not so, and we were entirely able to quit sin without the saving power of the Gospel, would not a different term other than "slavery" have been used by Paul if it was really just something one could easily quit?

In other words, if people before salvation are slaves to sin, do they in this condition have free choice?

It would make sense they don't, and then upon salvation, maybe then they have a state of mind resembling in some ways free choice. This free will may reside only in some aspects of our lives. I've known some who become Christians yet still remain addicted to smoking or alcohol. They clearly don't have free choice in all aspects of their lives.

On a positive note, I've known some to be addicted to smoking in their early days as a Christian. At some point they are then supernaturally healed of their addiction. This healing does not then place them automatically in a condition of free choice.

In contrast they are slaves to righteousness, and have the character of Christ to no longer suffer from the addiction. They now reflect the character of Jesus in this area of their lives. In such a positive condition, they also have no free will. Smoking is no longer an option.

Should I expect some to claim such character can only mean they are therefore robots?

I hope not, but that is the reasoning given by so many who think the ability to do both right and wrong is a virtue. I say this somewhat tongue in cheek.

What it really reflects is a lack of thinking about the implications of what we are saying. We subjectively think a life without free choice is a bad thing as it means we are no more than mere robots. To have sound character does not mean we are no longer living with a measure of free creative agency.

I think I understand this correctly. Am I missing anything here?

The verses from Romans 6 above then make mention of how we are set free. We don't set ourselves free. If we don't, is it a bad thing to claim it is God who does set us free?

To be set free implies strongly the one set free was not free to leave beforehand. It means we had no free choice in the matter. Ask any drug addict how free they are to quit from their addiction. They need outside help, just as we do to quit sin and live a life which reflects Jesus.

When it comes to conversion, and giving our lives to Jesus, we don't simply decide to do so. God himself is necessary for us to be set free. I don't see how we have any real free choice in this matter. I also cannot see how this is somehow bad, so therefore unsound theology.

I suspect some, if not many Christians, think the unconverted do have free choice here. Nevertheless, it just doesn't make sense from scripture to think we do. Neither does it make sense from observation. This is how I understand it. I would love to understand how else one should understand these verses if I really am incorrect. I'm open to correction. Please just be nice about it. ☺

Miracles Don't Convict

When I unpack this whole issue of free will and simply choosing to follow God, the story of Israel after they were liberated from Egypt is quite telling on the subject. It tells us we don't have free choice before we are saved, when it comes to salvation. It also shows us there is something about human nature whereby we don't get saved or convinced to accept Jesus as our saviour, by clever arguments or miracles.

If anyone had a reason to want to choose God and follow him, it had to be the Israelites. The God of Abraham, Isaac, and Jacob made a serious display of power in Egypt to get them out of there. A powerful nation had been brought to its knees by major calamity. The gods of Egypt were powerless to do anything. The God of Israel proved who was in charge. Miracle after miracle stood as proof pointing to the God who was most worthy of their worship.

After all the displays of God's power in Egypt, surely crossing the Red Sea, on dry land would have been the final word. With all the bodies of the dead Egyptians washed up on the shore beside them, after crossing, Israel really had to know who was God. There was no doubt. Or was there?

Somehow Israel just couldn't connect. They doubted God, no matter what he did, during 40 years of wilderness wandering.

God even made his presence obvious to everyone on a daily basis. By day he led them in a pillar of cloud. At night God manifested his presence in a pillar of fire. There was no mistaking where God was. He never left them for an instant. There was also no forgetting him.

Still they complained, grumbled, and at times, even rebelled and considered returning to Egypt. All this was done in the very face of God, if we understand his obvious presence by the pillar of cloud and fire. Does this tell us something about how easy or natural it is to just simply choose to follow God?

It isn't!

It just isn't natural or easy to follow God – not without a particular change within ourselves, brought about by God himself.

What about the following statements of God to Moses in Deuteronomy:

"Oh, that their hearts would be inclined to fear me and keep all my commands always, so that it might go well

with them and their children forever! " **Deuteronomy 5:29** (NIV)

> *"Moses summoned all the Israelites and said to them:*
> *Your eyes have seen all that the Lord did in Egypt to Pharaoh, to all his officials and to all his land. With your own eyes you saw those great trials, those signs and great wonders. But to this day the Lord has not given you a mind that understands or eyes that see or ears that hear."* **Deuteronomy 29:2-4** (NIV)

They had no mind or heart for it. The very nature of Israel - their heart - would not allow them to follow God. Following God for the average Israelite was as foreign a concept as getting my dog to play violin. It just could not happen.

There were some exceptions amongst the people of Israel. We read of Caleb as one of these exceptions:

> *"not one of them will ever see the land I promised on oath to their ancestors. No one who has treated me with contempt will ever see it. But because my servant Caleb has a different spirit and follows me wholeheartedly, I will bring him into the land he went to, and his descendants will inherit it. "* **Numbers 14:22-23** (NIV)

Why was Caleb an exception?

The verses above say he was different because he had a different spirit, or heart/attitude.

How did he have this different spirit?

Did he pick it up off the sand or stony ground during their wanderings in the wilderness?

Did he simply choose to have it when the others decided they didn't want to?

Maybe it was mail order?

I doubt it. Every Israelite, if they really were free to choose, had every reason to make the right choice. This is what makes sense to me anyway. Why chase after foreign gods when they are so obviously inferior?

A truly free person would surely fall down in wonder and adoration of such a God. This is no ordinary God. Why pick a loser?

This is a God who not only saves you from slavery in Egypt; he even splits the ocean as a final parting statement to your captors. This is no ordinary party trick.

Was all this coverage of Israel just to show us how bad this particular group of people was, and therefore how good we must be in contrast?

Is God keen to have us thinking how good we are in comparison to those rebellious Israelites?

Yes?

Really?

Or was God rather making a statement on the condition of mankind in general, and showing not even miracles on a grand scale are sufficient to bring about a conversion in someone?

I don't want to set myself up as both judge and jury. I will dare suggest if we answer yes to any of the first three of those last four questions, we have a problem. It's a problem called self-righteousness, and pride.

We need to understand external displays of great power do not change us, or give us a heart to follow God. Only God himself can bring about such a necessary change – a change of heart.

Choose Life.

There is a verse I hear about more than any other to justify believing everyone has free choice and so is now free to choose to follow God:

"This day I call the heavens and the earth as witnesses against you that I have set before you life and death, blessings and curses. Now choose life, so that you and your children may live..." **Deuteronomy 30:19** (NIV)

Many think God telling the Israelites to choose life was a clear statement showing they could. Why else would he tell them to choose if they couldn't?

I can think of a very good reason why he would.

Firstly, telling a people to try and do something they can't possibly do is a good way to drive the point home showing they can't. Simply telling someone they can never do something isn't nearly as powerful a statement as telling them to go ahead and try, and thereby finding out for themselves.

Harry Callaghan knew this well in the classic 1970's movie called Dirty Harry, where he said to the punk:

"Go ahead. Make my day." (Eastwood)

Harry was pointing a magnum revolver at the guy's head. The guy knew he couldn't try to pull his gun on Harry before Harry fired first. Harry knew this too. Harry was simply pointing out the obvious by telling the guy to try. There was no better way of making the point. To this day, I expect millions of people still recognise this classic, unforgettable statement:

"Go ahead. Make my day." (Eastwood)

I've already referred to statements in Deuteronomy chapters 5 and 29. They point out clearly God knew Israel would never be able to follow his commands perfectly. God even explained why. He made it clear it was because they didn't have the right mind or spirit from God to be able to.

I'll repeat a key verse again:

"Your eyes have seen all that the Lord did in Egypt to Pharaoh, to all his officials and to all his land. With your own eyes you saw those great trials, those signs and great wonders. But to this day the Lord has not given you a mind that understands or eyes that see or ears that hear." **Deuteronomy 29:2-4** (NIV)

Is this not patently obvious? Any normal person can be nothing but detached if not hostile towards God, without the miracle of a changed heart. We see this time and time again in scripture. Still, many Christians struggle to accept this. I can only suggest this is because the spirit of the world, which I view as a very religious spirit, does not want us to know this.

This influence reaches into many of our churches. We bring this thinking with us when we first start attending church. Religion wants us to think we can take credit for our conversion. It wants us to take at least some of the credit for our conversion and saved condition. It doesn't want us to know our conversion and salvation was 100% God. We end up reflecting a thinking whereby our salvation and conversion was perhaps 90% God and 10% us. Pick any percentage figure – the point remains the same.

I've learned over and over again in conversations with some Christians it is hard to understand people in their natural unsaved state do not have a mind or spirit which can follow God. No conversion or righteousness is possible without direct intervention of God in a person's life. This can be very hard to understand, depending on the prior dogmas we have been exposed to.

As we learned above, Caleb was different because he had a different mind or spirit. He didn't buy it in a shop or at the local mall. He was chosen by God to be given a different spirit from the vast majority of his people.

"For you are a people holy to the Lord your God. The Lord your God has chosen you out of all the peoples on the face of the earth to be his people, his treasured possession. The Lord did not set his affection on you and choose you because you were more numerous than other peoples, for you were the fewest of all peoples." **Deuteronomy 7:6-7** (NIV)

Can anybody see what I can see in the above 2 verses in Deuteronomy 7?

I might be wrong here, but it does seem to say it was God who did the choosing where Israel was concerned. True, it doesn't specifically say they couldn't then choose life once God had chosen them. He says that elsewhere. It does however shed some light on where rests the true capability to choose concerning the things of God. It is not with man. It is with God.

Dogmas don't die easy. I know how much many will struggle with this concept. Some will say things are different today. They might bring themselves to admit Israel was not free back then before Jesus came and died for us, but now all people are free to choose.

Great! If we now accept this, it is a huge step forward in our thinking. Still, I do have to ask a simple question:

If one thinks all people are free to "choose life" today, but they were not before Jesus came, why is the main proof text given by so many Deuteronomy 30:19?

So we really do believe the Old Testament record showing people were not free from slavery to sin except in a small number of exceptions (e.g. Caleb)? If we do, we cannot use Old Testament scripture describing the Old Testament state of mankind to describe the New Testament state of mankind.

The statements in Deuteronomy were made some 1400 years or so before Jesus came. If we believe everyone alive today is free to choose eternal life by accepting Jesus as one's personal saviour, proof is needed from the New Testament. Some do think they have such proof, and I will cover this.

Arminianism Again.

"No one can come to me unless the Father who sent me draws them, and I will raise them up at the last day."
John 6:44 (NIV)

The above words of Jesus indicate we cannot become a follower of Jesus without the intervention first of God the Father. I referred to this before in my brief discussion of Calvinism.

Calvinism had difficulty explaining its theory of how God would choose some for salvation and some for eternal damnation. Such theology didn't make sense to at least some people back in the 1500's. As a result, Jacobus Arminius re-evaluated the Catholic view of free choice. It was the prevailing view before John Calvin developed his particular salvation theology.

From the writings of both Calvin and Arminius, protestant Christianity formed two major schools of thought. They are with us to this day. I would suggest the majority of Christians today, whether Catholic or Protestant, follow a more Arminian "free choice" way of thinking in their concepts of salvation.

From my own observations, I see many Christians operate with a very open form of Gospel preaching. What I mean is if everyone has free choice to accept or reject the Gospel, then all one needs to do is just get the message out there. Get the message under their nose of an unbeliever, or in their face, and the Christian's job is done.

It won't matter who the message gets to as they all have an equal opportunity to embrace the message and surrender to Jesus. Bad luck if they are having a bad day. Bad luck too if the delivery of the message is less than stela. I do have to wonder how many must be burning in hell for want of a decent gospel message delivery.

The Arminian view of free choice holds God is now drawing everyone to Jesus. I don't see it in this way for a number of reasons:

For one I don't think Jesus would have made the 2 statements in John 6:44 and verse 65 about how we do not choose for ourselves to become a follower of Jesus. A clear distinction is made between those God is drawing and those he is not drawing at any particular time.

I also do not think Paul would have made his statements in Romans chapter 6 about the state of slavery for unbelievers, which I referred to earlier.

An Arminian would simply then quote:

Now is the time for judgment on this world; now the prince of this world will be driven out. And I, when I am lifted up from the earth, will draw all people to myself. **John 12:31-32** (NIV)

Full marks to my Arminian friends! Jesus said when he would be lifted up (crucified), he would draw all people to him.

I don't disagree with that. I just disagree with the timing of it all. Surely we can agree those born 2000 years after Jesus was crucified were not being drawn at the time Jesus spoke these words. We also have to conclude the same for those alive 2000 years before Jesus died.

Rationally we need to conclude Jesus was saying the result of the historical moment of his crucifixion would have an impact on all people so they could be ultimately drawn to him and saved.

This logic would then apply to all who had lived and died before Jesus lived and died, and also to all those who would live and die after Jesus lived and died.

The timing of the drawing to Jesus would be entirely in the hands of God. For many who have lived and died, such timing may not even be in this life. It may still be in the future. We will have to see what the Bible says about this timing later.

In the Arminian way of thinking, Jesus' statement from John 12:31-32 above is saying free choice is now on all people, or at least it was after the crucifixion. One could even argue now Jesus does the drawing, and not his heavenly Father, as stated in John 6:44.

If free choice began or was made possible just after the death of Jesus, then all I said about the fixed and hostile state of man's heart changes from that point on.

Great! Does this now mean everyone is free to quit the bondage of sin without God's intervention?

We certainly don't see this in real life.

But yes, one can say this is just my opinion. Such a statement is never a sound argument. More needs to be said. If it is just my opinion, I have to ask where this new heart condition in the unconverted and unsaved is seen today.

In fact, I don't see very many people freely giving their lives to Jesus. I've never seen any in over 40 years as a Christian. I've have seen people give their lives to Jesus, but it was never a process of free choice. It was always a fight, at least spiritually, just like Israel leaving Egypt. It was always obvious God had his hand in it. I even think God wants his role to be obvious. He doesn't want us thinking we get saved by ourselves.

Every conversion I've seen indicated the action of God to set them free from the bondage of the unsaved condition. It seems ridiculous I have to argue this stuff.

Maybe I only ever saw the hard cases. Perhaps there were many I never saw where it was just a simple walk in the park, leaving the life of sin (Egypt?), as a free choice to follow Jesus?

If it was so easy for so many, I do have to wonder why continuing the walk of a Christian is so tough at times. I don't know anyone who thinks the Christian walk is easy. For such a challenging path, was it really that easy to start it in the first place?

I'm sure many of my Arminian friends would agree it does take a fight to let go of the world and follow Jesus.

If they can admit to this, why not just give up on the free will idea? Forgetting "free choice" makes a great deal we see and experience make sense. Free will dogma contradicts so much of what we see and experience around us in the Christian walk.

Maybe it is a fear of thinking we must be a robot if God gets 100% of the credit for our salvation?

If God choosing us, and setting us free makes us a robot, is that really such a bad thing?

I've only recently learned I must be a robot, as it is obvious to me from scripture and experience how I did not choose God or set myself free from sin and the unconverted life. Knowing all this never changed the fact I was still a living being with some measure of free agency and creative ability.

I don't feel like a robot. Over time I can see I have a great deal of biological programming I can't necessarily change, but God does. I've been shaped and programmed by all manner of circumstances I've had no control over. I'm fine with this, if this really does mean I'm nothing more than a robot in the thinking of some. They are as much a robot as I am, with all manner of biological programming similar to mine.

If we really have to shun the idea of robots or puppets, can we understand everyone alive holds a unique character and personality different from everyone else?

We have no power to change how unique we are. Our programming in the manner of what makes us who we are, and different from everyone else, is very much fixed. It is fixed, much like programming in a robot. Is this really so bad?

There is also much about us which is not fixed. We all have a measure of freedom to make all manner of choices, depending on personal circumstances.

We also have a measure of freedom or free agency to express creativity in a manner way beyond any animal capability. This free will inherent to man, is something we have whether saved or unsaved. It is not something only available if we give our lives to Christ.

Back to the more specific subject of spiritual salvation, we also have to consider Paul spoke of the condition of the unsaved before they were saved. Remember the verses given at the beginning of this chapter?

So you are no longer a slave, but God's child; and since you are his child, God has made you also an heir. Formerly, when you did not know God, you were slaves to those who by nature are not gods. **Galatians 4:7-8** (NIV)

If the Arminian idea of freedom after the death of Jesus is to be believed, how could anyone still be a slave before conversion? Paul wrote these words years after Jesus died and rose again. He even told the Romans the same thing as we have seen in Romans chapter 6.

Paul wrote much on the condition of man before conversion. It was all about slavery to sin and Satan. After the death of Jesus, could someone be both a slave to sin and Satan, and also free to choose life as a follower of Jesus?

This would seem like an absurdity to me, but maybe I just don't get it.

I see far more consistency in the message of scripture by simply agreeing how even after the death of Jesus, the basic state of mankind was still the same.

Mankind needed a saviour before the death of Jesus, and still does today. This is because the fallen nature of mankind has been consistent since the Garden of Eden. The only thing which can change this is to be born again, or converted.

No change has come on mankind automatically because Jesus has died for us. His death did not automatically endow all people with a partial conversion or a new mind. We still need to be set free from slavery to repent and believe the Gospel. Nothing changes for anyone until they set free. None of this will happen without God's intervention. We can't do it out of "free choice".

We can do other things through the free will all humans have to various degrees. The process of salvation is not one of those things.

Knowing this takes a great deal of pressure off any Christian who has been burdened with a teaching saying the salvation of so many depends on them getting out there and saving the unsaved.

Some might thrive under the pressure of "doing it tough for God". I'm happy for those few. I've known far far more Christians unhappy and struggling under the burden of having to get out and save the world. Yes, at the end of Matthew we read how Jesus told his disciples to go out and make disciples. He did literally say this. I don't deny it. What we need to recognise is he didn't tell them to save people. The difference is huge, and we need to understand this.

Thinking of life in general, I don't walk by free choice much at all. When I get up in the morning is determined by my family responsibilities. As much as we in my family would all like to be on holiday in Europe, we just don't have the savings to do so. My kids have little free choice on whether they go to school or not. The same goes for their music practice.

Wisdom puts great demands on my life. I'm fortunate the discipline I learnt in my younger years has me far more a slave to wisdom than folly.

Fear of consequences and common sense has my life defined by fairly narrow boundaries. Am I really free to simply step beyond those boundaries at whim?

I'm not so certain I have such freedom. I don't even want such freedom if "freedom" it is. I'd rather lead a life of character and discipline as such leads to positive outcomes I value.

Yes, in theory, I know I could step out, but I'm usually not that stupid. A knock to my head might change that. For now, I have no real freedom with this.

How much free choice is there in my life?

Certainly, a lot less than if I had financial independence. If we didn't have to work for a living, the boundaries would not be so narrow. We are working to change this, but such changes are not happening overnight. For now, we live a fairly restricted lifestyle.

I do walk by faith, and this is a totally different thing from the treadmill of life. The faith I walk by is a gift from God, and a constant miracle and sustaining strength to keep me on this walk.

If I really try to think about the outcomes of this free will dogma, I don't see much to show for it. Few people are getting saved in this theoretical freedom to choose. The vast majority are going to their graves unsaved.

God, who performed such a masterful stroke at the cross, somehow seems incapable of getting many saved after such a huge investment. Is it any wonder John Calvin started thinking free choice didn't answer all the questions?

It Is For Freedom!

"It is for freedom that Christ has set us free. Stand firm, then, and do not let yourselves be burdened again by a yoke of slavery." **Galations 5:1** (NIV)

This verse on freedom above, quoting from Paul's letter to the Galatians is perhaps the second most quoted scripture to claim proof for a doctrine of free choice.

If it does support a doctrine of free choice, it certainly does not support the Arminian view people are somehow universally free as of the time of Jesus' crucifixion.

Notice how the end of the verse refers to the universal condition of slavery for the typical person. Paul warns the Galatian Christians to not go back to that condition of slavery. Would he make such a warning if such slavery no longer existed as of some decades before when Jesus died?

Still, the verse does refer to freedom. I have no dispute with that. I would even argue it is for freedom to no longer choose evil that Christ came. I would not argue he came to give us freedom to both not choose evil, and choose evil. Why would I rejoice over freedom to still choose evil?

I don't want such freedom. I know I have plenty of it in areas of imperfect character in my life, but I only want the freedom to reject evil. I don't want freedom to perform evil. -Still, many I know insist we have freedom for both, and it is good. In their view, Jesus came to give us both. Did Jesus really come to give us freedom to choose evil, as well as good? Why not just good?

I have to conclude so many making these statements really haven't given it much critical thought. I have to wonder if they really understand the definition of free will.

Perhaps we need to be thinking Jesus set us free to begin to choose good. He won't always remove the ability to choose evil in every case. If he did we might forget how much we need him. In some areas of our character, he does heal us or remove the slavery we were under to choose evil. When he doesn't, he does want us to know how much we need him to set us free even more. He doesn't want us thinking we can do it ourselves, when we can't. This makes sense to me.

It also makes perfect sense Jesus came to give us freedom from the consequences of sin, which is death, and also freedom from sin itself. The Christian walk, as I have always understood, is about growing empowerment to reject evil. Is this not the essence of character God is developing in us? I have never understood it to be about growing empowerment to both accept and reject evil. That would be just plain weird, yet so many insist on this and even get angry as they do when they meet someone who questions the logic.

Such empowerment does not happen overnight in all aspects of life. I sometimes wonder why. My best answer to such a question is it reinforces how much we are dependent on the power of Jesus not only for salvation, but also for transformation and becoming more like him.

The longer we live with our human failings, the more we realise we don't have the power in ourselves to perfect ourselves. This power can only come from God, and it does. God is always changing and shaping us for the better. I've seen this time and time again. It would not be good to ever forget this. Our struggle with imperfections ensures we don't.

So many people I know, whether of Christian or non-Christian persuasion really struggle to believe holiness is only achieved by the power of God at work in us. Too many think we have to somehow make it happen, and God helps us make it happen. In their view we are responsible for making change happen in our lives.

Some may then try to qualify this. Instinctively we know the role of God in our transformation is greater than we might be able to admit. The view is then we have a role to play in our transformation. Our responsibility is partial and not total. We do our part and God does his part. I hear in this a desperate struggle to claim even just a small part of the credit for the changes in us. Responsibility equals credit after all.

All I can suggest is we just let go the need to try and claim credit for anything in our Christian transformation. Just give it all to God. If we really want credit for anything, just let it be in the work he gives us to do. In this there is plenty of scope for us to hear:

"Well done my good and faithful servant!"
Matthew 25:21 (NIV)

This does not mean we should be complacent about our failings and bad habits. Am I now contradicting what I was saying before? Not at all!

To be careless about such is madness, even if we know we cannot change ourselves. Sin does lead to pain after all. Rather, we need to go to the source of changes for the better – God himself. Out of this is born our growing relationship with God as we interact with him concerning our weakness, and other issues as well. The closer we draw to God, the less likely we are to fail in our character.

God isn't just interested in changing us for the better. He is also interested in growing a relationship with us. A love for his creation points logically to a desire for relationship with his creation.

Free Choice Outside Theology.

If we step outside theology, is free will to be found anywhere else?

I will argue there is little to be found in Christian theology, except as an expression of weak or less-than-perfect character. By weak character, I mean when sometimes we behave well, and other times when we don't.

I will even argue there is little to be found in my own life, except where my character is less than perfect, or I express the general free will of all humans, which makes us distinct from animals. Perhaps then I should say there is way too much free will or choice expressed in my life as there are so many aspects of my life where I am not perfect.

Whether we believe in free choice in the world of theology or we don't, I wonder how much free choice we can find outside the realm of theology.

I hear people talk about it a great deal. It is like the ethos of our Western democracies. In the current relative freedom of the West, there is far more freedom in choices one can make than in more controlled economies, such as those under dictatorships or blatant communism. I do see these freedoms disappearing in the West at this point in our history.

Funny that. We think we live in democracies. We probably don't. Our forms of government look a lot more like oligarchy. That's how I see them anyway. If we struggle with this, look up the meaning of "oligarchy". It may surprise.

If I'm right about the illusion of democracy, is our belief in our power of free will no less a myth as well, or at least partially?

Yes, I did get to choose what jeans to put on this morning. I even chose my t-shirt. My clothing wasn't imposed on me. I'm not talking about that kind of free choice.

I am grateful I wasn't born in China under Mao. I wouldn't have had a choice over what I'd wear! Mao suits were the vogue, and hard luck on anyone who thought otherwise.

Interesting how those born in China under Mao had no say in it. I'd even argue they had no choice in how they viewed Mao. He was a hero, and most if not all were indoctrinated from a very young age to believe it. There was no other way to think made available.

As with any bell curve, there was always going to be a number of unfortunate souls who were real outliers in China. Someone always has to be different. Their destiny was re-education in a labour camp. There was just so much free choice going on in China back then. It's no wonder we all wanted to live in China at that time in history.

How lucky was I to be born in Australia? I certainly had no choice in the matter. When I was born had incredible significance too. If I'd been born in the time of my maternal grandfather, in the late 1800's, I could have spilled my blood with his and so many of his friends in France during World War One.

My grandfather chose to go to war in World War One. But did he have any free choice in the matter?

In theory he did, but most like him didn't hesitate to go. Did he have any say in the cultural mores he absorbed as a child that made him so ready to visit France back then?

I really don't think he did. He was a product of his time and had no control over how his thinking was formed.

For those interested, I will be publishing his diary from World War One. I'm working on it now, while I write this book. If you join my mailing list as detailed at the end of this book, I can let you know when it is available. It is an amazing project, going through pages penned now over 100 years ago.

How many of us really try to not be products of our time?

I can't think of anyone who ever has. Even the rebels of the 60's, or the punks of the 70's, were products of their time. They were all great conformers, thinking they were different, yet still very much products of time and circumstance. They may have chosen who they conformed with, but could they have chosen otherwise?

I don't think so personally, but this is just my view. They were still free moral agents in many respects, but perhaps less than they realised.

In so many ways I can't help thinking we have no control over what we believe. We think we are selective and discriminate over what we accept as true or false. Can we really change what shaped us to discriminate in the manner we do?

Sure, we can take a major step in life to go overseas and live in an ashram in India for a year. I've no doubt such a decision, freely chosen, will shape the way we think thereafter.

What has influenced us to choose to go to an ashram? Many would never go without the events in life to shape them to think going to one is a good idea.

For myself, I know I wouldn't go. However, who knows what may happen in the next few years to change my thinking so much so I would go and stay in India for an extended time?

Indeed, there are some if not many choices we make. This is part of what makes us distinct from animals. There are crossroads in everyone's life. Some decisions in life can be extremely hard. Still, behind every decision we have made "freely" there is so much which influenced our decision over which we had no control.

Perhaps I can liken our lives to a hang-glider on a particular cliff. We are only on this cliff because it was the best one we could reach from home for a good day's hang-gliding.

Some breezes we miss, and some we fly. We have no control over the strength of a gust, or its direction. The breeze is better on some days from others. We can't control the weather. How good a day's gliding depends on decisions we can make, but there is a great deal we have no control over.

If we don't like a hang-gliding analogy, for reasons over which we have no control in our thinking, perhaps the analogy of a card game is better?

We play with the cards with which we are dealt. We also play within the rules of the game we are playing.

If we receive from the dealer a bad hand of cards, can we suggest we change the game, or call for a re-deal?

Life, and card games, just may not allow for such flexibility.

Sometimes we have to play on regardless. We make the most of the cards we have, and the skill we have for the game. As I write, I could face the temptation to play solitaire on my phone, and take away from my focus on the task of finishing this book. I enjoy Solitaire on my smart phone, but for now I will make a relatively free choice to resist the temptation and keep writing.

This is how I see life for all of us. We all have some measure of limited free will. We probably do also with aspects of our imperfect character. Still, if we really think about it, there is so much over which we really have no control.

I've learnt to accept this. I'm not fatalistic by any stretch of my imagination. Maybe I am, but am unable to see the obvious due to so much I've had no control over in my life. ☺

I do work hard to change what I can change. I'm always working on my standard of living, trying to raise it where ever possible. I raise and love my kids as best as I can. I love my wife as best as I can.

I understand God as best as I can too. I understand all within the limits of what he chooses to show me, and allows me to find out about him in my personal walk with him.

Outside of the imperfections in my character, I do have some free choice. It operates in fixed boundaries over which I have little control. I keep pushing these limits where ever I can. That's just me, and I don't think I can change this and be someone else. I'm stuck with my body and my mind - a unique human being trapped in a Homo Sapien body. I could dare say I'm very much like a unique robot or puppet character, in so many respects. Does anyone really think they are any different?

Just out of curiosity, I asked a friend who is an atheist what he thinks of free choice. I really wanted someone with a view which was not shaped by church in any way. He was very obliging.

He spoke of someone in his family who thinks people who are overweight can simply choose to eat less. He knew such a view was far from reality. In his perspective, he could eat as much ice cream as he liked and never show it. Others were not so fortunate. Some could simply get the whiff of an ice cream and put on weight.

He was obviously speaking figuratively, but it did not change the fact he knew self-control was not a simple case of free choice for many people. He also understood fairness was not the lot of the average person. No two people are the same, and neither is how life deals with each of us. There are choices we all face, but how much freedom we have before each choice is made is very much subject to so many issues over which we have little or no control.

Funnily enough, from this conversation it was clear too how outside of church circles free choice was very much a subject of debate.

Does Anything Go?

There is a danger. It comes with understanding we have less free will than so many religious dogmas would have us think.

This danger comes from then deciding, stupidly, to let go of our will, our character and our minds, and simply live "come what may". "Anything goes" in this way of thinking.

We may have boundaries we can't control, but we better live responsibly within those boundaries. Scripture is full of admonitions in both the Old and New Testaments to reject bad behaviour and negative impulses. Good and sound character is a definite goal and objective. I seriously believe this. I also understand we don't achieve it by our own strength and will power. We do it by the empowerment of God.

If we let go of sound character, and live in a realm of "anything goes", we will suffer. It is that simple. Any sensible person, Christian or not, aspires to a life of character where suffering from poor choices is just a memory.

To question the validity of a doctrine called free choice is not to say we no longer need to reflect the character of Jesus in our lives. We do. It is the only way out of suffering which is founded on poor choices, however free such choices may have been.

There is enough suffering independent from so many of our choices. We know this when a drunk driver hits our car. We don't need to add to this suffering through outcomes we could avoid with sound thinking based on our Christian way of life.

I feel so pedantic labouring these points about free will. In many ways it seems rather weird for me to be doing so. I don't normally think about such things. Free choice has never been a part of my Christian walk or thinking.

Character and sound habits have been the things I have understood, thought about, and to which I aspired. They make sense to me in a Christian world view. I never needed to think of free will to have a sound walk with God.

As needless as it is to me, I'm only thinking about free choice as I've learned over time quite a few Christians do think it is a focus in their Christian walk. They think this, even though I can see they would be much better off in life without it. It really does strike me as pointless verging on harmful baggage in their thinking. A focus on imperfection does not lead to perfection. A focus on an ability to make wrong choices does not encourage right choices.

A Context For Free Will

With all this, I've tried to think of how free choice might apply to life. I've tried to imagine if there is a context in which it might exist. Fortunately I have found one. I have made mention of it already a number of times. It is worth a particular summary focus.

If character has not yet been perfected, is this when free choice exists?

I think I'm on to something here.

Every parent with teenage kids must wonder how things will go when their kids are finally 18 and can legally buy and drink alcohol. I hope by the time my kids reach this stage I will have had some opportunity to help build some character in them. My aim is to prepare them so they won't go crazy with alcohol when it is finally legally available to them.

One of the scourges of our nation is binge drinking. I know it often starts before one is 18. Sometimes it doesn't. Every new adult faces the challenge of what habits and character they will form with the new-found legal freedom with alcohol. For some I suspect they have a degree of free choice before their character is formed. They could go either way. Do they get drunk or do they drink in moderation?

Far too many choose to get drunk and in time it becomes a habit. If someone is under the control or influence of a really poor peer group, they may not have much free choice over whether they form a bad habit of getting drunk every time they go out. It may not be an addiction at this stage. They only get drunk when they go out, and going out might not happen too often. If it was every Friday night, I'm not certain a seven day frequency could be called an addiction. It could be called a habit.

Is the narrow realm of unformed character and habits the place where free choice exists? I'm happy to say it is. It may not last for long before habits and character for better or worse is formed. Still, it did or does exist at least for a short period in at least some of our lives. This has got to keep those determined to hang on to this idea at least a little bit happy. In keeping with the theme of this book, this has got to be good news for some of us. ☺

Our ability to reject bad character is really a measure of how much free will we have. On one extreme we have destructive addictions. There is little free will for someone with those. Addictions are a form of slavery. On the other extreme, we have perfect character. Jesus had perfect character. We want perfect character too. There is no free will in perfect character. Jesus never made room for doing the wrong thing. He was perfect.

In areas where our character is not perfect, we see how sometimes we do well, and sometimes we don't. This is the road to perfect character. It is fraught with free will. As we get better, we see free will in action less and less as we only choose to do right more and more. I could even argue free will is the opposite of character, whether it be good, or whether it be bad.

The Not-So-Free Choices

Personal responsibility is a value I hold dear. I really do believe the world is a better place for those who learn to take responsibility for their actions. Many won't, and pay the price.

Many around them pay the price too for those who won't take responsibility for their actions. Whether they like it or not, they are responsible for their actions as no one else can own them. Denial of responsibility can never change this, even if the legal system accommodates such thinking.

This is one of the tougher aspects of life. We suffer under the actions of others. We often get what we don't deserve. We didn't choose so many outcomes. Nevertheless, we <u>can</u> choose how we respond to all that is unfair in life.

Even this is a very unfair view of life as some people I know are so battered by life circumstances they have no real ability to choose how they respond to the storms in life. Their lives are akin to a ship with no anchor, caught in the middle of a storm beset with raging seas. Nothing can change in that department without outside help and intervention. The mast is down, the sails are shredded, and the rudder is detached and useless. They have no free choice in their circumstances, and such forms of affliction affect both Christians and non-Christians alike.

If someone becomes hysterical, are they ever free enough to slap themselves in the face to snap them out of it? A slap might be just what they need, but is usually only going to come from someone else. How free are we if the help we need can only come from some other person?

If we can't help ourselves in any particular situation, do we consider free choice is available for that specific circumstance?

Ask anyone who has suffered from depression how much free choice they had to climb out from the pit of despair. Those who have suffered from this know too well there is no simple snapping oneself out of it. The chains of depression are as hard and cold as raw steel itself. It is not a place to go looking for free choice.

Do we choose to be tough, or do we choose to fall over and not get up again when life deals us a hard blow? I've not had a nervous breakdown, but know some who have. They never chose that outcome. Perhaps events leading to it were a function of avoidable poor choices. I myself would not want to judge how easy it would have been to avoid such poor choices.

How many in this world are really good at learning from the mistakes of others? It irks me to think how often I have had to learn the hard way, even when I already knew better from the experience of others.

It won't be the case with everything we might do wrong. I never got into shop lifting like some I knew in primary school. I don't know why. Somehow I was shaped to reject such a temptation. I didn't shape myself to be that way. I'm sure my parents played a role. It is hard to imagine free choice playing a part in how I was back then, and am now.

I could say I'm now hard-wired where the idea of shop lifting is concerned. I just don't do it. It isn't a free choice. If it was, that would imply I could just as easily choose to shop lift as not shop lift. I really don't think I'm free to shoplift. It isn't an option. Is a free choice available to do right or wrong if there is only one option?

To some I might come across as too quick to make excuses for the follies of mankind. It is a fair question to ask. Am I too quick to make excuses for others and their poor decisions?

Bad behaviour is a lot like gravity. It pulls us down, and sometimes that pull, and the impact at the bottom, can be really harsh. It is no wonder the Bible says a great deal about making sound decisions in life. The God who loves us so much really wants us to become people who automatically make sound decisions that won't lead to pain and suffering.

Dare I say he wants the "programming" in our thinking to reflect that of a robot with sound character?

So do the constant admonitions in scripture to reject the ways of sin make it plain we have choices when it comes to sin?

If we have choices to make concerning sin, are they freely made?

Both are good questions. They need to be asked. They also need answers.

We all have choices when it comes to sin. When the alcoholic reaches for the bottle one more time after promising his or her traumatised family for the thousandth time they will quit, a choice has been made. The choice born out of addiction and habit is predictable. It does not come from a state of freedom. The choice is therefore not free at all. It is still a choice. It is a choice not freely made.

I referred earlier to shoplifting. For myself, if I'm in a shop and the thought enters my head to steal something, the simple response for me is a simple no. I have no habit formed in this manner. Some do.

Some of my friends in primary school formed a habit of shoplifting. I remember how one friend was so relieved when he was caught as he knew he wanted to break the habit and he needed help to break it. He is still a friend, and I'm happy to say he doesn't have that problem now. The habit was broken when he was young, through the outside intervention of getting caught.

My friend's decision to shoplift was perhaps freely made when he started. He was under some poor influences. Once the habit was formed, the choice was no longer as free as it was in the beginning. He is now free of that bad habit. His new habit is self-control, which he has had now for 40 years or so. I'm grateful we share the same habit.

We are both free from shoplifting. I would argue we are not free at all to shoplift. Neither of us wants this bad habit. We don't want it playing on our consciences. The temptation to shoplift doesn't come often. I'm too busy to really give space to such a thought, but I guess the kingdom of darkness will try to push the idea every now and then.

I hope it is clear my answer to those two questions posed a page or so before is "yes" for the first question. We really do have choices when it comes to sin.

The second question about choices freely made is not as cut and dry. Some choices are made out of addiction and bad habits. They are not freely made. Good choices are born out of strength of character. Therefore good habits are not freely made either, if we really understand the definition of free choice or free will.

Good choices may come out of freedom from a certain kind of sin, but freedom from sin is not the same as a free choice or a choice freely made concerning sin. Freedom from sin is sound character. There is no freedom to sin when we have sound character. I see this as good news!

Personal Responsibility

With the point made of how some choices are not so freely made, I return to the subject of personal responsibility.

I understand how we are not free to choose with many of the decisions we make in life. Tragically some will argue I'm therefore encouraging others to not take responsibility for their actions. Only poor understanding will lead us to this conclusion. Wholesale rejection of what I'm saying, without really listening to what I'm saying will also lead to this conclusion.

I've worked with many kids in primary school as a mentor. It is clear there is so much in their behaviour caused by circumstances totally outside of their control. They are children after all.

One day, when they are adults, it will be obvious to many how blaming their childhood is not going to solve the problems in character and behaviour they have carried into adulthood. At some point in life they have to take ownership of their character and behaviour. No one else will.

If they do, such action is called taking personal responsibility.

These kids I know may not be to blame for the wild character they demonstrate as children. They are not responsible for the shocking influences which have shaped them. Nevertheless they will need to face up to their lives and who they have become, even if the legal system won't encourage them to do so.

Whoever is to blame becomes irrelevant when we are adults and living with the consequences of our actions. Our actions belong to us, no matter who we can say caused them, or how they originated. Our bad habits, poor character, and addictions belong to us and no one else. We are the ones who have to shoulder the responsibility of looking for changes for the better. No one else can or will live our lives for us.

We see this demonstrated in the life of an alcoholic when they finally decide to go to an Alcoholics Anonymous (AA) meeting. They know the behaviour belongs to them, and they know they need help. They also know they can't help themselves and need help from an outside power.

This outside power to overcome alcohol addiction, or any other condition of addiction or poor character is called Jesus Christ. Jesus Christ is the way to freedom from bad character. Jesus is the way through the murky path of free choice as we reach for perfect character. Jesus is the perfect embodiment of perfect character, free of free will. His character is perfect, and we can be too.

I could only wish those who think a doctrine of free will is central to the Gospel message of Jesus could spend time with broken messed up people as I have. It takes serious effort to deny how little freedom to make good choices exists for seriously broken people.

Wading through the boggy mire of a subject like free will has not been easy. I know it will upset a lot of people. When they get upset it looks like they have no control over their responses. Such extreme responses emphasise to me the serious need for light to be shed on such a difficult subject.

There has to be a good reason why so many would react in such an unreasonable manner. Unpacking this will require a separate book focused solely on the subject of free will. I may go there when this book is finally finished.

Free will is real. It does exist. Many don't have much in their lives. They are enslaved in bad habits and poor character. I would argue I have too much and want much less as I aspire to the perfection of Jesus and his character in all areas of my life.

Many I know who espouse free will as an important pillar of their Christian faith have plenty of the same imperfect character. I can only hope in writing this they can learn their free will is at odds with the character of Christ we all aspire to. They need to stop wanting more of it. That's my opinion anyway.

Perfection in character, free of free will, is part of the hope Jesus represents for all mankind. This will not take away from the unique individual free will aspects of being human and distinct from animals. It took me a while to get to this understanding, but where free will is concerned in the lives of the broken in character, this is definitely good news!

We Can't Love Without It.

I really thought I was done with this chapter on Free Will. I knew there was much I didn't say, but there wasn't room for a book within a book. Still, one topic kept coming back to me. It was incessant. It is probably the biggest stumbling block keeping people hanging on to the idea of Free Will, and giving it far more place in their thinking than it probably deserves. I clearly needed to make some reference to it. Here we go...

I'm talking about the notion which says true love cannot exist without free will or free choice.

It is quite a compelling statement. It is also quite convincing, but only if we don't unpack it, or think too long on what it is really saying.

If this statement is true, it is really saying true love can't exist unless we can also not love, or perhaps more bluntly, hate. If this applies to us loving God; what about God loving us?

Do we know God loves us because he can also not love us?

I personally don't think so. After all, the most powerful adjective or descriptive noun we have for God is love. I don't know his love for me is genuine simply because he has a free will, and can therefore also not love or hate me. It is not in his nature to not love me. He just does.

Okay, yes, free will might not apply to God here, but it has to on the human level as we keep hearing about free will and love! Does my wife think my love for her is only genuine because I'm somehow free to not love her?

I don't think so. My love for Jane grew out of first meeting her, and having opportunity to get to know her. The freedom to not love her had not yet entered the equation. There was an initial attraction. I didn't have that with every girl I knew. It was either there or it wasn't. The attraction issue had nothing to do with will or choice.

Over time we both learned we were compatible and able to get on well with each other. The attraction continued too. Love grew over time so it was inevitable we married.

At no point in the process did we talk about whether our love was genuine simply because we were somehow free to not love each other. If I was to be really pragmatic about it, I would have to say neither of us was really free to not love the other. The way we are wired meant it was inevitable. In the right circumstances, we would marry, and so we did.

Obviously no one was holding a gun to either of our heads and demanding of us we love the other. There was no force involved. I think somehow understanding of free will gets confused by subconsciously thinking a lack of freedom to not love implies force is somehow part of the equation. It isn't.

Marriage does have its ups and downs. The times when I'm a bad husband are where I have free will, and therefore not perfect in my character. I hope over time I will grow to be a better husband for my wife. In that process there will be less free will displayed in my daily decisions involving Jane. I won't be living in a pattern where sometimes I get it right, and sometimes I get it wrong. I will simply love her because it is the right thing to do. I count on the power of God at work in my life to make this happen. There is no other way.

Taking this to our relationship with God, we don't love him because he forces us to love him. We love him because he loves us. When we encounter his love the natural outcome is to love him back. Our response does not come out of coercion. It comes because it is natural to love God when he opens our mind and sets us free from the bondage of Satan.

This is not to say us loving God is always instantaneous. It usually isn't. There may also be extreme resistance. Satan doesn't give up his slaves without a fight. There may also arise issues which seriously hinder our ability to maintain a relationship with God. God always deals with such issues in time in ways only he best understands.

I'm reminded of stories where someone adopted longs to know who their true father is. A first meeting with one's true father in such a circumstance will not always be easy. It is only ever hard to the degree to which we carry emotional wounding. When there is no emotional wounding, the reunion or first meeting goes well. We are wired to lean towards our natural fathers. This is the way we are made. It is also the way we are made on a spiritual level too.

Ultimately we are all made to be in a family relationship with God. The removal of our fallen carnal nature is the first obstacle needing removal for this to happen. Secondary to this will be the emotional healing we may need from life experience before we can fully receive God's love for us, and also respond in love to God. God knows how and when to heal us. He is in the healing business after all.

I have to say our view of love as portrayed by the media (Hollywood?) might have a significant influence on our thinking love needs free will to be genuine. This portrayal of love is so often in a love story between a man and a woman. I'm not so sure it is the best analogy to use in understanding the love of God towards us, and our response to him. The love between a parent and a child is a far better analogy.

Speaking for myself, I don't love anyone else's children the way I love my own. I just don't. Sorry if that bothers anyone, but I think I'm not alone with this. It is the way God has made me, and most other fathers I know. I have no free will in this at all.

Interestingly enough, my kids don't love anyone else's father more than me. This is normal, and free will has nothing to do with it.

Yes, in my 7 years of mentoring troubled youth, and many more years working at youth summer camps, I know not every kid gets on well with their parents. I also know some kids even hate their parents. Is this the natural order of things?

It is if there is human brokenness involved. Where there are healthy functional families, there is no free will in the love between parents and children. Parents always love their children, and children always love their parents.

It takes a seriously messed up parent to make a child hate them. I've known a few such parents. I've also known a few children who perhaps would be expected to hate their parents, but instead direct such hatred towards others. This is known as projection in psychological terms. It occurs particularly once they are adults.

Invariably, with all the kids I've known let down by failed parenting, there is always the wish things could have been better. Everyone with a bad relationship with a parent wishes it could be otherwise. Deep down we all long for a healthy bond with our parents. Some I'm sure are so badly wounded they may even claim they don't really care. Such denial is understandable given the depth of disappointment. The disappointment always precedes such denial.

In all this discussion of love between parents and children, free will has never played a part. We might try to force it into the picture of this reality, but then what we have is force, and that inherently stands against what the pushers of free will dogma stand on.

If free will really is part of the nature of true love, we won't need mental gymnastics to prove it. It is only when we misunderstand free will; we try to work it into our understanding of love.

My children are secure in my love for them because I have no free will to do otherwise. I'm not forced to love them. I love them because I'm their father. It is this simple. This is how we can learn to understand God's love for us, and our love for him, without needless distractions from dogmas around free will. Once again, I'm not claiming free will is not real. I'm just saying love for or from God is not predicated on free will.

The certainty of knowing love from God without free will means we can always be secure in such love. God is not free to stop loving us. He loves us because of who he is, and we naturally do the same back, when we are finally set free to do so.

This understanding has got to be good news in a world so confused and uncertain about love.

13: Infinite Exceptions.

I love this term "infinite exceptions". It came from a friend in Texas, Dave Presley. He referred to learning to dance in his reply to my second survey question about the fate of those who reject the Gospel.

What are "infinite exceptions"?

Basically they are all the excuses we get from people in church when thinking people, whether Christian or not, stop and say:

"This picture isn't right."

In other words, when some of our theologies are unsound, thinking people do at times see this. The result is an infinite number of exceptions which have to be made up to account for the logical inconsistencies in any flawed theologies and dogmas we may have.

It is very rare for people in general to simply see the inconsistency and change the flawed theology till it is sound. As a result we have no end of "infinite exceptions".

This Picture Isn't Right

There is a picture and it isn't right.

The picture I'm referring to is the one which may form when we present the traditional Heaven/Hell Gospel message with which I grew up. This message is:

> *"If we say yes to Jesus, we go to heaven. If we say no, or say nothing at all, we go to hell."*

It's that simple. It's quite a message too, and it's the standard theology of my youth.

Not everyone will say this message isn't right, or it begs questions. I'm certainly not saying I think someone isn't thinking if they don't. Plenty of smart thinkers are quite happy with the concept, or are thinking about other things instead. We won't all think the same. Still, plenty are thinking and know what I'm talking about.

Probably the biggest question to haunt many Christian thinkers is the one surrounding what happens to those who never receive the Gospel. These are the ones who "say nothing" to Jesus as they never got the Gospel to say yes in the first place.

I learnt at a young age we Christians had to get to as many people as possible through missionaries and the like so we could save as many as possible from the fires of hell.

I know I'm not just imagining this memory and making it up in my head. I recall reading how Bob Brown, a former Australian Green politician, left his Christian faith as he could not come to terms with a

God who left salvation in the hands of missionaries who may not be competent at reaching people with the saving message.

At least Bob Brown, and myself, grew up with this idea. I'd be surprised if we were the only ones. In fact, I know we're not, as I did refer to a church earlier which I've visited a number of times.

Each time I visit this church, we hear from the same elderly gentleman telling us of the urgent need to get out and reach everyone. Everyone knows why he is encouraging us to "get out there". We all know it is predicated on the idea if we don't, those not reached are doomed to an eternity in Hell.

It's classic "turn-off-Bob-Brown" theology. It's with us to this day. I'm fairly confident I'm not imagining it.

Logical Inconsistency

When we hold an unsound idea or worldview, over time logical inconsistencies will arise from that thinking.

Much depends on how deeply we hold to the worldview. Sometimes a logical inconsistency will not make us realise the fundamental worldview we hold is fraught with error. It will simply make us form an exception in our thinking. The dogma remains, with a growing list of attached amendments.

For many centuries people believed the world was flat. If one was to place a tall ship behind a row boat, one could position oneself back far enough on the sea on a calm day to make them look like they both had the same height. If one did, it might force one to question if the world really was flat. It might not too. In this case there is a logical inconsistency, but it may not be obvious for centuries.

When I studied French at university under an amazing teacher by the name of Dr David Wainwright, he had a saying:

"Il y a toujours des exceptions à chaque règle."
There are always exceptions to every rule.

Dr Wainwright was referring specifically to the French language when he said this. In many ways it was like a class joke. How many exceptions did it take before it was no longer a rule? French seemed to have many. So long as we knew the exceptions the rule was okay. Each rule wasn't perfect as they all had exceptions, but they would suffice to teach us French so we could avoid at least some dirty looks on the Boulevards of Paris.

Do our Christian theologies or worldviews present many exceptions? An exception is like a logical inconsistency. If we present too many, we have to realise eventually our thinking is unsound. We may not have a sound doctrine at all.

With enough awareness we ultimately find we have to change our views. Mankind could not continue thinking the world was flat forever. Eventually the logical inconsistencies the view presented overwhelmed the original viewpoint. The same is true for out theologies if they are unsound.

Hence my friend referred to "infinite exceptions". Some ideas are so unsound; there is seemingly no end to the exceptions required of us to continue thinking in such a manner.

I'm happy to say God really isn't an Englishman. I therefore think it safe to say neither is he French. If our understanding is sound about God, we won't have logical inconsistencies in our theologies. Some may wish to insist God is French. I'm happy for them if they do. It just won't work for me.

Creative Theology

It's not often we get to have conversations about "infinite exceptions" in church. When we do, we are often not aware we are. I've noticed this in 40+ years of being a Christian. We don't like to talk about uncomfortable subjects.

Remember, an "infinite exception" is the exception or theology we have to invent when we encounter the inevitable flaws if we hold unsound ideas or theology at the core of our Christian thinking.

I do remember one of those rare moments. It surrounded the question of what happens to babies when they die too young to say yes to Jesus.

Creativity came to the fore, and I'm so glad it did! No one slipped into dogmatic insistence that babies just have to go to hell. They knew God just could not be like that, even if their theology didn't tell them so.

Those with whom I was talking all believed salvation can only occur from our decisions made in this life. This is a fairly standard view many Christians hold. Still, with such a view, creative theology came to the fore. By creative theology, I mean to say it is extra-Biblical. This is to say it doesn't exist in scripture, without a strong creative flare or imagination necessary to justify it.

The common sense coming from knowing God in a personal relationship demanded we invent a theology to cover an "infinite exception" surrounding the idea of salvation for babies. The theology took the form of something akin to God having a special dispensation for children.

They didn't at that point wake up and start questioning if their overall theology was flawed. They simply added an "amendment" to the "constitution". Their theology begged some questions, so they had to plug an obvious hole with an exception they didn't find in scripture.

The basic "constitution" of so much standard theology has us thinking firstly there are only two possible destinations after we die. These destinations are heaven and hell. As with the US Constitution formed back in the late 1700's, Amendments were required to cover circumstances not covered by the original concepts.

The Catholic Church is well ahead of the Protestant Churches on this basis. They could see the begging of questions from the original dogma of two destinations. They came up with Limbo and Purgatory as extra possible destinations.

I can only guess most Protestant churches reject Limbo and Purgatory because they can't find the concepts in scripture. I tend to agree too. Their members are left with unofficial amendments one dreams up on the run, like the special dispensation God has for babies, referred to above.

Some of the more fringe protestant groups have a more clearly defined concept of heaven and hell. They understand the obvious problems existing in the fundamental thinking of much hell fire theology.

By this means they attract a large number of thinking people, and load them up with other forms of religious baggage which normally repels the average attendee of a mainstream church. Unhealthy religion will take whatever form it needs to in order to snare as many followers as possible.

This is one of my pet peeves with mainstream protestant churches. The after-death theology is so questionable; they give too many thinking people no choice but to accept certain fringe groups as the best option available for church involvement.

Fringe group theologies are sometimes harder to recognise as absurd, so a thinking person can fall under their spell more easily than they can under the more obvious questionable beliefs of some mainstream churches.

Members of these fringe churches can so easily see the flaws in the thinking of some mainstream churches. The errors "outside" are so obvious, it makes it easier to never question the less obvious flaws in their fringe church.

If people were less violent with their passions on life-after-death theologies, it might be easier for the mainstream churches to address these matters and openly discuss them. Silence on the topic has been the best option for too many for too long.

"Don't dare say anything or ask uncomfortable questions as someone might trigger."

I'm certainly grateful for some of the churches I know where pastors are open to the fact there are different views out there, similar to the points being made in this book. They avoid being dogmatic about certain theological positions, and make the congregation a welcome place for diversity of opinion.

Missing Missionaries

There could be many reasons to reject a salvation message from a missionary, with no fault on the part of the missionary. There could be many reasons too why a missionary would never reach certain people. Access to some tribes and locations would always be a challenge.

What a relief when the missionary finally arrives! At last people can be saved. Too bad for those of previous generations who had long since died before the missionary could get to them. They can be satisfied, even if they are suffering hell fire or eternal separation from God; their grand kids are doing fine.

Some fringe groups have an answer. We can baptise on behalf of the dead and save them that way. Poor mainstream theology makes some of these fringe groups look rather sensible. I wish it wasn't so. Perhaps God is happy we all look silly in different ways?

Creative theology is once more the order of the day if this topic is ever raised. What does God do with all the millions who died before they could have ever had a chance of learning about Jesus?

I've heard an argument drawn from the early chapters of Paul's epistle to the Romans. I won't quote whole chapters from Romans here. The theory holds people instinctively know right from wrong. Some do better than others at following their own moral compass.

Those who never heard of salvation through Jesus before they died can be saved by how well they did following their instinctive moral compass.

How cool is that!? We can still save ourselves! At least we can by this particular explanation.

It reminds me of how if we start telling one lie, we have to tell another to cover for the original lie. Creative theology is like that. If we start with a flawed theology, we have to come up with more flawed theology to cover it. It goes on and on. I'd much rather deal with the original flaws in our theology.

Is there a problem if people die before they have ever had a hope of receiving a salvation message about Jesus?

There is under much current thinking in many church circles.

Many believe the salvation message can only be received and believed in this life before one dies. If that was not the case, there would be no need for all the various forms of creative theologies we come up with.

If we don't get saved in this life, it's too late. No salvation is possible. It's now or never. Hence we add the necessary creative theology to whatever scenario confronts our thinking with obvious questions.

So many of these creative ideas are seriously flawed when compared with the basic understanding of Christian salvation most mainstream churches hold at their core, and need to hold at their core. I refer to salvation by grace as one of these core essential beliefs. I've heard a number of creative theologies which essentially promote salvation by works. We shouldn't have to go there.

Of course I'll be accused of creative theology by some when I finally present my case. I expect that. It's an occupational hazard in the Christian walk. I'm happy to let you, the reader, decide for yourself.

Bad Examples.

One of my favourite "infinite exceptions" is the consideration of Christian bad examples. I'm sure we have met at least one in our lives. I'd be a fool if I thought I wasn't one myself at times. Let's face it – we are all fairly flawed creatures, whether Christian or otherwise.

Somehow God still doesn't shy away from using us. I'm really glad he doesn't. It makes life so much more interesting. Still, there are times when I give myself cause for embarrassment.

Would it not be awful if someone's salvation depended on me!?

It's a scary thought. If someone unsaved meets me on a bad day, knows I'm a Christian and they are given every reason to not be one too, what happens if they die that night?

Life in the Middle Ages was tough, and particularly so if one lived on the Mediterranean coast of Southern Europe. The reason was simple – marauding Saracens. For some 400 years Europeans to the south suffered constant plundering and enslavement. Eventually they united sufficiently to respond, and from this began what is known in history as The Crusades.

Tired of the incessant attacks from the Middle Eastern Saracens, the European Christian armies marched towards The Holy Land. After 400 years of "bad days", losing friends and relatives to slavery, the Crusaders were not in a sound state of mind to present the Gospel message in the best possible light.

It is hard one thousand years later to really know how effective they were as evangelists. Depending on what one has read in history, the effectiveness of their Gospel message, if they even had one, was hardly a question. If my memory serves me correctly, when they captured the city of Antioch, they killed anyone they could lay their hands on.

They were very thorough. They were only really at war against the Saracens, but they killed Jews and Christians as well as any Saracens they could find in the city. That makes for a really effective salvation message.... or does it?

I've no idea what happened on a case by case basis. I'd be surprised if any particular crusader in his blood lust was busy trying to lead anyone to Jesus. But what if some were? How appealing would the message be?

"Yes, you too can become a Christian, just like me. However, please don't be put off by how all my Christian friends are busy killing all your friends and associates in the city, including the Jews and Christians. By the way, I'm also going to kill you too, so why not make a decision for Christ before I do?"

That's quite an altar call. Somehow I don't think anyone received a message quite like this before their blood was spilled.

Can we see the dilemma this creates?

The very so-called Christians the people of Antioch needed to lead them to Jesus before they died were not doing a good job of it. Too bad I guess, as they enjoy an eternity in hell fire, or separation from God, depending on how one wants to consider outcomes for the unsaved.

We either need to come up with some creative theology again, or reconsider the foundations of our existing theology. Something has to give.

One easy way out is to just consider there were already Christians in the city. These Christians should already have been active trying to save all the Jews and Saracens in the city.

Clearly, the resident Christians either hadn't tried hard enough to save everyone, or the Saracens and Jews had already made their choices. It would not matter then if they all died as they had already rejected Jesus. Even the Christians in the city could die too. They could die for not trying harder to save the unsaved. How neat is that?

Personally, I have a problem with all this.

If salvation really depended on getting a message out to people with freedom to accept or reject the message, how right is it so many lose out from a poorly delivered message?

Not only was the message delivered poorly, the Crusaders gave every reason for someone to reject Christianity before they met the steel of their swords.

If God really did love the world so much he would give his son Jesus to die for us, would it make sense for his plan of salvation to fall over so easily in the hands of such flawed people as Christians can be?

I'm not saying the Crusaders were necessarily Christians. Odds are many were not. Still, at least some of them could have been. They did represent Christianity, albeit poorly at least some of the time, whatever the truth may be to this question. War does have a way of bringing out the worst in us.

I certainly don't intend to present the Crusaders as somehow worse in conduct than their Saracen enemies. The Crusaders were only there because of 400 or so years of violent provocation from Saracen armies. There was no high moral ground on the part of the Saracens.

Thinking of another bad example, when we choose someone to babysit our kids, I take care to leave our kids in the hands of someone we are confident is capable and competent. The average parent would. Still, somehow, we have theologies which put the salvation of mankind in the hands of those who may not be so competent.

None of this stacks up with the God I've been getting to know over these past 40 years.

He is far too sensible.

He is far too capable.

He is far too intelligent to come up with such a poor plan.

He is also far too loving to leave so much to chance for those he loves.

Second Chances.

"But that would mean God was giving them a second chance!"

The affront was obvious from this elderly pastor I knew. He expressed this objection when I put forward the suggestion maybe some may get the Gospel message after they die.

It was only later I thought about it and realised they probably were not getting a second chance at all. If they never got any chance in this life, how could it be a second chance in the next?

For arguments sake, let's just agree some do get a second chance, even if it is only their first. How bad would it be?

Why are we so keen for others to get their just deserts when we Christians never got ours (assuming this is a purely Christian objection)?

For myself, I'm probably way beyond any thought of a second chance. I'm so not perfect, yet I'm saved. There would hardly be a day going by where I don't get my just deserts. God's grace is for me every day. I really need it too.

My elderly pastor friend also thought it was unfair for us to have to do it tough in this life as Christians, while others might sail through this life without knowing God, and then be saved after they died.

Did he never read Jesus' words about the last being first? Since when was fairness an issue in the Christian walk?

Maybe it is unfair? I don't know. Who said life as a Christian had to be fair? I'm only grateful I wasn't born as a Jew in Poland in the early 1920's. That would be one of the toughest straws one could ever draw in life. The fate for most Jews born in Poland in the 1920's was a slow painful death in a concentration camp, or the quicker alternative in a gas chamber.

Let's be really frank here. How much in life really is fair? I don't know of much at all. I was born in Australia. I have friends who were born in Uganda. I'm here, and they are over there.

Life's tough no matter where one is born – for most of us anyway. Still, both I and my Ugandan friends know I have it pretty good here in Australia. One would often say to me he wished Uganda had our problems in place of theirs.

"Fair" is for fiction writers and government Education Department bureaucrats, in my estimate of how life unfolds.

Just maybe, if God will save people after they die, it isn't unfair at all. This may be particularly so with the bigger picture in mind of how few are saved in this life time. I'll look at what scripture has to say about this in more detail later.

God Knows The Heart

Death is good at stripping the clouded veneer off our religious thinking. At least this is true for the season grief can represent.

Few of us will escape the grief from the passing of a relative. Many Christians will likewise experience the passing of an unsaved relative. Many would therefore wish they had been saved before they died. Inevitably, some will even ask their pastor if God really wouldn't save their unsaved relative.

It is not an easy question to ask. We fear the answer is no.

The usual answer given to this question is God knows the heart. I've heard this reply so often I could say it backwards in my sleep. God knows the heart!

That statement in itself is an "infinite exception".

Behind it, without our realisation, is a theology of salvation by the condition of our heart. Our relative was never a Christian, yet somehow the state of their heart makes up for it.

If this really is true, then many of us don't need Jesus to be saved.

The Bible says a great deal about the natural state of our hearts:

The heart is deceitful above all things and beyond cure. Who can understand it? **Jeremiah 17:9** (NIV)

I'm not trying to depress anyone here. I believe in good news probably more than many Christians I know. I will get to why eventually.

The point about the verse from Jeremiah above is our hearts are not good. Who can understand it? God can, and he doesn't need to kid himself in the ways we often have to. If our theologies are contradictory we have to kid ourselves in all manner of ways to resolve these contradictions, and we often do.

Yes, when someone unsaved dies, God does know the heart. He has no illusions about the state of the unsaved heart. It won't save anyone. Still, we hear the line so often:

"God knows the heart."

He really does, but we don't help a flawed salvation theology riddled with holes by plugging the obvious holes with porous filler. It will always leak.

Any creative theology we come up with supporting the notion of salvation by works, good unsaved hearts, or any other means than Jesus will sink a ship, or at least leave us shipwrecked.

In my view, once we really grasp how good the good news really is, we won't need to resort to so many of the creative theologies I've referred to in this chapter.

Everything will make sense without any awkward patchwork bandaids when we really understand the Gospel. We won't need to cover flawed logic with hastily thrown-together religious constructs which conflict with the core truth of salvation by faith in Jesus.

Suicide

In some religious circles, suicide is looked on as worse than murder. It is murder – murder of the self. I'm not sure why it is somehow worse than murder. If comparisons can be made, murder with consent just might be less bad than murder without consent. I guess there is no end to the value judgements we can make in a religious context. I personally don't understand how suicide could be worse. It must all come down to opinion.

In Australia we understand the problem is serious. We have high rates of youth suicide, and high rates of suicide in the countryside. Farmers are doing it tough, and some take their lives as a result.

A friend once said how she felt suicide was extremely selfish. I'm not so certain I could call it that. Who really understands the depths of despair which can grip a person in a hard place in life?

Sadly, the answer to this question is quite a large number of people do understand depths of despair. Depression is far more evident in our society than ever before. I can't say more people are getting depressed. I don't know. Maybe we are. I will say we are certainly more aware of the problem. That is clear.

I'm no expert on suicide. I can only surmise the path to such action is often likely to be via depression. Hence I do think many who have suffered or suffer from depression really do understand the depths of despair which can grip a person.

A number of friends have been in the grip of depression at various times. Some still are. For some medication is their means of coping. They all have something in common. They can't shake their depression on their own.

The "infinite exception" looms large over this subject. Is someone who suicides really responsible? Does their despair merit the punishment some have in mind for them?

I knew someone who I would deem to be responsible. She was an elderly lady who feared suffering the same fate as her mother, who had many years of dementia. Her mother's dementia was hard on the whole family.

She decided with the first signs of dementia in herself, she would take her own life. She did. The last thing she wanted was to inflict the hardship of dementia on others.

I'm not so certain her suicide was selfish. I don't have any questions on responsibility in this case. She knew exactly what she was doing. She was an anaesthetist. She knew how to do it painlessly and quickly. She also ensured minimal impact on others in a physical sense. I won't go into further details.

There was an emotional impact. I was not the only one with tears in my eyes at her funeral. Her children were certainly impacted. In particular, the one child of hers who was a Christian was troubled more than the others. I didn't want to probe with too many questions. I could already guess what was going through his head.

I can't help but see a paradox in this. With all the talk of good news, why was the Christian the most troubled?

I think we all know. Their mother was not a Christian. To make it worse, their mother had taken her own life.

Does good news of the Gospel kind have a place in this situation?

For many it doesn't. The wisdom of "infinite exceptions" has not messed with their thinking enough to start questioning theologies which are full of contradictions.

We rarely if ever hear about hell fire at funerals. If the service has any form of religious flavour to it, heaven is usually referred to as the destination. No matter who the person was who died, and whether or not they were Christians, the gentle assumption made at many funerals these days is heaven.

I'm glad our society has moved on from the former days when suicides would never be buried in the local church grave yard. If a suicide was not hard enough to take for a family, rejection by their church and the lack of a Christian burial was the last thing they needed.

In the previous chapter on free choice, I tried to make it clear being open to receive Jesus as our saviour is a work of God. I don't have any difficulty recognising in my friend who suicided, the lack of a saving work of God before she died. I may have missed it. If there was one, I've not been told.

Some will put forward the "creative theology" Jesus could have met her just before she died so she could choose if she wanted to give her life to him. He well could have. Whether he did or didn't, I doubt he needed to in order to save her. His power to save is bigger than any theology we may have saying he can't save her.

So many are fixated on the idea salvation can only be received in this life. I don't know why exactly, but I could guess it goes back to the parable of Lazarus and the Rich Man. In this parable there was a huge gulf separating the saved Lazarus, and the unsaved rich man. It could never be crossed. I've already discussed this in an earlier chapter, and why it does not refute my position.

I'm so glad many scholars realise it probably was just a parable shaped around the context of a popular story out of Egypt. Lord of the Rings would be a similar genre in today's contemporary scene, if one was tempted to tell a parable today.

We really would be well advised to check the sources of our theologies before we invest too heavily in them.

I can't blame anyone for thinking a salvation decision is only possible before we die. We have been indoctrinated with such thinking for many centuries. The questions it begs are so often silenced by the suffocating weight of religious tradition.

It suited well the power structure of the church in history to have people believe this salvation theory. Those for whom there was no escaping the obvious questions could then be silenced by burning at the stake. Fortunately it is not as easy to maintain the silence today.

My elderly friend who took her life was responsible for her actions. She made sure of it by ensuring she did it before her dementia progressed too far to stop her.

Jesus might have saved her before she died, but I don't think he had to. He isn't limited by our cumbersome and sometimes contradictory theologies. This is definitely good news!

I'm so glad I can understand enough to realise for suicide, where despair has taken personal responsibility far out of the equation, or even when it hasn't, there is still a hope of salvation. I can easily see this hope is founded on a sound, logical, scriptural and academic foundation.

I'll get to this foundation eventually. In the meantime, please be assured there is every reason to believe in good news in the midst of the too frequent tragedies suicide represents for us in society today.

14: Knowing God.

For you granted him authority over all people that he might give eternal life to all those you have given him. Now this is eternal life: that they know you, the only true God, and Jesus Christ, whom you have sent. **John 17:2-3** (NIV)

A Purpose for Eternal Life.

Quite a number of people I know have shared how even after many years of marriage to their husband or wife; they are still learning new things about them.

I can say for myself I've experienced the same with my wife. Human beings are far more complex than what may immediately meet the eye. If people are complex, made in the image of God, what of God himself?

Would it take a lifetime to really know God? Would a lifetime be enough? I would think not. In my 40 plus years now of getting to know God myself, I'm finding there is so much more to learn and know. I find myself realising more and more how little I really do know about God.

It would be fair to say there is never a dull moment where knowing God is concerned.

With this in mind, I want to consider the above two verses from the seventeenth chapter of the Gospel of John, referred to above.

The first of the two verses seems somewhat straightforward in its meaning. Jesus was given authority over people from God the Father. This was so he could give the gift of eternal life to everyone God the Father drew to him.

The second starts to sound a little mystical to my reasoning. It is like he is giving a definition to the meaning of eternal life, as if it is something other than just living for a long long time, with no end. It reads like Jesus is saying eternal life is knowing God the Father, and Jesus his son, rather than just an unlimited span of time.

Does this then mean eternal life is not living forever, and Jesus was straightening out a misconception here?

Given the tiny bit I already know of God, I would have to say the answer to the above question is no. Rather, I suspect these verses are more figurative than literal in their meaning, and particularly verse three.

Language doesn't always have to be dry and crisp in presentation and meaning. Sometimes there is a value in couching a concept in obscure terms to hopefully make us think – to make us stop and pause.

I can look back at nearly 2000 years of Church history. I see so much of what I understand and take for granted was not always clear in previous centuries.

Salvation by faith alone was certainly understood in the beginning, when the apostles originally presented the Gospel message. That central and critical point in the message was soon lost however. It was not until another 1400 years or so before it came back to our attention with Martin Luther, and others with a similar understanding.

I recall some years ago reading how the forgiveness of sins was not very well understood. Apparently some 200 years ago, according to whatever the book was I was reading, people would be forced into the British Navy as a punishment for believing their sins were forgiven.

I am unable to verify if this really was true without doing extensive research on the history of the understanding of forgiveness. Maybe I should do such research one day. For now I'm happy enough to believe it is likely given how many I have met over the years who struggle individually to believe God really has forgiven their sins.

Some people really struggle with believing they are forgiven. It is a witness to me of how hard it is to really believe the Gospel message. It can seem way too good to be true. If it is still hard to believe today, I suspect it also was 200 years ago. For now I can spare myself the extra hours in research.

If I reach into my own life for an example, I recall how for many years I would ask God to prove to me he really loved me. I could read he did, but I wanted to know it personally.

After some years of seeking this personal revelation, it did begin to hit me. He showed me he had been showing his love for me through so many of his people in the Church. I had no doubt these people really did love me. It was unmistakable.

Over time, the revelation of his love for me advanced and deepened. Initially I understood and knew God's love as something reaching me from other people. Over time I began to know his love for me through direct relationship.

This personal revelation of his love for me is not something which has now arrived and been finalised. It is ongoing. I know there is more. I keep seeking it too. It is all part of the mystery and wonder of knowing God. It is a truly amazing journey, and in so many ways I keep thinking it has only just begun.

So, back to this rather mystical statement of Jesus saying eternal life is knowing God. The point I think Jesus wants us to grasp, not superficially, but with deep reflection, is it takes an eternity to really know God. If anything can make sense of this verse, this explanation does!

But how does this relate to the Gospel - the Good News?

Could it mean our historical understanding of the Gospel is still primitive because our understanding hinges on really knowing God?

Could it mean there is still more to learn about how good the Good News really is, because getting to know God can take so long?

God is Love.

A number of times I've alluded to how our view of God shapes and informs our thinking. How well we know God is behind every example of "infinite exceptions" mentioned in this book.

For most our theology tells us a baby is too young to give their life to Jesus. Many also believe if we die unsaved we are doomed. If we put the two ideas together with a fairly healthy view of God's love, we then find we have to resort to creative theologies to make sense of the obvious disconnect.

In the middle ages many theologians knew enough to resort to such. The creative theology then formed concluded there was an alternative to Hell called Limbo. It would do as a place for babies as they couldn't stretch their understanding enough to find heaven in the equation.

Over many years looking at various belief systems in different church denominations, I've come to a basic conclusion. How we view God reflects how we understand scripture. Given this, what shapes our view of God can be many things.

Scripture is certainly one source of how we view God. It does and can inform our opinions, even though I've said our understanding of scripture will be influenced by how we view God.

> *Whoever does not love does not know God, because God is love.* **1 John 4:8** (NIV)

The above verse from the first epistle of John describes God in really simple terms. God is love! How clear could it be?

Unfortunately, saying God is love is not necessarily a clear statement. The first part of the verse above sheds some light on this fact. It says if we don't love, we don't know God.

I've referred to the wicked nature of the human heart in a previous chapter. Many who don't know God likely struggle to understand the true nature of their unsaved heart. I can understand this. If I replace the word "wicked", which can sound a bit extreme, with a more gentle term like "imperfect", it might be easier to understand what I'm saying.

Few non-Christians I know run around thinking they are perfect people. One of the outcomes of an imperfect heart is we don't love too well. Selfishness gets in the way of loving others. We don't need to be Christians to know this.

The understanding each person can have of love can vary so much. Hence our view of God can vary so much, and therefore how we interpret scripture and form our doctrines can vary so much.

Just listen to a popular radio station for a week, and this should be abundantly clear. I can't say for sure, but I have to wonder if love is the most common theme in songs from at least the last 50 years or so. So many songs create so many different pictures of love.

If I try to draw a number of themes from different songs in my head, it doesn't take me long to come up with a number of descriptions. Love hurts to some, and one even considers love is a battlefield. Some wonder if love has anything to do with anything, while others think it is all we need.

Do we get the picture? I have to wonder if many of us are confused about love. No wonder the realm of religion or spirituality can seem confusing.

I cannot speak for all these song writers who have left their imprints on my mind. I hardly know their names. I have to surmise they have formed their views of love from experience. The same could well be true of our views of God.

We can read God is love, and experience so much in life which will influence our view of love. I know I certainly did. I'm not surprised the menu for religious dogma is extensive.

Perhaps the greatest influence I've seen on how we view God is our relationship with our own fathers.

It's no surprise I have seen many with a poor relationship with their father struggle to have a healthy view of God, let alone a personal relationship with him. My human father was largely absent. No wonder I had to struggle to know God loved me.

Fortunately God is bigger than our personal dysfunctions. He understands us well too. He is pretty good at breaking through the barriers we unwitting erect between us and him because of the failings of our human fathers.

Still, there is also plenty of religion to stand between us and a healthy relationship with God. All the religion mankind has managed to stuff into Christianity over 2000 years has also played a factor in distorting our view of God.

Fortunately again, God is bigger than our religious construction projects and philosophies. He can reach us through the religious smog, smoke, and haze, and sometimes he does.

This must be why my own views of God and my understanding of scripture have changed so much over the past 40 years. God has always been bigger than the mess of me. He has also been bigger than the tangled web of religion which has held me in its thrall for much of my life.

I'm slowly waking up and coming to life. It makes for an interesting journey, even if I say so myself.

Moses' Argument.

The LORD would speak to Moses face to face, as one speaks to a friend. **Exodus 33:11** (NIV)

I love the above statement. How many of us are this comfortable with God? Are we so at ease in our relationship with God we can speak with him like talking with a friend?

I hope so. I know for many it is a hard concept. For whatever reason, they have not moved beyond the "fear" of God. Sometimes, as I've previously alluded, it can be a function of how well we could communicate with our earthly fathers. It can be so much harder for us to relate to a heavenly Father if we have not been close with our direct physical father.

It can take time to overcome our baggage standing in the way of us relating well to God. Remember it took me years to really know I knew he did love me. If I was asked how many years, twenty would be a decent estimate.

The relationship Moses had with God was certainly one to aspire to. I'm sure it took time to get to that place. Moses was in so many ways no different from you or me.

We can read through the journey of Israel under the leadership of Moses, in the second to fifth books of the Old Testament. In this journey we read of some really interesting exchanges between Moses and God. From these we can learn certain things about God and how he thinks.

One particular example comes from the exchange Moses has with God after Israel gets the dumb idea to smelt a golden calf. This happens while Moses is up on the mountain receiving the Ten Commandments. God was really unimpressed with Israel falling back into idolatry so soon after leaving Egypt:

> "I have seen these people," the LORD said to Moses, "and they are a stiff-necked people. Now leave me alone so that my anger may burn against them and that I may destroy them. Then I will make you into a great nation."
> But Moses sought the favor of the LORD his God. "LORD," he said, "why should your anger burn against your people, whom you brought out of Egypt with great power and a mighty hand? Why should the Egyptians say, 'It was with evil intent that he brought them out, to kill them in the mountains and to wipe them off the face of the earth'? Turn from your fierce anger; relent and do not bring disaster on your people. Remember your servants Abraham, Isaac and Israel, to whom you swore by your own self: 'I will make your descendants as numerous as the stars in the sky and I will give your descendants all this land I promised them, and it will be their inheritance forever.'"
> Then the LORD relented and did not bring on his people the disaster he had threatened. **Exodus 32:9-14** (NIV)

Moses made an interesting point to God. If God was to destroy Israel over the golden calf issue, then the Egyptians might view God in a certain way. They might impute an evil design on God's part in leading Israel out of Egypt.

Moses proposed God's reputation was on the line. What would the Egyptians think if they hear Israel was destroyed by God in the desert?

Was this great God, who brought Egypt to her knees to deliver Israel, just another psychotic power-freak god? Was this God of Israel just like the Egyptian ones?

Moses raised a good point. God was at this stage in human history investing in his reputation. I'm sure it wasn't for his sake. He isn't insecure. He was investing in the record of scripture certain signature events to reveal himself and his nature to mankind.

What I gather from this event, and how God responded to Moses, is simple. God is and was neither a fundamental Calvinist, nor an Arminian.

I use the term "fundamental Calvinist" to distinguish between so many Calvinists I know who would say they cannot hold to all the ideas of fundamental Calvinism. They know they cannot accept God really is harsh in the manner fundamental Calvinism portrays.

This then leads me to an important question:

Would a fundamental Calvinist God today have "the Egyptians" say it was with evil intent to bring someone into being, knowing their fate was eternal damnation and torment in the fires of Hell?

Do I have to answer this question?

In case I do, the answer is "yes".

A fundamental Calvinist God has no problem with his reputation for bringing people to life knowing the only future for them is suffering for eternity in Hell.

This is the nature of a fundamental Calvinist God. Hence, it would not be strange to a fundamental Calvinist God to rescue Israel from Egypt knowing they were destined for destruction soon after in the desert.

Similarly:

Would an Arminian God today have "the Egyptians" say it was with evil intent to bring someone into being, knowing the odds of them ever receiving the saving message about Jesus were minimal at best?

Is the answer to both those questions as obvious as I think it is?

Like Moses, I could ask the same of God myself concerning his bringing people to life, only so they can end up with an outcome of eternal punishment. In my view, God would not allow "the Egyptians" to draw such a conclusion indefinitely. At some point in time He would want the record straightened so mankind did have a sound view of His nature.

I say "at some point in time" because at this stage the message is very clear to quite a few "Egyptians" who I know or know of, about the mercurial nature of the so-called love of the Christian God.

The fact so few seem to understand this problem in our theologies is more a reflection of the state of mankind with religion, than God himself. It would have to suit His purpose for a season for mankind to form these perspectives under the many and varied influences of religion.

Our historical experiences with religion are important for informing mankind on the various ways the problems beginning in the Garden of Eden are expressed to this day. Saying this, I do have to wonder if the time of this season is drawing to a close now. I hope it is.

In summary, God saved Israel from his wrath by indulging Moses for the purpose of the necessary written record of His true nature.

This encounter with Moses was therefore instructive in revealing something of God's nature. The same lesson can equally apply to us today. We need to think about the theologies we hold and what they say to the world about our God.

Would it be appropriate to close with "for those who have ears"?

Psycho God?

This is a difficult topic to talk about. I have friends who have invested heavily in the Calvinist creed. I'm grateful they all will say they are not totally Calvinist in their thinking. I therefore hope they will not see themselves in my references to "fundamental Calvinists".

In deference to them, I can say in many respects, I have certain Calvinist views myself. One of my Calvinist friends was able to point this out to me, and fortunately my mind was open enough to hear him.

One area where I cannot claim any allegiance is the belief God brings people into being, with the express design they will be predestined to eternal punishment. This is not the God I know. He has not revealed himself to me as having such a nature. Neither can I see this idea in scripture. Respectfully, some friends think they can, and I hope our differences in perspective will never separate us as friends.

No one has any say in how, when, where, or to whom they are born. I don't mind if the outcome is ultimately good or bad, to understand the Gospel to mesh perfectly with this hard reality. If it didn't, I would have a hard time myself viewing it as good news.

The Gospel can't be good news in my view if it is only good for a small minority.

To me, bringing people into existence with a direct purpose which will see them suffer for eternity is something out of a horror movie. I'm sorry to say this, but the way it comes across to me, it is basically psychotic.

How comfortable can we be if our theology is saying to thinking people our God is like a psychopath?

I'm sure this is never anyone's intention. I dare say there is a certain embarrassment thinking about it too if we can recognise we hold theology like this. Please keep reading. I will explain why one can safely discard such thinking and still be faithful to scripture. To no longer have to make excuses about a presentation of God I can prove to be false has got to be worth the time to keep reading this.

Pick any leader in history who was a tyrant. In most cases they were probably psychotic. Adolf Hitler certainly was. So was Joseph Stalin. In both cases, they were kind to a small number of those close to them. How far such kindness extended is anybody's guess.

Does this sound like a certain theology?

Eva Braun, who married Hitler just before they killed themselves, I'm sure adored Hitler. What was their personal life like together? I don't know. Was it a wholesome relationship? I doubt it, but how would I know? Maybe they both enjoyed S&M?

Some people are comfortable being abused. They can be so close to the abuser they fail to realise they are being abused.

Religion can be like this too. I've seen it so many times myself it is sickening. I've had face-to-face encounters with a number of cult leaders. These were people revered to the point almost of worship. Their followers could not say a negative thing about them. This was not only because they were constrained. They really did believe the sun shone out of...... you know where.

I've tried communicating with the followers of certain cult leaders. They were incapable of any acknowledgement anything was wrong with these leaders, or the ethos elevating their leaders.

I even was witness to some fairly intense physical abuse of one particular cult member. There was no telling anyone it was dysfunctional. Such words would not have been heard, let alone understood. After all, I was only a child when witness to the abuse.

Religion can have a way of closing the minds of people. Some of these followers would outwardly seem to be quite intelligent and well educated. Still, not all expressions of religion are as intensely abusive as I've observed in certain cult settings.

The point I need to make is how under the guise of religion, all manner of strange creeds can be respected and accepted, with rarely any thought as to what they say about the nature of God.

Does it make sense any kind of theology which presents God as having the nature of a psychopath just may not be good news?

Stone Them!

I've pointed out before how fundamental Calvinism is not without scriptures they can use to try to support many of their positions. I've also made it clear this does not mean the Bible is full of contradictions. It isn't. It is just misunderstood.

The Bible is also written in a manner to allow us to interpret all manner of conclusions to show us (or others?) much about ourselves and our view of God. The way the Bible does this gives me more reason to be in awe of its inspiration from God, than to discredit it.

The death penalty was a frequent event in the Old Testament. It even had its place in the New Testament. There were moments in both testaments where God was very heavy handed in his treatment of sin, and not just amongst his own people, the Israelites.

Today, many nations which have developed a strong Christian heritage have turned from the death penalty as part of their legal code. I used to think the aversion to the death penalty was rather strange as God did not seem to have had a problem with it in the Bible. Why would all these nations with cultural values so strongly influenced by the Bible be turning from the death penalty?

Back in the late 1980's, I was living in England. Every now and then I would catch up with a good friend of my father. He was living in London, and a practicing Psychiatrist. I always enjoyed these visits as catching up with someone who knew my dad so well was a way of feeling just a little closer to home.

I don't recall how the subject came up, but I remember saying how puzzled I was when I heard Christians express abhorrence to the death penalty. My father's friend was fortunately able to explain it to me and it made a lot of sense.

His explanation was given this life is the only time one can be granted salvation, if we sentence someone to death, they have less time for someone to convince them to receive Jesus as their saviour.

If we end their life early, odds are they will be consigned to eternal torment in hell. If we give them a life sentence, there is more chance they might repent and be saved. It was only a chance they might be saved, but at least one can say we gave them every opportunity.

Reading between the lines, I can see this viewpoint was very Arminian. It was all about free choice, and helping someone to make the best decision, if at all possible.

There was also an underlying belief people somehow could be responsible for the salvation of others to a greater or lesser extent.

Personally I would not be comfortable carrying such a responsibility. I always thought Jesus did the saving - not me, even though he could use me in some manner as part of the process. To think I might be critical in someone's salvation is absurd to me if salvation is through Jesus and no one else.

Regardless of how we looked at the death penalty from our human perspective, God didn't seem concerned about the issues bothering us. This lack of concern does in some ways fit with the fundamental Calvinist viewpoint.

As much as we might think the fundamental Calvinist portrayal of God is rather heartless and cruel, a Calvinist can point to events in the Bible which portray the same, but only if we believe salvation can only be attained in this life, and never after we die.

Fundamental Calvinists can argue God can come across as quite callous when dishing out death on so many wrong doers, including their innocent family members.

This would then be at odds with my view of a God who does not have such ambivalence in the manner of the fundamental Calvinist view of God.

I'll draw on one particular example to illustrate this point. It involved the sin of an Israelite called Achan, and how he hoarded some valuables after the battle for the city of Jericho.

God had given specific commands any gold or silver had to be given to the holy treasury. It could not be kept for oneself in the sacking of the city. This story can be followed in Joshua chapters 6 and 7, in the Old Testament. The penalty on Achan, for his disobedience was particularly severe:

Whoever is caught with the devoted things shall be destroyed by fire, along with all that belongs to him. He has violated the covenant of the Lord and has done an outrageous thing in Israel!'" **Joshua 7:15** (NIV)

Then Joshua, together with all Israel, took Achan son of Zerah, the silver, the robe, the gold bar, his sons and daughters, his cattle, donkeys and sheep, his tent and all that he had, to the Valley of Achor. Joshua said, "Why have you brought this trouble on us? The Lord will bring trouble on you today." **Joshua 7:24-25** (NIV)

Notice how it was not just Achan who suffered for his disobedience. His family was also executed. To make the point even stronger, even his livestock were executed. It is hard to consider a more extreme form of punishment than this.

It might be argued the family members colluded with Achan in some measure, so therefore were party to the crime. That may be true. We don't really know. Neither do we know the ages of the children to determine if they could have been realistically responsible in some way. The livestock were clearly responsible. Cows, goats, sheep, and donkeys usually are.

Really?

Depending on what one wants to read into these events, much support can be drawn for the fundamental Calvinist position on a superficial level. I can understand the argument their view of God comes from scriptures like these. Such views might have a great hold on ones thinking so long as we avoid getting into philosophical arguments about contradictions which follow from such thinking, and considering the need for more "infinite exceptions".

I can certainly respect the effort to hold scripture as sacrosanct and beyond question. I really am happy to join with my Calvinist friends and hold the same position towards scripture.

Where I differ is I don't think we need to hold to our interpretations of scripture as sacrosanct. I also differ in my understanding of the bigger picture behind these events where God can seem to be so harsh. The fundamental Calvinist view presents way too many contradictions. We either live with these contradictions and the "infinite exceptions" they force on us, or we reconsider our fundamental viewpoints in our theology.

The scriptures are fine. We and our understanding and interpretations may not be. This is how I am able to differ from the fundamental Calvinist view. They are certain they have their view of the salvation process correct, at least in the main details concerning predestination to salvation or damnation. There is however too much saying to me they are not correct on these major points concerning God's plan of salvation.

Clearly, if we view death and salvation from the perspective of my dad's friend in London, then what happened to the family of Achan was a huge deal. By his view, the sin of Achan had an eternal impact on his whole family, with no opportunity for later repentance.

At stake is the reputation of God. This is the same God with concerns about how the Egyptians would view his actions some 40 years before.

Somehow God wasn't worried this time. Was he fickle? Had his nature changed? Maybe he was just tired of the Israelites?

Yes, I know I have to be careful about being too certain of my views on God and his personality. All I can say is I've formed an opinion from 40 years of getting to know him, and I may yet find I have to change my perspectives all over again. I have had to change my view a number of times in various ways on this journey already.

I don't think God was tired of the Israelites. Nor do I think he had changed his personality. I've held the view for a long time God does not need to change and hasn't. What I do believe is our view of death is probably far dire than God's view of death.

We run around with the idea salvation is only going to happen in this life only, and hence get so easily offended by so much death God allows or directly causes.

We could think God doesn't care much about saving people. Maybe just saving a few will do?

Personally, I look at the price he paid in Jesus, and can't reconcile such a view. I think the suffering of Jesus proves God is far more invested in the salvation of people than many of us are able to believe.

If we had a clearer view of the depth and reach of God's good news, in the Gospel of Jesus, would death seem so bad?

I think that's a good question. I won't answer it yet.

Something I do understand about death is it comes on us all.

For some, life is much shorter than for others. Much of this can be due to simple time and chance without God's involvement at all. This can seem so tragic from the confines of our brief existence in time and space. It may not for God who lives outside of time and space. One day we likely will too, and time will make better sense.

God did not ask us if we wanted to join him in this existence we call life. This can seem to be very unfair. I get that. Some of the lives we lead are simply terrible. There is no escaping this fact. I suspect this is true for the vast majority of people who have lived throughout history.

Most get a very raw deal, then, at the end of it all, we die. Great!?

God can seem to be so above it all – so above all we go through. Even so, I do see an important distinction shining through.

God, in the form of Jesus, left behind all Godly glory and power, to come and live with us. Not only did he live with us, he died with us too.

It wasn't a merciful natural death - he didn't take the easy way out. He died by our hands in a display of unjust extreme human brutality. It endured for some 15 hours or more.

From God's perspective, is a shortened life so bad?

If death was all about burning forever in a tormenting hell fire, then getting there sooner would be a big deal. No one would want that. I doubt God would either.

I suspect God is not so callous towards death in the way he may seem to be in his administration of the death penalty. He knows the good news better than any of us.

He also knows death does not represent the end it does to so many of us in our imaginations and religious dogmas.

A brief window into this clearer understanding of death perhaps can be gleaned from this statement of Paul to the Corinthians:

> *It is actually reported that there is sexual immorality among you, and of a kind that even pagans do not tolerate: A man is sleeping with his father's wife. And you are proud! Shouldn't you rather have gone into mourning and have put out of your fellowship the man who has been doing this? For my part, even though I am not physically present, I am with you in spirit. As one who is present with you in this way, I have already passed judgment in the name of our Lord Jesus on the one who has been doing this. So when you are assembled and I am with you in spirit, and the power of our Lord Jesus is present, hand this man over to Satan for the destruction of the flesh, so that his spirit may be saved on the day of the Lord.* **1 Corinthians 5:1-5** (NIV)

We have here the teaching of Paul to the Corinthians on what to do with a Christian who has become consumed by a sinful lifestyle.

I draw our attention to the statement he makes in verse 5. Paul was saying the guy needed to be put out of the church so his "flesh" could be destroyed.

There may be a number of ways to understand "destruction of the flesh", but the one making most sense to me is the guy was expected to die or at least suffer significantly from the degenerate lifestyle he chose.

The reason was not so he could then hurry off to an eternal torment or separation from God. Rather, it was so he could be saved at a particular time in the future referred to as "the day of the Lord".

I'm not too comfortable with rushing off into the sunset with one verse clutched tightly in my hand, thinking I've got the big picture on something in scripture. Still, this verse just might open a window of understanding. It may well shed light on a serious issue concerning death and how God views it from his vantage point.

From the human perspective, death is very terminal.

From the religious perspective, death is very dire. It's fraught with uncertainty over destinations either extremely bad, or blissful.

From God's perspective, death just might be far more about redemption for all manner of people. This redemption may be hard to perceive with all the foggy religious dogmas clouding our brains.

This is what I'm learning over time, and this is, once again, good news.

Needless Pain?

I've blown the lid on Calvinism. If this is too strong a statement, at least I've challenged some major pillars on which it stands.

I hope I haven't lost too many friends in the process. I can only hope and pray level heads will prevail and if there really is serious affront from the points I've made, I hope we can talk about it with open hearts and minds, with any malice and offense left out of the equation.

I've also said how I view the two main pillars of protestant theology as both Calvinism and Arminianism. My view of how I see Calvinism portray the nature of God is already on the table.

Now it is time to peer under the lid on Arminianism. Once again I hope I don't lose any friends over this. I know how much some of my friends have invested in it.

Fortunately most of us don't have any idea we are in this particular camp. The reality in most church settings is the majority of us in a congregation have no real idea of what is behind the theologies under which we sit. In some ways this is a good thing. There is less to muddy our thinking.

Still, when we carry dysfunctional theology, it does eventually affect how we live our lives as Christians. This is definitely not a good thing. Hence I write on these topics.

I'm not a great fan of pain at the best of times. Needless pain pains me even more. If I can shed light on certain topics and so remove a source of needless pain, then my job is done, even if I do have to lose some friends on the way.

Group Think & the Natural Mind.

And so we come to Arminianism. This represents the pillar on which rests in my estimation the majority of Christian salvation thinking.

Simply put, Jesus died for our sins so we can be saved from the penalty of death and all that might follow, whether hell fire or simple separation from God.

This penalty can only be avoided if we freely choose to accept Jesus as our saviour before we die.

What could be wrong with that?

Nothing, if a couple of conditions were in place:

- Everyone is truly free to make such a decision.
- The message is clear and available for everyone to act on it.

I can't say it should be obvious by now. Nothing is ever obvious to everyone where spiritual concepts are concerned. Religious thinking has a way of getting in the way.

Still, I hope I've made it plain to at least some that people today are naturally not free to make a decision to follow Jesus. Freedom is not the state of the natural fallen state of mankind. Slavery to Satan does not equal freedom.

I've already shown it was very much the case in the Old Testament before Jesus came. There was no free choice in the Old Testament. I've also tried to make it plain it is no different after the death and resurrection of Jesus.

Arminian scholars may try to argue things are somehow different with people now Jesus has died for our sins. All I can suggest is to get out of the seminaries and try talking with a few people.

Nothing has changed. People and our ability to relate to God are no different today from how we were during the Old Testament times. It takes a major intervention from God to be able to start a relationship with him. There may be exceptions, but I don't know of anyone where their conversion did not involve some measure of spiritual struggle.

The apostle Paul certainly agreed with this:

The mind governed by the flesh is hostile to God; it does not submit to God's law, nor can it do so. **Romans 8:7** (NIV)

Does the above verse refer to everyone who has not been converted?

I actually know many Christians who think it refers to them too, at least in some measure, even if they acknowledge they are converted. By whatever extent our minds are governed by the flesh, it is fair to say it does refer to born again believers too.

Whatever disagreements may exist on who this verse refers to, does it not make sense if we are unconverted (i.e. not having God's Holy Spirit dwelling in us, as per standard Christian understanding), then we really are not free to be anything but hostile towards God?

Considering the second condition above – how universally available and clear is the message of Jesus and his saving power?

In fairness to the Arminian free choice position, I have heard of a number of cases where people in non-Christian countries received direct personal visits from Jesus himself. No missionary was necessary, and they did indeed convert.

On a personal level, an ardent atheist cousin of mine received a personal visit from Jesus and converted on that basis. The change in her mental outlook was staggering.

There is nothing to say every human being does not have such an experience before they die. I can only say it does not seem to be the case from scripture, but how would I know?

I can't know really as I've not had an after death experience as some few people have. Even then, an after-death experience is extremely subjective. I'm not sure if it is wise to prove anything from an individual's claim of an after-death experience.

What I mean by an "after-death" experience is where the person has died physically, perhaps on an operating table, and then come back to life after being determined to be dead through lack of breathing and no heartbeat.

No after-death experience I've heard of does indeed speak of receiving a Gospel revelation before they died. This may be because they were already Christians.

For all we know, everyone not already a Christian does get this personal revelation before they die, and somehow they either accept or reject it. In my view, it would be hard to refuse such an offer if we knew we were on the verge of death.

As with most if not all flawed theological constructs I'm aware of, I can see the onset of more "infinite exceptions" coming to the fore.

Does a soldier leaping out of a trench in World War 1, running into a machine gun, have time to receive a message from Jesus and accept it before he is killed instantly by a bullet in his head?

Maybe these are the unfortunate ones who do get to go to hell. Did they die before Jesus could explain anything to them?

Sorry to sound so cynical. It does my head in thinking of all the questions arising when I'm presented with theologies struggling to stand up to a modicum of scrutiny.

Am I leaving myself wide open to the same critical scrutiny once I present my picture of what I think is going on here?

I hope I remember to ask this question once I do. It should be interesting to play devil's advocate and see if I can pick holes in what I think makes sense.

All this is a result of trying to make sense of the Arminian idea where the Gospel has to be accepted in this present life, and all are currently open-minded to receive it. There is no second chance, or first chance, after we die, according to all the Arminian dogmas I've heard.

I should add the Calvinist position holds salvation is only available during this current life too.

Final Second Salvation

Perhaps I can skip all the mental gymnastics the Arminian free choice position requires of me. Does the typical Christian labouring under Arminian dogma (usually with no idea they are under such a dogma) think every non-Christian gets a visit from Jesus before they die? Hardly, if their actions are anything to go by.

I've mentioned before the common angst following the death of a non-Christian relative or friend of a Christian. The concern stems from the notion they had to be saved before they died.

"Hell is burning while the church sleeps" is a slogan I've heard all too often in church circles. It is a catchy phrase, and a powerful marketing tool to get evangelists out there on the street to urge people into church.

The consequences of inaction are obvious. If we don't save people, they're going to burn!

It all looks very messy to me. In history I see the urgency of missionary endeavour as discounting the idea Jesus didn't need missionaries to save anyone.

The obvious answer to this point I raise is Jesus commanded us to make disciples of all nations. This is all the missionaries were trying to do. Right?

Not if we understand the strength of the argument given in many churches. This argument usually takes the form of our need to get on with it because the salvation of so many depends on us being active in making new disciples.

They would not put such pressure on their congregations if they believed the case was otherwise. With no alternative viewpoint to consider, most Christians have no other way of looking at the problem.

I'm still left thinking most Arminian-influenced Christians do not expect Jesus to show up at everyone's point of death.

Wimpy God?

So why do I claim the Arminian position is so untenable?

I've already covered the observation and scriptural position showing free choice is not such a "free-for-all" as some may think. Regardless of whether people in general can actually grasp the message of salvation or not, few really seem to, in spite of our best efforts to explain it.

This is not necessarily a flaw of the church. History certainly presents one possible problem. Way before any missionaries could find new lands to spread the Gospel message, many thousands had already lived and died without the Gospel message. They were hence doomed with no say in the matter.

So just how effective is God at saving people?

In my view, he is really good at it. He really knows what he is doing. Arminian dogma, when I unpack it, is really saying to the world God is failing badly.

We may as well say he doesn't know what he is doing as his plan of salvation is brilliant up to the point of Jesus' death on the cross, but then it fails badly. Putting salvation into the hands of the church was and is a losing proposition if we follow Arminian thinking.

This doesn't mean the church is somehow useless or redundant. It isn't. We just need to understand the Church is not given the primary role of saving people.

A huge problem arises when we adopt Arminian dogma, whether we realise it or not. It stems from thinking the Church has a huge task of getting the message of salvation to the world so the world can be actually saved.

Many many Christians I know think this is their mandate and responsibility. If it really is, then God has seriously failed a world which cannot save itself. Surely God is much smarter than this?

I don't think God is an Arminian. I think God is much much smarter than the Arminian position allows for. It is such a tragedy to me so many churches present to the world a God who is basically losing. They present him as a wimpy God. I hate it!

Struggling To Be Heard?

I'll never forget the day I heard on a local Christian radio station a particular Gospel advertisement. It basically followed this line of argument:

"God is trying to reach you. He is trying to reach you with a message of how much he loves you and longs to enjoy eternity with you. The trouble is you cannot hear him. He wants you to hear him, but you can't."

I wanted to throw up when I heard this. How pathetic must God be in their estimation if he wants us to be able to hear him, but we can't?

Does he have a voice?

Doesn't he know how to reach us so we can hear him?

Is his whisper that weak?

Does he even have to whisper?

Of course he knows how to reach us if he really wants to! If we are not hearing something from God at any particular time, the reason, and the only reason, is because he isn't trying to at that or this point in time.

When God wants us to hear him, he will be heard. It is that simple.

Every Christian who has been called by God probably realises God reached them in the exact manner he needed to. God always knows how to draw a response. I don't know any who would claim God did not know what he was doing when he saved them.

There must be something about the plan of salvation that caters for the fact so many died before the Gospel message ever had access to them.

To say otherwise would imply a God with really poor planning skills. I don't see poor planning evident in his creation, so I don't expect to see it in his plan of salvation.

Similarly, there must be something about the plan of salvation that caters for the fact so many are not naturally free to receive the message, let alone respond to the message in a positive manner.

Arminian dogma, under which the thinking of most Christians resides, does not allow for this understanding. If something gets in the way of our understanding of the Gospel, is it too much to ask we toss it in the bin?

Please?

I really don't think there is anything in scripture requiring God has us saved now or never. If we begin to understand this, a whole new vista of good news possibilities begins to open before our eyes.

Just how good could the Good News be?

Love Meets Judgment.

The message began well enough. A speaker was describing how a man he knew met his wife at a church he was invited to visit. He saw his future wife and decided to chat with her. She asked him what he thought of God and he suggested he showed up the next day to talk further. Her question then:

"What if you die tonight?"

I think we all know why she asked such a question. People die every night for all manner of reasons, at all manner of stages in life. Death is not just reserved for the elderly. In her thinking and in her persuasive reasoning, if she didn't pitch Christ to him that night, the next day might be too late.

Sure enough, he committed to Christ that night and potential doom was averted. Is this really an accurate picture of what God is like? Does it correctly portray the nature of God's plan of salvation as one so precarious?

I'm referring to the salvation process theory this girl had, which speaks volumes about the god she believed in, and the effectiveness of his salvation process.

We cannot separate our view of God from our ideas on salvation. At some point we have to ask questions if the two don't match. For many, sadly in my view, there is no disconnect. I'm trying to fix this by means of this book, even if only in a small way.

The message beginning with this story of a man's conversion continued. It covered the topic of God's judgment. I may have been wrong in my understanding of what was said. The message seemed to be saying God is as much a God of judgment as he is a God of love. God's need for justice and judgment is balanced perfectly with his need to love, at the cross, where Jesus died.

On the surface it sounds plausible. There was a powerful ring of truth but the message didn't sit right. It was only in the wee hours of the morning as I lay in bed thinking about it that the clarity came to me over why the speaker could say what he said.

He believed salvation really is hinged on whether someone lives or dies overnight before getting the saving message the next day. His view of God allows for such risks, and it may be too late for some, if not many.

The teenager in the message could have died that night without giving his life to Christ if he couldn't hang around long enough to hear his future wife present the gospel. How lucky was he that he could? We will never know.

Such an outcome could be reconciled in the mind of the speaker as God will have his justice if his love is not sufficient to move someone to be saved at any particular moment.

Is love really so delicately balanced with judgment in the mind of God?

How did Jesus refer to his heavenly father?

The clue is in the question. Jesus referred to God, while he was on earth, as a father. The God of Jesus is a father! My God is a father! Hey, I'm a father too!

I understand too well, and I will speak on this further in Chapter 16, how imperfect father experiences can shape a distorted view of God. I'd be a fool to claim

I'm a perfect father myself. I don't know of any, except for my God in Heaven. I think he is an outstanding father, if anyone is wondering.

One of the many things I have learned about my Father in Heaven from being a father myself is how my relationship with my own creations (my kids) is not equally a relationship of judgment as well as love.

There are times when discipline is needed, but judgment and justice are not defining values of my relationship with my children. If there is one word which does define my relationship with my children it is love, and only love, as imperfect as I am.

Do we really think there is another defining term equal with love to describe how God relates to his creation?

I know many do, and as a result, they can find all manner of scripture to match their thinking, as this is how scripture is written. It is like a mirror, but it is usually not the person looking into it who can see what the mirror is showing. It is usually others looking at the reflection of scripture in the life or thinking of an individual who can see the individual in ways so many, including the individual in question, can't.

If we really can't see God as fundamentally a God of love because our earthly fathers failed us badly, can we at least consider how we wish our earthly fathers could have been?

Poor father figures are not the only things which shape our views of God. Simple poor teaching is a culprit I'll name as the number one cause. Other factors come into play too.

Does our view of God as a father really line up with our theology?

What is our view of fatherhood? Does it shed any light on how we know and understand God?

This is what I hope we can consider as a closing comment on this chapter discussing the need to know God to really understand his salvation process and the good news hidden (for too many?) within.

15: Back To Basics.

I'm going to present a really simple argument from scripture. I think it will make sense to at least some reading this book. I've no illusions what makes sense to me may not make sense to someone else.

Nevertheless, if we all understood the following point, it may in some way reduce the conflict so many have over disagreements between respective perspectives.

I know this is too much to ask of everyone as it can take time for the simple truth to sink in that:

"We are fallible, and we can be very wrong."

I Can Be Wrong.

I've been confronted by this simple truth so many times in my life. I hope I never forget this important life lesson. My hope here is if I can be open and honest about my fallibility, then anyone reading this may be a little more open to at least hear me out.

I even hope we can find a common bond from a mutual understanding we all can be wrong. If we can achieve this, we might embark on some serious learning and discovery.

We can also discover disagreement does not require hostility.

False Prophets (Profits?)

"Watch out that you are not deceived. For many will come in my name, claiming, 'I am he,' and, 'The time is near.' Do not follow them." **Luke 21:8** (NIV)

Can lead to...

"If you don't agree with me on what the Bible says, then you have to be a false prophet!"

Since Jesus gave the above admonition to be careful about being deceived, nearly 2000 years have passed. No doubt many millions have been deceived, just like Jesus said they would. I'm sure I'm not the only one to learn things I once believed about my Christian walk were not really true, but who knows – maybe I've got that wrong too?

Two thousand years is a fair time for people to get things wrong on all manner of subjects. History has certainly shown this to be true. There are so many different opinions on theology, and they can't all be right.

People carrying a deception have more than one thing in common. The first thing in common is the deception. I dare suggest the second is the belief the other guy with the differing view has to be wrong.

It is a rare person who can truly have an open mind. An open mind leaves one open to the possibility of change in one's thinking. Change is something most of us resist. Human nature does tend to be "change averse".

We understand the Reformation as a time in history some 400 years ago. Much began to change in Church thinking at that time. We don't usually think of us being in a period today called "The Reformation". What if The Reformation never ended? If it didn't, are we not still in it?

I tend to think the Reformation of the Sixteenth Century never really ended. All my Christian life I've continued to learn. I've sometimes had to change my mind completely on certain theological ideas. I'm certain I'm not the only Christian who experiences this. We keep learning and growing in our understanding of what Jesus was teaching.

Is there a good reason to think we know it all today, and have "arrived" at final and total understanding?

I've learned from my work in the realm of science the guy who thinks he knows it all and must be an "expert" usually knows the least. I also have to wonder if the guy who rushes first to the accusation of "false prophet!" might be suffering under the same resonance of self-delusion.

We are probably all affected by indoctrination from our cultures and life experiences. It can take time to unravel the misconceptions coming from life experience and the interpretations we put on it.

Indoctrination can lead to the hard wiring of ideas. I've certainly experienced this in my life.

Sometimes we need serious shaking before we can let go of certain ideas.

I certainly don't want to presume a right to shake anyone here. Fortunately the digital world allows for safe distance where personal space is concerned.

Let's begin.

Again, God Is Love.

I've covered this point before under the chapter, Knowing God. It bears repeating. I say this because this point about the Gospel is the beginning and end of the story for me. I hope it will be for you too, if it isn't already.

We cannot presume we all understand what it means for God to be defined by love. This is particularly so for the love of a father. I do mean a good father. As a father, I know I'm not perfect. I'm human - all too human. God isn't. I'm glad.

> *"All things have been committed to me by my Father. No one knows who the Son is except the Father, and no one knows who the Father is except the Son and those to whom the Son chooses to reveal him."*
> *Then he turned to his disciples and said privately, "Blessed are the eyes that see what you see. For I tell you that many prophets and kings wanted to see what you see but did not see it, and to hear what you hear but did not hear it."* **Luke 10:22-24** (NIV)

The point I want to draw from the above verses from Luke is knowing God the Father is not common knowledge. Jesus said we can only know God the Father if Jesus chooses to open our minds to know him.

> *But when the set time had fully come, God sent his Son, born of a woman, born under the law, to redeem those under the law, that we might receive adoption to sonship.*
> **Galatians 4:4-5** (NIV)

We can start to get to know our new heavenly Father, once we become part of the family through adoption as sons and daughters (as revealed above from Paul's letter to the Galatians). From my own experience, I know this can take time. I suspect it will take an eternity.

As I've said before, we haven't all had perfect father role models. This can affect how we relate to God the Father. I can only hope I have made enough of a positive impact on my own kids to give them a head start with God the Father.

One day, they may even tell me how I did. Until that time, I'll do my best to represent him in the best possible light.

Filters.

"Filters" is a term I use for the things affecting how we understand the Bible. If we have really negative perspectives on the meaning of love, it will have a serious negative impact on how we understand God as revealed through the Bible. If we have a positive and constructive view of love, then this will also affect how we understand what we are reading in the Bible.

Regardless of the risk involved with such a potentially highly misunderstood filter, I see love as the primary filter through which we need to understand scripture and the true nature of the Gospel.

Saying this, we need to understand the state of our perception of love and how it might influence how well we understand scripture. This is critical if we really want to understand the depth of the good news I'm discovering is in the Gospel.

God So Loved.

For God so loved the world that he gave his one and only Son, that whoever believes in him shall not perish but have eternal life. **John 3:16** (NIV)

The above is arguably one of the best known verses in the Bible. This may be true, but I still find myself wondering if we really grasp what is stated in the term *"so loved"*. In other words, he loved us all so much. He loved us to a degree which many of us may not yet be capable of understanding!

This rich and abundant love of God is the first main filter through which I interpret scripture to form my understanding of the Gospel.

It is worth mentioning too the Greek word for "world" is "Kosmos". If we think of this term directly in English (cosmos), we get the impression the world God loves so much is not just a small group within the world, or a tiny portion. He is indeed a God who loves the whole world, and not just a small or select part of it.

This is where the whole premise underlying the predestination theory of Calvinism falls flat on its face. The predestination of Calvinism leaves a huge proportion of mankind under God's choice for damnation. It does not fit within the understanding of a huge love for everyone in the cosmos, or world.

How could a God of love bring so many people into existence so they could be tortured for eternity in the fires of hell? In addition, how could he when they have no choice in the matter?

That is plain psychotic.

It makes sense as the nature of Satan, but not of God. Would it also make sense Satan would love to deceive us into thinking God is so much like he is?

It would make sense he has achieved such a deception, at least with a few Christians. If we can learn what such a theology represents, I do hope it will open at least a few eyes to what is going on in such thinking. Does it make for a sound Good News message from those carrying such theology?

It sounds like the type of plan a devil could come up with. In contrast, would a God of love have a better plan?

Obviously, I'm viewing this through my understanding of love. I suspect this is the same understanding which has many of my friends who lean towards Calvinist predestination admit they cannot accept the full Calvinist position.

Their growing relationship with God is beginning to tear apart their theologies. This is a great thing in my view. It's been happening to me too, for much of the past 20 years.

Even Arminianism?

As our minds are opened to the depth of God's huge love, some questions arise for my free-choice Arminian friends too. Could Arminianism also be flawed?

If God loves everyone so much, why would he limit the saving power of Jesus' sacrifice to the choices people make in this life alone?

Such a question is particularly important given how few people in history ever heard of Jesus. This question also applies when we fail to understand the foundational hostile-to-God nature of the human heart before conversion.

The Arminian position does not match with the God I know. It just doesn't. Call me ignorant. Call me a fool. Throw all the scriptures you like at me. I've seen plenty. From what I've seen, there is nothing convincing in the scriptural argument of the free-choice believers. Either sound English comprehension is seriously lacking or scriptures are set up to contradict other scriptures, in every case.

I've held all manner of unsound theologies in my lifetime. I thought they were rock solid until I found out they were not.

With all due respect, I suspect the same will come for my free-choice and predestination friends. As it stands, those two camps stand in direct opposition to each other. They cannot both be right.

Saying they can't both be right does not then automatically mean one has to be right either. It just may be they are both wrong. Wouldn't that be interesting!

God Wants What?!

I want to introduce the second foundational filter I lean towards in my understanding of the Gospel:

> *I urge, then, first of all, that petitions, prayers, intercession and thanksgiving be made for all people -- for kings and all those in authority, that we may live peaceful and quiet lives in all godliness and holiness. This is good, and pleases God our Savior, **who wants all people to be saved and to come to a knowledge of the truth.** For there is one God and one mediator between God and mankind, the man Christ Jesus, who gave himself as a ransom for all people. This has now been witnessed to at the proper time.*
> **1 Timothy 2:1-6** (NIV)

I've pulled out six verses from The New Testament. They are found in the first letter of Paul to his protégé, Timothy. The verse I want to draw our attention to is verse 4. I've included all six verses above to show I'm not taking my interpretation of verse 4 out of context.

Verse 4 reads like an addendum or afterthought to the previous urging of Paul to be praying etc. in verses 1-3. What he says may be an afterthought, but it is huge in its consequences.

What Paul says is God wants all people to be saved. It is quite simple really. God wants to save everyone. This is my second foundation filter through which I view scripture to form an understanding of the Gospel.

I'd dare say in the time of Paul's writing, it was not a big deal. It was probably obvious, and understood by most if not all Christians. The Gospel - the good news of salvation through Jesus, was by then about 30 years old. Hence he manages to throw the statement in as an afterthought to his main point. I'm so glad he did! Paul probably thought this was obvious.

In the context of today, perhaps 99% of Christian theological thought has God either does not want to save everyone, or God is incapable of saving everyone, even if he would like to. Paul's afterthought stating God wants to save everyone is huge.

Do I understand verse 4 correctly?

Is it possible I don't?

One way to check on the meaning of a verse is to compare it in different translations. It is wonderful to have software that can do that for me. I've used my e-Sword (Meyers) software to compare the same verse with fourteen different Bible versions, including two French ones. The meaning is the same in every one.

Do I have to spell it out here? I hope not. It is easy to look up a host of different Bible versions on-line, and the Bible software I use is free too. Please do have a look on-line if you are curious. I think you will be impressed with how similar all the different translations are with this particular verse.

What about context? It could be possible I've got the context all wrong.

There is no end to the mental gymnastics a typical human being can perform. The variations in theologies out there, just under the Christian banner, are proof enough to me on that point. To be fair, I have pointed out the Bible does seem to be written in a way to allow for that.

The Bible, to its credit, does seem to be quite good at exposing us for all we are and represent. I appreciate that quality more and more as the years go by.

At the end of the day, if someone doesn't want to accept this scripture for all it is worth, they will find a reason not to. I can say I've understood the scripture in its context, and someone else can and will simply disagree. It is ultimately in the hands of the reader to decide.

I will make this point to help illustrate why I think I do understand this verse correctly. I've already referred to my first filter through which I understand the depths and reach of the Gospel message - the love of God.

By my understanding of God's love, and what he has revealed to me personally as my heavenly Father, his love makes it obvious he wants to save everyone.

Could good news be any plainer?

But wait a minute! Didn't the Apostle Peter say something about how the writings of Paul can be hard to understand, and people do indeed twist the meaning of what Paul wrote?

Bear in mind that our Lord's patience means salvation, just as our dear brother Paul also wrote you with the wisdom that God gave him. He writes the same way in all his letters, speaking in them of these matters. His letters contain some things that are hard to understand, which ignorant and unstable people distort, as they do the other Scriptures, to their own destruction. **2 Peter 3:15-16** (NIV)

This is the perfect out. If ever our theology does not line up with statements of Paul in his letters in the Bible, we can simply play the "Peter" card, and ignore it. We can claim Paul is simply dropping another line which is hard to understand.

Of course very few would do this intentionally. The vast majority of us are really sincere with our beliefs. It is however very easy to find a justification for holding on to anything we want to believe. Our minds are good at fooling us. If we really want to believe something, or hold tight to a dogma, mental gymnastics with scripture is normal practice, or we can simply read right over a challenging scripture and ignore it.

I've done it plenty of times myself with former beliefs I've long since discarded, but held for years in the face of all manner of scriptures saying I was wrong. Many friends can attest to the same. We all know of scriptures we have been reading for many years, and then finally it leaps out at us to reveal something we have never before considered.

But what if Peter agreed with Paul on this point of God wanting to save everyone?

If he did, just maybe, we could allow ourselves to let go of just one cherished concept. We could discard the option of playing the "Peter" card referred to above on this point alone:

But do not forget this one thing, dear friends: With the Lord a day is like a thousand years, and a thousand years are like a day. The Lord is not slow in keeping his promise, as some understand slowness. Instead he is patient with you, not wanting anyone to perish, but everyone to come to repentance. **2 Peter 3:8-9** (NIV)

There it is! Even Peter thinks God wants to save everyone. Could it be any clearer?

Following on, many would say they know God wants to save everyone. It's obvious. Nevertheless, it isn't going to happen. God knows this and is able to accept it. We should too or at least try harder to minimise the damage by trying to get more people into church.

Damn! Did I just hear good news flee out the door?

Saviour of Who?

Back in the days when Jesus walked the earth, the common view of God's dealing with mankind was simple. Back then, there was no New Testament of the Bible. There was only the Old Testament. There was only the Old Testament and the only people who had possession of those sacred writings were the Jewish people.

The Jewish people, in terms of historical record, were the only conscious remnants of the descendants of Israel or Jacob, who was prominent in the Book of Genesis.

Maybe other people groups did exist in other parts of the world who knew they were of Israelite descent. I'm sure plenty of people in other parts of the world were descendants of those Israelites the Assyrians took into captivity as described in 2 Kings 17, in the Old Testament. I'm not so sure they knew they were descendants. This could be true even today. We just don't know for certain. Maybe some think they do know. Perhaps they do?

In the Jewish worldview, in the time of Jesus, as the only descendants of Israel in possession of the Old Testament, they knew they were the chosen people of God. The ministry of Jesus, and the record of the New Testament was to change all this.

God was no longer interested in just one small people group. His interest, because of Jesus and his death and resurrection, was to expand way beyond the Jewish people. Non-Jewish people would now become people of God.

Just as the Jews of Jesus' day resisted the idea of God's loving reach beyond just them, different Christian groups today can resist believing the Good News can reach beyond certain circumstances.

The biggest limitation I can think of is the reach of the Gospel beyond the grave. Many Christians I know believe there is no Good News message available for anyone after they die. It doesn't matter if they never knew of Jesus before they died. For whatever reason, God's saving power is unable to reach beyond the grave. If anyone doesn't get the message and respond to it before they die, it is too late – way too late!

So Jesus is the saviour of who?

Some?

The lucky?

Maybe some of those blessed to be born in a Christian nation?

Maybe the specific ones God set up to be saved?

Maybe the lucky who for whatever the reason were in the right place and time, in the right frame of mind, in receipt of the message, and so got saved?

I'm sorry if I sound a bit cynical. It only comes from thinking about different ideas out there on salvation, for many years. It almost sounds cliché to ask, as so many pose the same question, but what does the Bible have to say on this?:

> *For physical training is of some value, but godliness has value for all things, holding promise for both the present life and the life to come. This is a trustworthy saying that deserves full acceptance. That is why we labor and strive, because we have put our hope in the living God, who is the Savior of all people, and especially of those who believe.* **1 Timothy 4:8-10** (NIV)

Okay, the living God, who I can only assume is Jesus, is the saviour of all people. It isn't some; it isn't the lucky, or a select few. It is everyone.

The point about those "especially who believe" I suspect is an emphasis on those already believing, and therefore saved at the time of writing. When Paul wrote this he likely understood there were many who had lived and died still to be saved. There were also many still to be born and saved.

Is Jesus the saviour of all if not everyone is saved at any particular point in time? I guess he is if the unsaved are to be saved in the future. This would even extend to those not saved when they died. God must have worked out a way, a place, and a time, to deal with this. I'll unpack these details in a later chapter.

And so God not only wants to save everyone, Jesus is actually the saviour of everyone. He is not just the saviour of a select few. If he was, he would not be the saviour of all. This is not what I would describe as a filter, but more a fact – Jesus is the saviour of all, if not now, eventually.

Maybe we still can believe in Good News after all.

It's All Too Hard?

My third and final filter through which I understand the Gospel is quite simple. God is supreme. He is big - really big! It's another way of saying he is capable.

If anyone I know is a problem solver, it has to be God. Jesus is the saviour of all because he can. He knows how to save everyone because of how great he is.

Some like to use the term "sovereign", which basically means God gets his way no matter what; much like a king would in former days. Those who lean towards the predestination of Calvinism tend to understand this well.

Sovereignty is why some have mistakenly assumed I was a Calvinist. I had been saying a fair bit about the greatness of God. When they did, some years ago now, I had no idea what they were talking about, except in very vague terms.

That was the reason I started to study Calvinism and find out what it was all about. Naturally I then had to study the free choice dogmas of Arminianism to fill in the bigger picture of what most Christians today believe, even if they don't know it was Jacobus Arminius who influenced them so much.

Enough preamble - let's find out how capable God is:

> Then the Lord said to Abraham, "Why did Sarah laugh and say, 'Will I really have a child, now that I am old?' **Is anything too hard for the Lord?** I will return to you at the appointed time next year, and Sarah will have a son." **Gen 18:13-14** (NIV)

I love this question, as posed above by God to Abraham. Is anything too hard for God? Given the certainty God had for Sarah to deliver a son in a year's time, I think not.

Perhaps my free choice friends will protest what happened to Sarah was purely biology. They don't have any doubts God can manage biology. The free will, if such a beast really does stand in God's way, is an entirely different matter.

Is it?

The protest given by the free-choice Arminian believer is God won't influence our thinking lest he end up with robots. The thinking goes that it cannot be real love expressed by us unless God is entirely hands off. Otherwise, all God has is a herd of "yes" men and women. Who wants that?

This does make perfect sense. There is a weakness in this argument however. No conversion has ever taken place with God playing completely "hands off". In fact, where he is hands off, people remain as they are - slaves to sin and Satan - hostile to God.

I'm not so sure God is really that interested in a hands-off approach. If he was, Israel would never have left Egypt. Even when Israel was out of Egypt, we saw they had a fundamental problem - their natural heart was not inclined to follow God. Fortunately, God did have a solution in mind for this problem:

> *I will give them an undivided heart and put a new spirit in them; I will remove from them their heart of stone and give them a heart of flesh. Then they will follow my decrees and be careful to keep my laws. They will be my people, and I will be their God.* **Ezekiel 11:19-20** (NIV)

Taking a non-capable person, and making them fully capable (of obedience) seems like full-on hands-on to me. I do get a strong impression from scripture God is not really into the free-choice, hands-off, Arminian way.

Given there is not a Christian I know who was able to make a decision to follow Jesus on their own, I have to wonder if this is so bad after all.

No one I know seems to be complaining. In fact, they all seem to be really glad they are converted. We were made ultimately to be this way after all.

There's no free choice in being slaves to sin and Satan either. People make fairly willing slaves too, until God sets them free. For all the talk of free choice, where exactly is it?

Maybe this whole free choice "God doesn't want us to be robots" theory is just that - it is just a theory.

Theories are fine, but they need some reality to back them up.

My kids had no choice about their parents. Apart from the typical rough patches of parent/child angst, they don't seem to mind. Come to think of it, we really had no choice on who we got as kids.

We wanted kids, but desire was about as much say in the matter that we got. We don't mind who we ended up with, and didn't mind from the moment they were conceived.

Taking this further, we had no choice on giving birth to humans. We were stuck with human babies. If we'd wanted to give birth to zebras, we were not so free to do so. Even though it was predictable we would only give birth to humans, with no other option, we never minded.

When God does open our hearts and minds to be able to receive and accept him as our heavenly Father, no one seems to mind. It's funny that. The free choice believers seem to want to insist somehow it's a bad thing we have no say in it.

I probably should unpack this sovereignty subject a little further:

> *The Lord Almighty has sworn,*
> *"Surely, as I have planned, so it will be, and as I have purposed, so it will happen."* **Isaiah 14:24** (NIV)

I love the common sense in this statement from Isaiah in the Old Testament. Isaiah had no illusions about God having his way. This is the nature of God. No one can withstand him or stop him.

No theology can constrain him, no matter how scholarly we may think we are.

If God really does love us so much he wants us all to be saved, why even consider somehow God has been limited in some way from achieving what he wants?

> *Whom did the Lord consult to enlighten him, and who taught him the right way? Who was it that taught him knowledge, or showed him the path of understanding?*
> *Surely the nations are like a drop in a bucket; they are regarded as dust on the scales; he weighs the islands as though they were fine dust.*
> *Lebanon is not sufficient for altar fires, nor its animals enough for burnt offerings.*
> *Before him all the nations are as nothing; they are regarded by him as worthless and less than nothing.*
> *With whom, then, will you compare God? To what image will you liken him?* **Isaiah 40:14-18** (NIV)

What if we really took at face value these statements showing how great God is, and how nothing can stop him or stand in his way?

Can people really stand in the way of God?

Can we, with our imaginations fired up, and flaring nostrils with the idea of free choice, really stop God?

Somehow I don't think we can, but that's just me. Who am I to speak for others?

Understand too I'm not thinking or suggesting God is going to force salvation on us. Part of his greatness is the depth of his understanding and wisdom to know how to deal with each of us with the necessary sensitivity to see us healed of any dysfunction keeping us from the natural decision to choose him when he opens our minds.

It makes perfect sense to me God is big enough, powerful enough, and sufficiently wise and sensitive enough to make the Gospel seriously good news for all people.

Prodigal Love

The subject of the Prodigal Son has been playing on my mind for some time as I've been working on this book. It eventually forced me to come back to this section to say something about it as part of this chapter on "basics". It serves as an addendum to the first filter for understanding which is the extravagance of God's love. The more I think about it, the more it makes sense I have to say something.

The meaning of the word "prodigal" is interesting in itself. I did a Google search and came up with a couple of definitions. One spoke of reckless spending or wasteful extravagance, and another spoke of giving on a lavish scale.

The Prodigal Son is a well-known parable of Jesus. We can read about it in Luke chapter 11 in verses 11 to 32. For the sake of convenience, I'll include it below:

Jesus continued: "There was a man who had two sons. The younger one said to his father, 'Father, give me my share of the estate.' So he divided his property between them.

"Not long after that, the younger son got together all he had, set off for a distant country and there squandered his wealth in wild living. After he had spent everything, there was a severe famine in that whole country, and he began to be in need. So he went and hired himself out to a citizen of that country, who sent him to his fields to feed pigs. He longed to fill his stomach with the pods that the pigs were eating, but no one gave him anything.

"When he came to his senses, he said, 'How many of my father's hired servants have food to spare, and here I am starving to death! I will set out and go back to my father and say to him: Father, I have sinned against heaven and against you. I am no longer worthy to be called your son; make me like one of your hired servants.' So he got up and went to his father.

"But while he was still a long way off, his father saw him and was filled with compassion for him; he ran to his son, threw his arms around him and kissed him.

"The son said to him, 'Father, I have sinned against heaven and against you. I am no longer worthy to be called your son.'

"But the father said to his servants, 'Quick! Bring the best robe and put it on him. Put a ring on his finger and sandals on his feet. Bring the fattened calf and kill it. Let's have a feast and celebrate. For this son of mine was dead and is alive again; he was lost and is found.' So they began to celebrate.

"Meanwhile, the older son was in the field. When he came near the house, he heard music and dancing. So he called one of the servants and asked him what was going on. 'Your brother has come,' he replied, 'and your father has killed the fattened calf because he has him back safe and sound.'

"The older brother became angry and refused to go in. So his father went out and pleaded with him. But he

answered his father, 'Look! All these years I've been slaving for you and never disobeyed your orders. Yet you never gave me even a young goat so I could celebrate with my friends. But when this son of yours who has squandered your property with prostitutes comes home, you kill the fattened calf for him!'

"'My son,' the father said, 'you are always with me, and everything I have is yours. But we had to celebrate and be glad, because this brother of yours was dead and is alive again; he was lost and is found.'" **Luke 15:11-32** (NIV)

In the NIV (New International Version) translation above, there is no mention of the word "prodigal". The term is still well-known in Christian circles. It is primarily used to describe the wayward son who finally returned to his father.

This wayward son is referred to as the "prodigal son" because of how he squandered his inheritance on wild and reckless living. We don't normally use the term to describe the father in the story. Would "The Prodigal Father" sound right?

If we look at the reaction of the older son and his perspective, just maybe we could refer to this parable as the one about the prodigal father. Consider the way the father celebrated the return of his lost son - it was lavish, and wasteful from the perspective of the older son.

Consider also the love of this father. The older son could have viewed the love of his father for his wayward younger brother as wasted extravagantly on the wrong cause. This is indeed a story of "prodigal love".

We understand Jesus was speaking in this parable about the love of his heavenly father towards anyone who is as yet unsaved, or in other words, lost. It tells me the love of God is "prodigal" - lavish or extravagant, even towards the undeserving.

This is a critical understanding I need to carry through the rest of this story as we unpack how good, good news can be, in the Gospel message of Jesus.

16: Basic Objection Filters.

There are other mental filters one can employ. They make it hard to see through my critical core filters of:

- God so loved;
- God wants to save all; and
- God is great enough to achieve what he wants.

The big challenge for all of us is to recognise we have filters through which we form our understanding of scripture (or anything for that matter). Some of these filters can be really hard to see for ourselves. It is often easier for an outsider to see our filters.

I'm going to discuss a number of those filters here.

I Can't Be Wrong

It makes sense the first one I should look at is the opposite of the first filter I want at the core of everything I think I understand. I certainly don't want to claim I really live by the creed of understanding my fallibility perfectly. It is so hard to do.

I once met a fairly new Christian at a church men's breakfast. He gave his testimony and shared a number of perspectives on his beliefs.

After the breakfast I shared with him there were some other ways of looking at one of the points he had raised. I did my best not to be confronting so we got on very well. As a result, he wanted me to meet a friend of his.

A few days later, I met them both for coffee. This friend he introduced me to was basically his mentor. His mentor had introduced him to Christianity. It didn't take long for the mentor to realise we had different views on certain aspects of our Christian walk.

He then didn't hesitate to point out I was therefore a false prophet!

Perhaps I could have taken him to task for calling me a prophet. I had in no way made any claims on future events. Still, I had a different perspective, so therefore I represented a great evil in his presence.

I was somewhat floored someone could be so dogmatic, and belligerently so. He had been a Christian for many years. Surely he knew there were all manner of disagreements in church circles. Few disagreements, if any, warranted such blatant animosity.

We were sitting at a small table, but I tried to help him picture what it would be like if fifteen different Christians could be sitting with us, and all from different denominations.

I proposed it could be possible for all fifteen individual Christians at the table to differ from everyone else on certain perspectives. I then asked if all these Christians would then be false prophets.

This mentor once again did not hesitate. He had the answer. Indeed, it was the final word. If all of the other fourteen at the table with him differed from him on any points of doctrine or theological perspective, they all had to be false prophets.

Needless to say, I was relieved when this meeting with such a charming man ended.

I'm glad to say the guy who introduced us was a little perplexed after. He figured I was a decent enough person. It just didn't make sense I could think differently on a particular subject in the Bible. He told me he feared I was reducing the authority of the Bible.

All I could do was ask him who told him anyone was able to do such a thing. I'd always found the Bible stood above all our foibles.

Clearly he was very much under the thumb of his mentor. It wasn't a healthy relationship by any means, but there wasn't much I could do about it.

The mentor was clearly locked up in the idea he could never be wrong. He had no idea he could read the Bible through his own particular filters, and be totally unaware of his filters. He lived under the delusion of infallibility.

I've been certain of all manner of perspectives in my Christian walk. In the thick of it, it can be really hard to conceive of any possibility of error. As a case in point, I used to be under the belief that I had to keep the Sabbath by not working on Saturdays.

I'm glad I'm over that one. It made life needlessly difficult. I see it in a whole new light now. I'll have to save that topic for another book perhaps.

I do want to say I have quite a number of friends who still think they should not work on Saturdays. I in no way think of them as false prophets, like the above mentioned mentor. They just have a different perspective from me and I'm fine with that.

I'm grateful for the experience of coming out from a particular set of beliefs. It has shown me how much my thinking can change if given a new perspective.

I really do understand how fixed we can be in our thinking and cling to our pet scriptures and arguments, to the exclusion of all others. I hope I never forget these lessons. It is so liberating to be at least somewhat free of the delusion of infallibility. I only want to say "somewhat" as I don't want to kid myself there is probably more still to learn.

To shift me out of the particular theology on the Sabbath took a long time. My neurones were very hard wired in my thinking. It taught me not just about myself, but about people in general. People don't shift their thinking easily.

Some have a fear of acknowledging their potential for error. They think it prevents them from taking a strong stand for truth.

I don't think it has to at all. All I say is I hold to my position based on what I currently understand. If there is something I'm not aware of which will change my perspective, I'm open to hear it.

I in no way simply accept the so-called evidence someone may then put forward for any viewpoint. It needs to be tested. They may have simply made it up.

Back at university when I was studying engineering, I used to visit one of the Bible study groups on campus. I recall how on one occasion the minister made a comment I didn't agree with so I asked him how he could justify such a position.

He answered by shooting back a list of scriptures he claimed gave full support to what he had said. I was fortunate a friend was sitting next to me and he wrote down the list of scriptures.

What we found later was none of them had anything to do with the topic I raised. The minister shot the scriptures back at me like a smoke grenade to shut me up. For most sitting there, they just naturally assumed the minister was right and I was wrong because he hit me with a bunch of scriptures.

We can see such a smoke grenade technique used in many different settings, be they political, religious, scientific, or whatever. Just bring up a heap of dribble in response to a challenge no one has time to check up on in the short time frame of the interview (or whatever the setting).

Most people will be satisfied. With the right voice of authority, all manner of dribble can pass as fact. Just don't rock the boat. Most people are kept happy that way.

Whatever it is we find ourselves believing, it is natural to think the matter is settled. Few of us are trained to challenge our own thinking. We might challenge the thinking of others, but rarely our own. Why bother with the discomfort?

Many can go through their whole lives and never be seriously challenged over what they think. We sometimes choose our church denominations because we are born into them and are comfortable with the doctrines. There is nothing wrong with this in so many ways. Why would we choose the discomfort of surrounding ourselves with people we could never agree with?

If there is a problem with camping in the denomination in which we find ourselves, it is we may never have a chance to find out there are other perspectives which may be better than the ones we hold. We can be born, live, and then die, surrounded by dogmas which never serve us well.

Father Figure Filters.

Father figures can present a major filter on our thinking. A poor father example can at times influence how we understand the Bible. Our experience with our own earthly father will quite often shape how we understand God and his love. I've already referred to this in a previous chapter. It bears repeating under the subject of objection filters.

Films portraying family relationships from a previous century hold a certain fascination for me. I can't say they truly represent the cultural norm from a previous age, but so many do have austere father figures.

Even movies of the period surrounding World War Two often portray fathers with very limited emotional expression. So many fathers saying goodbye to their sons, going off to war at a railway station, will only shake their hands. They didn't hug them; they didn't say they loved them – they shook their hand, and said goodbye.

Even if this was only true for maybe fifty percent of the fathers back then, it is still a large proportion.

Such a large proportion of the population could then be viewing God through a similar filter, shaped by their life experience.

I'm currently reading the original war diary of my maternal grandfather, Clive Muir, and typing it up for my family so it is easier to read. The first page covers his embarkation on the transport ship Aeneas, on 20 December 1915 (Muir).

He mentions "Mother", and even Mrs Wood waving them off, but no mention of his father. I can only but wonder about his relationship with his dad. What could be so important he would miss seeing his son off to a war?!

My own dad fought in World War Two. I have no doubt the war itself might affect the ability of a man to show his emotions. I certainly loved my father, and I know he loved me. I just don't remember ever hearing the words "I love you" from his lips. I have to question if he ever heard the same from his father. It is sadly too late now to ask him. Even if it wasn't, I would hesitate as I'm not sure how he would have handled such a question.

There's was a generation where kids were often packed off to boarding school. This comes through quite clearly in the Famous Five children's book series I used to read with my kids. I also read them when I was a kid too.

Distant fathers do make for a distant God. I'm not surprised I spent years searching for a clear revelation God really did love me. I'm grateful my search was not futile.

Is it any wonder the theologies passed down to us from previous generations portray a God with a less-than-loving personality?

I've no idea how often someone would question the idea of sinners burning forever in hell fire from the judgment of a loving God. Such a God might have seemed to be quite normal two hundred years ago. I'm sure it seemed normal 3000 years ago when some people had no problem sacrificing their own children in flames to a pagan god called Molech.

Such is the power of a father-figure filter. We all have one. The only question is how much light it reflects or allows through?

Church and Culture Filters.

If we are thinking about filters capable of affecting how we perceive our religious dogmas, the obvious one to call our attention to has got to be our church background.

It may not be that common today, but back when I was a boy, some fifty years ago, it was rare to not have some kind of church affiliation. It was obvious to everyone in Primary School. We all had religious education of some form. Only one of my friends at school was an atheist. I still remember this detail to this day. I even remember his name. It was so unusual to be an atheist.

The default religion for most of us was The Church of England. We were part of the British Commonwealth of Nations after all. Australia was an Anglican country as our Queen was the head of The Church of England. We had both church and culture rolled into one.

It went without saying we all learnt from a young age how good people went to heaven, and bad people went to hell. This was the same for any of my friends in other religious education classes, except for maybe my Jewish friends. I don't know what they learnt about life after death back then.

The natural outcome of learning something from such a young age is one just might hold this belief for the rest of their life. Culture is like this. Other perspectives may exist, but sometimes our culture can keep other ideas right out. If we don't know there is another viewpoint, we may carry the same one all our lives.

This is not necessarily a bad thing. It is just how things work to influence our thinking to either change or stay the same.

If a new idea comes along, our immediate value standards as set by our church background and culture will quite often raise a flag warning we are in unfamiliar territory. Depending on our personality, the warning flag of the unfamiliar will be sufficient to completely close the mind from listening.

I have my own world view with all this. Namely, there is no way a new revelation on aspects of Christianity will ever get any traction without a move of God first to open our minds.

This may sound simplistic, but it is the only way I have to explain why I can now work on Saturdays, while some of my friends still think they are breaking the Sabbath if they do.

Understanding to me is a gift. The fact it comes from God, according to my world view, is part of the good news. If I look back over the last 2000 years of

Christian thought, I see a slow evolution of thinking and spiritual understanding.

God doesn't seem to be in a hurry to break through the barriers our cultures and religions have imposed on our thinking. Nevertheless, the barriers do come down. Over time it would seem to me He gives us new filters by which we can understand the world and his revelations to us in the Bible.

If two hundred years ago Christians struggled to believe their sins were forgiven, I do wonder how we will view current hell fire dogmas in another 200 years.

Resistance to Change

The final filter I wish to draw our attention to is a really basic one – resistance to change.

It is not easy for people to change. Hence, our minds and our thinking often won't change. Change is a stress, and sometimes we resist any addition to the stress levels we already manage in our lives.

I might have a hundred different books in a list of books I really want to read. A friend might come by and say with great enthusiasm I have to read a book he or she has just read. I know already my immediate reaction would be a friendly resistance, unless my friend was particularly skilled in selling the reading of the book to me.

I'm already overwhelmed by the weight of books calling for my attention. I just don't have the time. If someone was to really insist I read a particular book, I just might snap and get defensive. I know the stress.

New ideas can work in the same manner. It is much easier to maintain the status quo. Changing thinking may mean changes in other areas. Why disrupt a happening church social culture by no longer keeping a no-work-on-Saturday Sabbath?

If you start working on Saturdays, you stand out a mile in a Sabbath keeping church. Changes like this don't come easy. I speak from experience and as a witness to many broken relationships.

Some changes can have a church lose all sense of direction and purpose. This can be quite troubling for the leadership of a church. When my understanding of Sabbath keeping changed, it was a change already reaching into the highest levels of the administration of the church. I was not the only one changing my thinking.

Strange as it may sound, being different was a hallmark of the church I was in. It helped give us a sense of identity. Changing the view on the Sabbath would mean we were not so different after all. Our sense of identity was at risk.

I'd been prepared for such a shift in thinking for some years before it came on the church itself. Many hadn't been prepared like I was. I believe God prepared me for such changes in advance. I doubt it was just time and chance. God has always been very active in my life.

Quite a few in the church denomination couldn't understand the change in thinking. They formed other churches to preserve the former thinking. It was probably the best thing they could do. I don't think anyone should think harshly of them for leaving and following their consciences.

Of those who remained, the speed of change in thinking varied from person to person. Some never changed. They stayed out of loyalty to the organisation.

If there was one common factor to us all, it was we all felt the pain of change. It wasn't easy on anyone. Change can be painful, and our church felt it deeply. Families were divided; friendships torn apart.

Change management was a skill sorely lacking in the leadership of the church, but who could hold such against them? Few have such skills in the corporate world. It is unrealistic to expect the necessary skills to just miraculously appear in a church. God clearly chose not to perform such a miracle. I could suggest he didn't because it served a purpose in teaching us so much about ourselves as we negotiated change. I feel I've learned and benefitted from the experience, however painful it was.

The bottom line for all to understand is even if change may be necessary, and change may make sense; it won't be easy or without some disruption and pain.

If change in our thinking can equal disruption and pain (not always, but certainly sometimes), is there any wonder there is resistance to change?

We Lose Our Leverage

In some ways I'm getting ahead of myself here raising this point. It is already obvious I'm clearly talking about a change in thinking on the whole hell fire subject, and maybe even more.   I'm sure this should be obvious by now.

For some church organisations, a shift in thinking on hell fire and all it implies involves a shift in thinking on the overall church culture.   I've already discussed how culture represents a filter that can prevent us seeing something that may be true.

There is however a specific aspect of some church cultures that would be severely impacted if such a specific change in thinking on hell fire would occur. It bears making mention of this at this point in the discussion.

Fear is a powerful motivator. It has been used in political and religious spheres for thousands of years. The threat of hell fire has been at the core of much religious and political motivation for centuries.

The fear of hell fire has been a great incentive for obedience and conversions.   What motivation do we have if we lose that?

This is a serious question some churches will have to face if they are to ever confront their thinking on hell fire. Most won't. I'm sure of that.

Organisations are too big and secure to cave in to a change in thinking that easily.   It is usually the individuals who respond first if a certain truth begins to shine through the haze of long-held dogmas.

Some of my friends are dedicated evangelists. They are driven by a strong sense they have to get out there and save lost souls from the inevitable.

As much as I've personally felt sorry for them, the energy such fear inspires has kept attendance up at their churches, and maintained growth to a certain degree (no pun intended).

The threat of hell fire is not a strange topic to many who are not Christians. It is an aspect of many of the world's religions. The idea is not foreign. The whole world is in many ways familiar with such thinking. Such is the impact of religion on the world at large.

I'm not saying all church growth is purely from fear, and therefore of questionable sincerity. I will say I've heard it said a number of times how taking away a concern for the lost takes away motivation from a congregation.

Is this such a bad thing?

I've seen all manner of hard sell approaches in my life. I've been involved in a few myself. I've not just observed them.

They don't inspire me. I know they lead to burnout. I know plenty of burned out Christians.

But didn't Jesus tell us to make disciples of all nations?

Yes, he certainly did.

Making disciples of all nations has been understood to mean we have to go out and get every man, woman, and child saved. It could mean something else too. It could be understood to mean we are to make disciples from every nation, without having to ensure every single individual is converted.

Even if there are only two disciples made from any particular nation, then we would have fulfilled this responsibility.

I'm not saying we should have a minimalist approach. If more are to be converted, so be it. This is not in our hands. Only God converts someone. We just have to cooperate with the different ways the Holy Spirit leads us to reach people.

Some see certain countries as their calling. I get that. What does not help is if dogmas get in the way of what one thinks Jesus wants them to achieve in a certain country.

If a missionary thinks they need to be seeing the salvation of everyone with whom they come into contact, they will suffer great disappointment. This is particularly so if the thinking is governed by unsound dogmas. If our understanding is sound, our effectiveness will reflect it in the mission field.

Personally, I see any established congregation as a potential mission field. Making disciples reaches far beyond just seeing someone converted and becoming a Christian. I see discipling as far more about what follows conversion than the conversion itself.

Leading people towards spiritual maturity is at the core of making disciples from my perspective. This can happen in a local church congregation without ever going overseas. We all have different jobs to do.

If we shift motivation away from urgency to save the lost, we may well see a shift in momentum. If our motivation has been wrong all these years, this is actually a reflection of poor discipling. That will mean we haven't been doing it right.

In my view right motivation, founded on right discipling, comes from teaching Christians to learn to individually follow the lead of the Holy Spirit. It has much to do with individual empowerment, rather than corporate allegiance and toeing the line.

If it means some will just stop attending our churches, fine! Maybe they were never called in the first place. Who knows? We don't need to judge such matters.

What matters most is we understand who does the calling. It isn't us. We just need to be available to cooperate with whatever part in the process Jesus wants to share with us. He isn't stingy. He loves to share what he's doing. He doesn't want to keep all the fun to himself.

He does want us to be effective, aided with sound understanding of what he is trying to do. If we really have no idea what he is doing, how can we really be a part of the process? How can we then help in that process?

Is there a risk if we don't understand that we may even get in the way? That bears thinking about.

*There is no fear in love. But perfect love drives out fear, because fear has to do with punishment. The one who fears is not made perfect in love. **1 John 4:18 (NIV)***

The point made by the apostle John above also bears some consideration. If love drives out fear, what are we doing using fear in the first place?

Fear in fact stands in the way of the perfecting of love in the people of God.

What if the Gospel message had far more to do with the love of God, than anything to do with fear?

Would that be good news?

An Open Door To Sin

If losing leverage to get derrieres on seats was not sufficient reason to stoke our rhetorical fires of hell, then surely the threat of unrestrained sin should!

It's bad enough to think we may have fewer members in our churches if we can't scare them. What if those who are left lose their incentive to stay on the straight and narrow?

Even worse, what if the church then loses its sting in desperate calls to the world to forsake its ways of sin?

I'm sure it worked well in the past. At least to some extent it did. In the Christianised West one could argue a healthy dose of hell-fire preached quite often could present a sober case to restrain the worst of our human tendencies. I would not want to argue against this premise.

Still, without true repentance brought about by God's intervention in our hearts, crime was as prolific back then as it is today, if not worse. Australia could be grateful for that, as could any nation with a penal background.

Those here prior to white settlement may not agree, but if Europeans other than the British had settled Australia, would things be better for the Aborigines? I suspect not.

I'll never forget being part of a fairly law-based church some years ago. The focus on the Ten Commandments and doing the right thing was a strong focus. There were certain benefits that came from a clear understanding of sin. Grace however was not well understood. The focus on law gave a strong tendency towards salvation by works rather than faith and grace.

New leadership brought about a change in focus. The church realised its focus on law was not the right focus. It tried to make its focus more Jesus-centred, rather than commandment-centred. The results were interesting.

Within months, quite a number of marriages blew apart. They seemed like stable loving families under the focus of law. When the focus changed to grace, we began to see what was really going on.

Many pastors could not believe the changes they saw coming over some people. It wasn't everyone, but it was a significant "some". The force of law was sufficient to provide a veneer, but the heart of the matter was something else.

I understand a law focus is not the same as a hell-fire focus. I will argue the effects can be similar. A church with a strong hell-fire focus will have the same significant "some" as the church I referred to above. The threat of hell-fire may be the only thing keeping some in church, or maintaining a certain appearance of "good".

Is appearance sufficient for the outcomes we seek to achieve in our Christian walk, or the churches we pastor? I don't know anyone who would say it is. I'm fortunate my church social circles are not so shallow.

Would much change if the message got out to the world there was better news than the standard heaven or hell outcomes with which so many of us are familiar?

I dare say if anything did change, it may not be for the worse. I'm not saying all we need to do is just soften our message to get people saved. I've already made it clear (I hope) salvation is a function of God moving on someone, and not a good argument or a "nice" sounding story.

If anything, for those of us still moved by God to be a part of his Church (and I definitely am), the presentation of a positive Gospel message is much easier to put forward.

Having a message without the weird bits about God being somewhat psycho, or rather limp-wristed has got to be better for us Christians. We would never have to worry about encountering someone intelligent ever again. There wouldn't be intelligent arguments we couldn't credibly answer.

I don't like persecution, but it certainly is easier to take if it doesn't come from presenting God as a little weird (or maybe really weird, depending on the theology).

If "weird" really is truth, then so be it. I've stood up for plenty of "weird" in my Christian walk over the years. I'm only glad over time my mind was opened to learn so much of what I stood up for was just religion, and nothing to do with Christianity at all.

Does a change in thinking on hell-fire really mean sin will then break loose in both the world and churches?

Things are fairly bad in the world, even if so many are conditioned by a fear of hell-fire. Fear does not produce righteousness. Only the power of God does. It does so by acting from within the converted individual.

Hell-fire is common to many religious dogmas outside of Christianity. As I've stated before, it does have some effect, but this effect is not sufficient to bring about a world which does not need saving. We still have a mess. As my brother-in-law once stated quite candidly:

"I wonder if we aren't in hell already."

The fear of hell-fire and all its consequences will not create a better world. We have many hundreds of years with all manner of religions to prove this.

Removing a certain incentive from people to keep them from sinning does not mean it is OK to sin. It isn't. Sin has consequences. Many are really bad.

I've noticed God does not do much to lift a hand to stop us if we really want to sin or do something similarly stupid. We learn the hard way if we have to.

I tell my kids home is a safe place to make mistakes. They know I don't want them to. They also know there are boundaries.

They don't test the boundaries in any measure to indicate my focus on grace is an encouragement to go off and sin.

They still do make mistakes, as do I. So far, the overall results do seem to be quite positive. I only hope they always will be. Maybe I'll be able to report back in a number of years to update on how its going? There are no guarantees in this life.

Is it time to consider something different from hell-fire punishment dogmas?

Is it time to consider if alternative views might be far closer to the truth?

Would this not be good news indeed if it was?

Let's read on and see how it might be possible.

17: Outside the Box.

Take any theological dispute one can think of. At times I liken them to tennis matches, with scriptures being hit back and forth between opposing players.

The usual form of so many of these debates is for one to present a scripture to support their position. Often then, without unpacking the scripture presented by the opposition, the opposing player then fires off their scripture which suits their position. The assumption is the alternative scripture renders the one presented before as null and void, as if it no longer has meaning.

Is this hypothetical neutering of scripture really the best way to show our respect for scripture?

Do we really wish to argue in a manner where we make so much of scripture meaningless?

This is the impression I get when we start tossing scriptures back and forth with no serious consideration of scripture presented by those with an opposing view.

Perhaps it Is more like an artillery duel than a tennis match?

Artillery Duels

An observer could easily form the impression the Bible is full of contradictions. Those in debate ignore scriptures not supporting or possibly contradicting their position, and cling passionately to those which do.

Is this not a presentation of contradiction to any observer?

I'll never forget a friend of mine turning up at church one day very troubled. He told me how he had been reading about both free choice Arminianism, and predestination Calvinism. He was seriously confused.

If both positions really were in the Bible as valid alternative positions, then the Bible was just one massive contradiction.

My answer was to point out certain perspectives of both positions were in error. The way out was to recognise there had to be another way of understanding it all so all the scriptures were understood in harmony.

We would need to think outside the bounds of our long-established theologies. That is not an easy thing. Our brains get hard wired when we imbibe of any form of teaching for long enough. We can only hope we have enough hard wiring of the right understanding to avoid being too led astray.

The challenge now is to present a view of God's plan of salvation finding harmony with all of scripture. Somehow a message needs to be found to account for who God really is, as best as we can understand and know him.

With this we need to be able to understand all the references in scripture to love, hell, Heaven, predestination, and choice.

This may seem like a big ask, but is it really?

Perhaps I'm too idealistic?

I can't be sure. I do suspect making sense of it all may not be so complicated. What we need is the right set of filters through which we can begin to understand scripture.

For myself, I'm confident the Bible does not contradict at all. It can still give sufficient room for many to think it does. I suspect God wants it that way. It allows people all the rope they need to hang themselves. In doing so, there may be a lesson for them in time to come.

I say this as I don't think the Bible was originally inspired to prove how clever we all are. A far greater purpose is realised if it demonstrates otherwise.

The Big "When?"

Perhaps the biggest block to making sense of all the apparent contradictions our theologies present is the question of when salvation has to take place.

The standard view is a decision for following Christ has to be made in this life. It follows then once we die it is too late, if we haven't already been saved.

I could follow with an intense philosophical discussion on whether anything can be too late for God. Speaking for myself, I would think not.

Others would resort back to the parable of Lazarus and the Rich Man and say indeed things can be too late for God. Good for them!

My views may be simplistic, but I do perceive far more dogmas rely on this one parable than the questions surrounding it warrant.

Perhaps we should focus on basic absurdities one can use the parable of Lazarus and the rich man to prove, like salvation is only for the poor. This should help us view the parable in a more balanced and nuanced perspective.

We know salvation is not just for poor people. One could argue from the Lazarus parable that it is. I hope we know enough to not make that error.

We can hang on to ideas we think are supported by a parable about a rich and a poor man, but we still have to account for all the contradictions to follow as a consequence.

Do we support a view presenting God as a psychopath?

Do we support a view presenting God as a loser?

It won't be hard for anyone who disagrees with me to say he is neither. Even then they still hang on to the logic their views point to and indicate he is one or the other.

People will try to justify and defend whatever they want at the end of the day, and simply refuse to acknowledge the logical end of what they are saying. I'm used to that.

I only wish people would put more focus on the parable of the Prodigal Son when it comes to salvation thinking, than they do on the parable of Lazarus and the Rich Man.

I'm not trying to say the latter parable is of less value in scripture or question its authority. I'm only asking we not rush to misunderstand it in order to defend theologies of questionable veracity. Is there an unhealthy negative bias at work here if we do?

By negative bias, I'm referring to an insistence on holding to the more negative theological view. This is the one where far fewer can ever be saved, which in my view is a very negative outlook on God's ability to save.

For anyone who has read this far and still understands what I'm saying, then I suspect you won't have any problems with what follows. Now back to the "when?" of salvation...

Is there anything in scripture covering in some way the life of the typical unsaved woman or man after death? I think there is:

> *I saw thrones on which were seated those who had been given authority to judge. And I saw the souls of those who had been beheaded because of their testimony about Jesus and because of the word of God. They had not worshipped the beast or its image and had not received its mark on their foreheads or their hands. They came to life and reigned with Christ a thousand years. (The rest of the dead did not come to life until the thousand years were ended.) This is the first resurrection. Blessed and holy are those who share in the first resurrection. The second death has no power over them, but they will be priests of God and of Christ and will reign with him for a thousand years.*
> **Revelation 20:4-6** (NIV)

The whole of Revelation chapter 20 is sprinkled with insights on the future of the typical unsaved man and woman after death.

I didn't want to quote the whole chapter lest the reader get too distracted by other elements and questions on other topics which may arise from such an interesting chapter. Hence I'll make reference to just two distinct sections of the chapter.

In the above three verses we see how Christians are resurrected to live and reign with Jesus at his second coming. He told them of this second coming after they saw him resurrected and alive with them on earth, before he ascended to Heaven.

We also see an important reference to "the rest of the dead", which has to refer (well, to me it has to) to those who died without being saved.

What I love about this reference is how it removes the need to somehow imagine a mechanism where Jesus reveals himself to everyone before their point of death, so they can make a decision for salvation or not.

To me it is clear there are those who die saved, and those who die unsaved.

It is also important to note those who died unsaved will be under the power of an event called "the second death".

Those saved before they died the first death are resurrected at some point in time. Their freedom from the power of the second death is what salvation is all about, including the gift of eternal life.

Everyone is born under the power of death. This is why we need the saving power of Jesus. This is a core element of the Gospel, or Good News. The power of death is broken in a general sense because of Jesus.

All we are waiting for, to see a total end to the power of death over men and women, is to see all mankind accept Jesus as their saviour. When and if they all do accept Jesus will be the end of death and its power over mankind.

Now on to the second part of Revelation chapter 20:

> *Then I saw a great white throne and him who was seated on it. The earth and the heavens fled from his presence, and there was no place for them. And I saw the dead, great and small, standing before the throne, and books were opened. Another book was opened, which is the book of life. The dead were judged according to what they had done as recorded in the books. The sea gave up the dead that were in it, and death and Hades gave up the dead that were in them, and each person was judged according to what they had done. Then death and Hades were thrown into the lake of fire. The lake of fire is the second death. Anyone whose name was not found written in the book of life was thrown into the lake of fire.* **Revelation 20:11-15** (NIV)

The timing of this section of scripture is after a thousand year period of Jesus and saints ruling over the earth. Some view the "thousand years" as figurative for a long period of time with a fixed duration. Others view it as a literal thousand year period.

Whether figurative or literal, it doesn't matter for this discussion. Near its end, there is a brief period where Satan is allowed to lead a general revolt on earth near the end of the literal or figurative thousand years.

After this final satanic revolt we come to verse 11 above, from Revelation chapter 20. The dead referred to in verse 12 are the same referred to in verse 5, in my first reference to Revelation 20. These dead are those who originally died unsaved. They are resurrected to meet their maker at this point in history.

The culmination of history is found here. All who ever lived and died are finally together. They are now alive in one place and time.

At this point, all our theologies are finally reckoned and resolved:

- Who was right?
- Who was wrong?
- Were any of us right?
- Is the question of "when?" finally to be settled here?

It would certainly be good news if it was.

Judged According To?

With my tongue held firmly in cheek, I can say all the justification for all the various dogmas of salvation by works can be found here (in Rev 20:12)! Here indeed, the dead, now brought back to life, are judged according to what they had done.

Verse 15 then alludes to the notion some, after this judging by works, are to have their names written in the Book of Life. It would seem at least superficially our works have finally saved us, or some of us. But is this really how it works (no pun intended)?

Will the works of some really qualify some for eternal life?

Rather than let the religions of the world, and all the religious people of the world, have reason to celebrate, I want to spoil their fun. Sorry!

Does judgement of all we have done really get our names into The Book of Life?

Not if Jesus' death and resurrection plays any part in this. What need would there be for a Gospel if judgment of our works was the way to salvation and the end of the story?

Only the deluded think they are so good to warrant saving. If I can make sense of anything in this world and all I've seen in my brief 55+ years, the obvious outcome of judgment on our works is why we need Good News.

So here we have all who had ever lived in history who died unsaved, standing before the White Judgment Throne of God. Books are opened. In these books everyone gets to see the sum total of all they did and the judgment to go with it (with fries?).

The sentence is death. This should be obvious. If it wasn't death, then Jesus never had to die for everyone. At least some of us could have saved ourselves.

At this point I'm open to speculation. We have all of mankind who died unsaved gathered at this judgment. From verses 12 to 15 it would seem somehow some make it into the Book of Life. If not, then all would be thrown into the fire.

The sense of how it reads, and I know this is subjective, does not indicate all are thrown into the fire. Somehow some of these who died unsaved end up saved. Only the residual unsaved from this resurrection of all unsaved, and what follows, experience the second death.

We know it was not because they were so good at saving themselves. It had to be because of Jesus and what he achieved at the cross.

Is this a fair speculation? I hope so. If it isn't, we may as well throw out our Bibles and forget all we ever learnt or should have learnt about salvation by grace.

Would it not be amazing if at this point in history, God is somehow able to reach beyond the shackles of all the humanly devised theology and preach the Gospel to all these people after they actually died?

Could God be bigger than our theologies?

What about our dogmas?

What about our narrow-minded perceptions of what we think and have decided God just wouldn't do?

I certainly don't know everything, and I could be wrong here. The obvious conclusion to me is as follows. The God I know has no problem with giving all who ever lived and were unable to accept the Gospel message, let alone receive it, an opportunity to hear the message and finally understand it at the time of this White Throne Judgment.

How else would additional people end up with their names in the Book of Life?

That Isn't Fair!

I can still hear my pastor friend saying how unfair it would be for people to have their opportunity for salvation after they have died.

Did he think he was somehow more deserving of salvation because he had "done it tough" as a Christian in this life?

Fairness and what we deserve has no place in a Gospel message centred on grace. Such terms don't compute with grace.

The computer crashes every time we try to resolve an equation computing equivalence between grace and fairness. It does the same when we try to resolve what we deserve and grace.

What does the parable of the Prodigal Son tell us about God's view on fairness?

It says a great deal about fairness. It tells us in very plain language God's desire to see those he loves saved is far greater than any need to be fair.

How badly do we want to be like the older brother towards any prodigal son? This parable was written for us if we do.

God is not worried about fairness. He isn't worried about justice either. He is still a just God, but the death of Jesus took care of justice once and for all. Every requirement for justice has been satisfied. The same is true for fairness.

Second Chances?

As I said before, some, including this particular pastor friend, think salvation at the White Throne Judgment means some get a second chance at salvation.

Firstly, I think it is worth repeating myself and stating the vast majority of people lived and died with no first chance of salvation at all. The message never got to them.

Secondly, even if the message got to them, and the missionary or whoever was fairly decent in his or her presentation of the message, God had to move their heart to be able to receive the message. They never had a hope in hell (or anywhere else) of salvation unless God moved first.

It is one thing to hear the message. It is entirely another thing to be capable of acting on it. People in their natural state can't. Only God can save us from the fallen condition and open a mind to receive his message. So far he has not been doing that with many people.

If the past is an indicator of the future until the White Throne Judgment, God's intervention with people will be limited up to the time preceding the White Throne Judgment. The verses which follow from the Apostle John make this very clear:

> We know that we are children of God, and that the whole world is under the control of the evil one. We know also that the Son of God has come and has given us understanding, so that we may know him who is true. **1 John 5:19-20** (NIV)

Just think for a moment about all the thousands of people who heard Jesus preach in the flesh, when he walked the earth before his crucifixion. Only a few hundred had their minds opened to believe.

God only gave understanding back then to a few. It was not in God's timing to save everyone then. They may have heard the Gospel message, from Jesus himself, but it never constituted a first chance, or being given understanding. Their minds were always closed.

God had to have had a future time in mind. Is there any other way of reconciling all the "infinite exceptions" I've earlier noted?

Is there any other way to reconcile all the possible interpretations of "Hell", and the God who "so loved", and the God who wants everyone to be saved, out of his prodigal love?

What First Chance?

Maybe we should unpack the idea of "first chance" a little more.

The theology I grew up with (heaven, hell, and Arminian free choice) would allow for a first chance for receiving salvation of varying effectiveness. It all depended on the circumstances surrounding how and from whom you got the message about Jesus.

I'm sorry to be really blunt here, but in some churches (not all by any means), ministers or priests have been known to be of blatantly obvious questionable moral standing. This does not make for a high quality opportunity for receiving the Gospel.

In fact, there would be all manner of sound logical reasons to reject the Gospel because the person delivering the message had no credibility. That's tough, if all you get is one chance to hear the message and respond.

I know the Arminian free choice argument where it takes hearing the message sometimes many times before one is ready to receive it.

What if, in this world of "abundant" free choice, time and chance had someone die before they had any chance of hearing the Gospel message the number of times they needed to? They died before they were ready to accept it!

Yes, I know. I'm presenting another one of those annoying "infinite exceptions". If I was to give my Arminian protagonist enough time, I also know he'd be able to come up with another "creative theology" to match it.

But does it really matter if one does get a second chance to hear and respond to the Gospel message at the White Throne Judgment of Revelation chapter 20?

It is in the Bible after all. Why not be just happy they do?

Remember the older brother of the prodigal son?

How badly do we want to think like him?

I personally don't think the opportunity they will get does represent a second chance. I've explained why it is more like a first chance, but who cares if I'm wrong?

So what if God's love is so big it is in his nature to "so love" (John 3:16)?

So what if he gives some a second chance because he desires to see everyone saved? Prodigal love is like that.

I don't know too many people in this life who have not been given a second chance at something who did not appreciate a second chance. Thinking of all the times in this life as a Christian where I've missed the mark (sinned) in my daily walk, I think I passed my second chance many years ago.

I don't know what chance I'm on now, speaking hypothetically. All I know is I'm saved, and I didn't save myself. I'm saved by grace, and the sacrifice of Jesus.

Given most if not all Christians I've ever known are living saved way beyond their second chance, why not be happy for someone else to receive the same?

Would this not be good news?

A Lake Of Fire

There is still one burning question remaining for me when I think of the statements made in Revelation 20. I referred to them earlier:

Then death and Hades were thrown into the lake of fire. The lake of fire is the second death. [15]Anyone whose name was not found written in the book of life was thrown into the lake of fire. **Revelation 20:14-15** (NIV)

If God really wants all people to be saved (1 Tim 2:4), what's going on with this lake of fire in Revelation chapter 20 above?

At this point in the "who gets saved?" question, I'm ready to give God a passing grade. He scores greater than fifty percent as it looks like he will save at least 50% of mankind.

Before I knew about the potential for salvation occurring at the White Throne Judgement, God was saving so few, he couldn't get a passing grade (i.e. >50%). He started so well with the death of Jesus, then somehow lost momentum with the follow through.

This is what I learnt in childhood Arminian-based Sunday school once I was old enough to think about it and start asking questions.

With some understanding about the White Throne Judgment, surely many more can be saved than we could previously consider with our standard theologies.

The plan of salvation with this particular detail now looks so good; we just might even give God a High Distinction (HD). The HD would come in with a score greater than ninety percent, if my time at university is anything to go by.

Still, I think we are allowing God to grade below par. He does actually want to save everyone after all. Look at the parable of the lost sheep in Luke chapter 15, if we have any doubts about this.

I don't think I'm pushing the bounds of understanding or interpretation too far with this one. I really do think God wants to save everyone – not just ninety or ninety five percent. He is known for his prodigal love after all.

I say this as a father myself. I love all my kids. Is God selective in who he loves? I don't think so. I've also been a witness to love with a depth I have never had to muster for my own children.

All my kids are basically healthy. I have extended family with kids who are not. Imagine if both of your two children had cerebral palsy (CP). My extended family has this issue to face. It isn't easy. Their lives are full of disappointment for what their kids can never be in this life.

Nevertheless, their love for their two CP kids knows no bounds. There is so much their kids will never be able to do. It is tragic, but we get to see a glimpse of the reach of God's love in the midst of this heartache.

Without a miracle, my CP relatives will never walk, never talk, or ever be able to take care of themselves, let alone give much in return. They are totally dependent on their two devoted parents. Their example is one where love is no respecter of persons.

Knowing this, I have to wonder about my God who "so loved". Could he have a plan even for the hypothetical "five to ten percent" who are so dysfunctional they don't somehow make it into The Book of Life at the time of the Great White Throne Judgment in Revelation chapter 20?

We can talk about free choice all we like, but what makes someone want to miss out on The Book Of Life?

I don't know myself. All I know is there can be a lot of messed up people. They didn't start life this way, but life had a way of happening.

I know a number of bitter messed up people. I know their circumstances too. Would I have been less bitter in the same circumstances? Probably not. I think God knows these circumstances too. Duh!

I doubt God is callous towards how unfair life can be, and how weak we can be in processing it all. God chose to live in the very mess of life with us, in the person of Jesus. It would be a lie to say he doesn't know and understand.

I know too God saved me. I didn't save myself. Yet here some are, not in The Book of Life, facing a lake of fire. I've no idea really how many would be in this position. I would expect very few – probably far less than my hypothetical five percent. I hope so anyway.

But still they are there, still messed up and hurting from all the mess of life that pointed them in the direction of those outcomes. They get thrown into a lake of fire.

Good news?

Refining Silver

I could say "they end up" in a lake of fire. However, I'm not so certain it is the end. So many of our theologies have us think a lake of fire has to be the end of the story.

This is no wonder given our thinking is shaped by years of standard hell-fire theology, with the add-on where salvation can only be given in this present life. But is there another way of looking at it?

As silver is melted in a furnace, so you will be melted inside her, and you will know that I the Lord have poured out my wrath on you. **Ezekiel 22:22** (NIV)

This third I will put into the fire; I will refine them like silver and test them like gold. They will call on my name and I will answer them; I will say, 'They are my people,' and they will say, 'The Lᴏʀᴅ is our God.' **Zechariah 13:9** (NIV)

In the above verses, taken from two different sections of the Old Testament, we see the reference to silver going into fire, or a furnace (a lake of fire?).

I'm not saying these verses are speaking of the lake of fire at the end of the book of Revelation. They do however speak of the thinking behind such practice.

Would any of us throw silver into a furnace to get rid of it? Not likely, unless we were trying to hide it. Is there any point then to throwing silver into a furnace?

Ask any silversmith. There is!

A silversmith throws silver into a furnace to purify, or make it perfect. The last thing on his mind is destroying it. The silver is what he values. He knows a furnace can bring even more value to the silver. Does God know this?

In the verse from Ezekiel above, God speaks of Israel going into a furnace as silver. He does not send Israel into a furnace as rubbish to be destroyed. He valued and still values Israel.

Obviously the language employed here is not literal. It is symbolic. By use of such imagery, I think the message is made very clear. How good for Israel is it to be likened to silver?

The verse from Zechariah above uses similar imagery. Look at the end, or reason, for such "furnace" refining to which God subjected Israel. The clear reason is not for their destruction. The refining is so this "third" of Israel will say, finally:

"The Lord is our God!"

How good is that?

If this is not a picture of salvation, I don't know what is.

We need to remember too this fire was not so good people would be made better, thinking about Israel. This was so incorrigibly wicked people, as God described Israel so often, would be made perfect.

We understand God can subject wilfully sinful Israel to a hypothetical furnace for their salvation. We also understand the same God wants to see everyone saved, and "so loves". He loves extravagantly. We do understand this! Do we?!

Would he not employ a lake of fire for the same positive outcome?

Sure, the Bible doesn't make a direct statement after the reference to the lake of fire in Revelation 20 about the outcome. It doesn't state how everyone then proclaims the Lord is their God because they have been refined like silver. It says nothing. The subject changes completely as the text moves into chapter 21, changing the topic completely.

By the end of the Bible, does the outcome need to be spelled out?

Isn't it obvious, if we really understand the Bible?

It would seem God leaves it to us to work it out, if it isn't obvious already. I like this. As I've said before, he continues to give us all the rope we need to hang (figuratively) ourselves.

God probably isn't so interested in labouring the point about his love at this point in the scriptures. He said enough already. By the book of Revelation, we should already know, if our minds have been opened to understand.

Yes, I know in reality, it is a miracle if we do know God's love by the time we read the Bible right through to the last book, Revelation. After nearly 2000 years, we still find it hard to understand.

This is partly because of who we are. It is also because of what is working against us in this world – a spiritual kingdom of darkness. This kingdom has all the religion it needs to throw at us to keep us confused.

Some of us also don't know God's love because God has not yet revealed his love to us in its fullness. We are all on different places in this journey of discovering his love.

At the end of the day, all understanding is a gift – a gift from God. That's my view anyway. We can try to understand it any other way if we like.

I can't pretend to have the final word on this. All I can present is what makes sense to me, and hope it helps lend clarity to what others may be thinking.

When I first started writing these last few sections on the lake of fire, I was really thinking it was a fifty-fifty proposition. Either the lake of fire was for final destruction of the unrepentant, or for refining.

I was quite open to either possibility. I was happy looking into the subject of the White Throne Judgment gave scope for far more to be saved than was allowed for by current standard theologies.

Now I've started writing about this lake of fire, and searching the scriptures for references to silver and refining, I can now see a perfect synergy with fire, refining, a God who "so loved" with prodigal love, and salvation for all.

It just makes sense.

And so all Israel...

I do not want you to be ignorant of this mystery, brothers and sisters, so that you may not be conceited: Israel has experienced a hardening in part until the full number of the Gentiles has come in, and in this way all Israel will be saved. As it is written:

"The deliverer will come from Zion; he will turn godlessness away from Jacob. And this is my covenant with them when I take away their sins." **Romans 11:25-27** (NIV)

The verses above speak of the hardening of Israel, and in essence, all of mankind. The hardening is another way of saying they could not of themselves turn to God. God designed this hardening outcome to only be temporary. This condition was not on everyone. The exceptions include Moses, Samuel, and King David, to name a few.

Does free choice figure in this equation?

I can't be too sure it does. I mean, who has a say in who gets hardened or not?

What comes after the hardening?

I think it is quite plain. All Israel will be saved.

Too good to be true?

Maybe.

Still, I don't think it is too hard for God. Yes, perhaps I should not be taking it so literally. Much of scripture is figurative. Maybe it means "most" of Israel?

Really?

I've said this all before. How we want to understand this scripture will depend on how we view God.

Do I need to repeat myself?

18: Unpardonable Sins.

The Chorus

I can hear the chorus already. I've come this far, with a proposal God just might get one hundred percent of what he wants. But there are still questions from those who really know their Bibles.

"What about the unpardonable sin!?"

That's a big one. I cannot ignore such a question and hope it goes away if I just shut my ears and eyes long enough. The elephant in the china shop doesn't leave the shop intact easily.

So what is this unpardonable sin?

There is not much in scripture shedding light on such a concept. The first I'm aware of in the New Testament comes from Matthew chapter 12:

> *And so I tell you, every kind of sin and slander can be forgiven, but blasphemy against the Spirit will not be forgiven. Anyone who speaks a word against the Son of Man will be forgiven, but anyone who speaks against the*

Holy Spirit will not be forgiven, either in this age or in the age to come. **Matthew 12:31-32** (NIV)

Those are heavy words. I would not want to take them lightly. The simplest way of understanding them is to conclude there is sin God is prepared to forgive, but there is a more specific kind of sin God is not prepared to forgive.

If a sin cannot be forgiven, is there any redemption possible for such a person?

This is the simplest interpretation I can think of. I'm aware this is what many Christians think it says. Is the true meaning really this simple?

Is truth always couched in simple terms?

I would have to say from my 40+ years of reading the Bible truth is not always simple or easy to perceive or uncover. I've been so wrong in my understanding of the Bible in years gone by; I do hope to have at least learnt that!

Are there any other references on the unpardonable sin which might shed more light?

There is one in the Gospel of Luke:

And everyone who speaks a word against the Son of Man will be forgiven, but anyone who blasphemes against the Holy Spirit will not be forgiven. **Luke 12:10** (NIV)

The verse above from Luke says basically the same as the first of the two verses in Matthew chapter 12. The fact the follow-on statement given by Matthew concerning "ages" is omitted is interesting, but not necessarily significant.

Further into the New Testament we read from the Epistle to the Hebrews:

> *It is impossible for those who have once been enlightened, who have tasted the heavenly gift, who have shared in the Holy Spirit, who have tasted the goodness of the word of God and the powers of the coming age and who have fallen away, to be brought back to repentance. To their loss they are crucifying the Son of God all over again and subjecting him to public disgrace. Land that drinks in the rain often falling on it and that produces a crop useful to those for whom it is farmed receives the blessing of God. But land that produces thorns and thistles is worthless and is in danger of being cursed. In the end it will be burned.* **Hebrews 6:4-8** (NIV)

These verses do seem quite straightforward to me in Hebrews. They seem to be saying if one turns away from his faith in Christ, then it is not possible for them to be turned around.

I know this is how I have always read such verses. It is how I always understood them. Was I conditioned to misunderstand them?

I do know of cases where someone has walked away from following God, and has returned to the faith. Does such "reality" fly in the face of what these scriptures are saying?

Could it be that those who think they have come back really haven't, but don't know it?

Is this what these verses are telling us?

I would prefer to think those I know who fell away then returned, never met a hypothetical point of "no return". If I understand Hebrews 6 in the light of "unpardonable sin" it makes sense there must be such a point from which one can never recover. If so, I don't know how to define such a point of no return.

Perhaps my preference in how I would like to understand these verses is only that – a preference, far removed from the harsh reality of these scriptures and the truth therein.

How many might I know in churches today who think they are saved only to have in reality a burning of "thorns" to look forward to?

It is such a lovely thought – all these friends who may be holding to hope, yet have no hope at all. Have we here the makings of a serious good news story?

Is this as good as good news can get?

The Epistle to the Hebrews has more to say on the subject:

> *If we deliberately keep on sinning after we have received the knowledge of the truth, no sacrifice for sins is left, but only a fearful expectation of judgment and of raging fire that will consume the enemies of God. Anyone who rejected the law of Moses died without mercy on the testimony of two or three witnesses. How much more severely do you think someone deserves to be punished who has trampled the Son of God underfoot, who has treated as an unholy thing the blood of the covenant that sanctified them, and who has insulted the Spirit of grace? For we know him who said, "It is mine to avenge; I will repay," and again, "The Lord will judge his people." It is a dreadful thing to fall into the hands of the living God.*
> **Hebrews 10:26-31** (NIV)

Once again, we do seem to have a powerful statement about those who decide they still want to live a life of sin after what we assume has been a true conversion to be a follower of Jesus.

To be fair, it doesn't say anything about leaving the faith. It does at least infer there is no coming back from such a state. Doom would seem to be the end for such a person.

It could in theory refer to those who simply are Christians yet find they still sin in a deliberate manner, rather than by accident.

I can't say I deliberately premeditate sin in my human condition, but do have to question if some of my failings are not deliberate. I'm certainly conscious of many times I do miss the mark, even if I'm not pleased with myself.

For all the times I've been angry with God, in particular seasons of life, I have to be honest and say my anger was deliberate. I'm sure I'm not the first to be disappointed with God in my walk as a Christian. So far I've always recovered from my disappointment and frustrations. I've seen the same in my children towards me.

Is Hebrews chapter 10 really saying I'm kidding myself?

Is it really saying I'm a fool if I think I have recovered, when the hard fact in scripture is I haven't?

If so, then I have nothing to lose by saying I really don't think so. I'm damned no matter what. Fortunately the God and Saviour I've come to know really isn't like this.

So, with all these scriptures apparently saying God can or won't ultimately redeem certain people, is everything I've said so far really just demonstrating scripture is full of contradictions?

I really hope not. Perhaps deeper study is necessary to ensure we understand how much the Bible really is in harmony with all its inputs from so many diverse writers.

To unpack this subject of sin never to be forgiven I'll begin with the verses in the Epistle to the Hebrews. I'll then consider the Gospel references in Matthew and Luke.

Context, Context, and Context.

I've referred to context a fair measure by now.

Sometimes I find the best way to unpack scripture and find its deeper context is to sit and read the specific Epistle over and over again. The specific verses in Hebrews which seem to refer to unpardonable sins have certainly challenged me and what I've written so far in this book.

I'm not talking about just reading a few scriptures over and over. Context may not become clear by such a focused reading. The bigger picture or context of an Epistle may only be found by reading the whole Epistle, and many times over too.

Obviously I can be accused of trying to read my own interpretation into the Epistle. I get that. The problem of data bias can also rise to the fore. Data bias is when we subconsciously identify points supporting a previously held position, while ignoring points which don't. I'm sure we have all done this and probably still do. Such is human nature.

However I may be flawed, it becomes a zero sum argument as no person alive is devoid of such potential. I can only do my best and let the reader decide by the conclusions I draw and how well I argue them. At least I recognise I have these weaknesses, and do seek to tame them.

Whatever my flaws, I resolved to immerse myself in the reading of the Epistle over and over again, asking myself constantly questions like:

- Who is this written to?
- Who is this about?
- What is the setting of what I'm reading?
- What is this about?
- How can this be understood so it does not contradict other parts of the Bible?

I was not disappointed with what I found....

Written to Who?

It may seem like a simple question. The Epistle, or letter to the Hebrews would appear to be written to and or for a group referred to as Hebrews. It would also seem to be addressed specifically to Hebrews who were in the church.

I have no argument with this. The Hebrews could also be referred to as Jews, or Jewish people – the direct descendants of Judah, who was one of the sons of Jacob, or Israel.

At the time of Jesus, the Gospel message was originally given to the Hebrews, or Jews, and then went to other peoples. Those who originally received this message were living in the Roman province of

Palestine/Judea. The disciples carried the message way beyond the borders of Palestine, and it was presented to Jewish people and others living far from Palestine, as the New Testament describes.

Given there were groups of Jews, or Hebrews spread far and wide across the Roman Empire, one has to ask if the Epistle was addressed to Hebrews all over the Roman Empire, or more specifically to Jews in one particular region.

Written to Where?

I've heard of some who suggest the Epistle to the Hebrews was written by Paul to the Jews in Rome. I don't know why they believe this.

To me, thinking it was written to the Jews in Rome is strange as there is a greeting from those in Italy to the recipients, right at the end of the letter:

"Greet all your leaders and all the Lord's people. Those from Italy send you their greetings." **Hebrews 13:24** (NIV)

If the Epistle was written to those in Rome, would those in Italy send greetings when Rome is actually in Italy?

Maybe they would. It might be those outside of Rome, and still in Italy were sending greetings to those in Italy who were specifically in Rome. It sounds strange, but might not have sounded strange 2000 years ago. Once again, I really don't know.

I would not be surprised if it was written from Rome, but find no reason to conclude it had to be written to Jews in Rome. I'm happy for someone to shed more light to me on this.

I will avoid going into these questions too deeply at risk of someone saying if I avoid such detailed research I risk missing the true point of the Epistle and the critical verses I'm discussing here in the book.

This might be true.

Still, it may also be true such a study would have me risk learning more and more about less and less. There is risk in every endeavour, and only so many hours available in any day. I'll choose to save some time at this stage. The points I'm making do not require the detail of a PhD submission.

Written When?

At the time this Epistle was written, the destruction of Jerusalem in 70 AD was much closer in time than when Jesus was speaking of the same fate in Matthew 24, Mark 13, and Luke 21.

Remember how the points made by Jesus, with his references to "Gehenna" and the Valley of Tophet, were all likely within a context tied to the judgement on the city of Jerusalem?

This Epistle to the Hebrews was conceivably written to those still in Judea, before Rome destroyed Jerusalem. The Catholic Encyclopedia (Fonck) dates the Epistle to around 63 AD.

I'd be surprised if there was universal agreement on the date, but give or take a number of years; I can't avoid noticing a powerful context here.

If it really was written only a few years before Jerusalem was destroyed, and the author had some idea of what was coming, just as did Jesus, would this awareness of pending doom influence the tone and content of the Epistle?

Written About What?

As I engaged in this immersion reading exercise, certain points began to emerge concerning the content of the topics covered in the Epistle to the Hebrews.

One thing I noticed was the numerous references to Old Testament events. The author of the letter also understood or expected the recipients were familiar with these same events. This reinforced my impression the letter was written to a primarily Jewish audience. This demographic is what one would expect to find in Judea. I would not expect the church in Rome was predominantly Hebrew.

Just as it would be correct to say the Epistle was written to Hebrews; I found the subject matter was predominantly about Hebrew people.

In the Old Testament there was only one group of people who God was dealing with as "his people". In the New Testament, with the advent of the New Covenant, there were two distinct groups with whom God was dealing. One group was the church, comprising both Hebrews and gentiles. The other group was the physical descendants of Israel still living in Judea.

The "physical" (non-Church) people of God, after the death of Jesus, were under judgment. This judgment was fulfilled with the destruction of Jerusalem and the temple in 70 AD. Jesus was very clear on this in Matthew chapters 23 and 24:

> And so upon you will come all the righteous blood that has been shed on earth, from the blood of righteous Abel to the blood of Zechariah son of Berekiah, whom you murdered between the temple and the altar. Truly I tell you, all this will come on this generation. **Matthew 23:35-36** (NIV)

Jesus referred to the destruction of Jerusalem many times with his references to Gehenna. Does it make sense the pending fate of Jerusalem and the Hebrews in Judea was on the mind of the writer of the Epistle to the Hebrews?

Further, is the fiery Gehenna judgement referred to by Jesus so often in the Gospels synonymous with the fiery judgement referred to in Hebrews 6:8 and 10:27?

> But land that produces thorns and thistles is worthless and is in danger of being cursed. In the end it will be burned. **Hebrews 6:8** (NIV)

> … but only a fearful expectation of judgment and of raging fire that will consume the enemies of God. **Hebrews 10:27** (NIV)

If it is, we know who this judgement is directed to – the Jewish people who rejected the message of Jesus and killed him.

This pending fate of Jerusalem was in fact another point which emerged from my "immersion" study of the Epistle to the Hebrews. I could see how the Epistle was sprinkled with allusions to pending calamity. It also made sense how for years I'd been reading this part of the Bible thinking it was pointing to a different calamity in a future second coming of Jesus. I had been completely missing the point and context.

I'd been raised with a common worldview on the return of Jesus known as "Pre-millennialism". This view proposes for nearly 2000 years the church has been living with constant expectation of the imminent return of Jesus. Such thinking says we don't know when it will be, but we have to live as if it is inevitable in our life time.

I'm not saying I completely disagree with this. I will say such thinking can distort our comprehension of scripture. By such thinking it is easy to think what we read in scripture today is with a context directly relevant to today.

In many ways many parts of scripture can be relevant to today. I do understand this. It is one of its qualities which I love and appreciate. What was written nearly 2000 years ago can have application today just as it did when it was first penned.

The problem arises when we unwittingly use this thinking to miss entirely the original context, and then form distorted dogmas the scripture would never point to with correct understanding.

My "programmed" thinking from years of "pre-millennial" teaching made me miss the likely context of the destruction of Jerusalem I can now see is throughout the Epistle to the Hebrews.

What Enlightenment?

Some may say the context of the references to unpardonable sin in Hebrews looks far more like it is directed to Christians who have fallen away. They would argue the Jews who were not believers in Christ could not be called "those who have once been enlightened" (Heb 6:4) or those who have "received the knowledge of the truth" (Heb 10:26).

This is a fair point and a sound argument in some respects. Even so I would suggest the warnings in Hebrews refer to both Hebrews in the church, and Hebrews outside the church.

The Israelites under the Old Covenant were living with all manner of enlightenment and knowledge within the Old Testament. Such enlightenment and knowledge was given by God to no other people.

Further, when Jesus came, all manner of people knew Jesus was like no other prophet. Many recognised him to be the Messiah. Thousands were in attendance when he spoke. Thousands were fed by him and saw his miraculous healings. These same thousands turned against Jesus when his time came to die for them, and all mankind.

It was not just the common folk who knew Jesus was different. The leadership, at least in the sect of the Pharisees did too. Consider the words of Nicodemus, who came to see Jesus in secret early in the Gospel of John:

Now there was a Pharisee, a man named Nicodemus who was a member of the Jewish ruling council. He came to Jesus at night and said, "Rabbi, we know that you are a teacher who has come from God. For no one could perform the signs you are doing if God were not with him." **John 3:1-2** (NIV)

Is it possible the harsh words of Jesus about Gehenna, and about fire and burning in the Epistle to the Hebrews were reserved predominantly for those who put Jesus to death, and then persecuted the Church after Jesus' resurrection?

I don't know how many times I immersed myself in the Epistle to the Hebrews before certain scriptures began to leap out and tell me something. A certain verse in Hebrews chapter 10 gave me one of those moments:

If we deliberately keep on sinning after we have received the knowledge of the truth, no sacrifice for sins is left, but only a fearful expectation of judgment and of raging fire that will consume the enemies of God. **Hebrews 10:26-27** (NIV)

The context finally hit me. In verse 27 above, it refers to "the enemies of God". It further states a few verses on:

For we know him who said, "It is mine to avenge; I will repay," and again, "The Lord will judge his people." **Hebrews 10:30** (NIV)

A footnote is given to this verse referring to the Lord saying he will judge his people, in Deuteronomy 32:36. I cannot escape the sense these verses, and the whole Epistle in many respects, are written with the context in mind of the Hebrews still in Jerusalem. Many of these were essentially the same who not only crucified Jesus, they also persecuted the church and were thereby "enemies of God".

This persecution of the Hebrews in the church is then referred to right after:

> *Remember those earlier days after you had received the light, when you endured in a great conflict full of suffering. Sometimes you were publicly exposed to insult and persecution; at other times you stood side by side with those who were so treated. You suffered along with those in prison and joyfully accepted the confiscation of your property, because you knew that you yourselves had better and lasting possessions.* **Hebrews 10:32-34** (NIV)

Yes, Jews in Rome did give Christians a hard time, or so I have heard from my reading of Church history over the years, but this Epistle was written primarily to Hebrew people. The church in Judea is the only place where I would expect the church to be comprised mostly of Jewish people. Anywhere else there would have been a mix of different peoples – Jews and gentiles, or non-Jews.

If we read Hebrews with the imminence of the destruction of Jerusalem in mind, all allusions in parts of scripture to perceived unforgiveable sins begins to make sense. It is not referring to unpardonable sins for the people of God at all.

I could now see there was a Hebrew people who crucified Jesus, wholesale rejected his message, and then persecuted the church in Judea. They could be viewed as people who had indeed been enlightened. They had tasted of the heavenly gift. They had also experienced the Holy Spirit, and the powers of the age to come, just as stated in Hebrews 6:4-5:

> *It is impossible for those who have once been enlightened, who have tasted the heavenly gift, who have shared in the Holy Spirit, 5 who have tasted the goodness of the word of God and the powers of the coming age...* **Hebrews 6:4-5** (NIV)

I could also see those same people, though never eventually born again like the disciples, could be seen as ones who had fallen away. Many had followed Jesus for years. Only a few of those who followed him did not eventually turn on him and participate in his crucifixion. Their tragic future fate in the fires of Jerusalem was sealed.

The Old Covenant ended with the death of Jesus, just as a marriage is over with the death of one or both spouses (see Romans 7:1-2). This is why in Hebrews 10:26 it speaks of there being no more sacrifice for sins. The Old Covenant was over, so one could no longer deal with sin through animal sacrifices:

> *If we deliberately keep on sinning after we have received the knowledge of the truth, no sacrifice for sins is left, but only a fearful expectation of judgment and of raging fire that will consume the enemies of God.* **Hebrews 10:26-27** (NIV)

The writer of the above verses could use the term "we" as he was a Hebrew, as were the people he was writing to in the church, and as were the people facing destruction with Jerusalem.

He was essentially saying that if we were like those in Jerusalem, we would be facing the judgment and fire coming on Jerusalem. Those Hebrews who were not Christians were trapped in sin by the rejection of their Messiah, Jesus.

It is also interesting to note the mention of no more sacrifice for sins. Anyone in the church had long since given up on temple sacrifices to cover sins, knowing Jesus was the only real sacrifice of significance. The context in this mention of sacrifices is once again pointing to non-Christian Hebrews as the subject of the specific statements.

In verse 39 following, the writer makes the essential qualification:

> *But we do not belong to those who shrink back and are destroyed, but to those who have faith and are saved.* **Hebrews 10:39** (NIV)

We then see the same qualification given in Hebrews 6:

> *Even though we speak like this, dear friends, we are convinced of better things in your case—the things that have to do with salvation.* **Hebrews 6:9** (NIV)

In both of these qualifying verses the writer is saying those in the church don't match the description of those who are slated for destruction. Where ever we read in Hebrews about so-called unpardonable sins, there is a qualifying statement showing the writer is not talking about the church.

In the past, before Jesus put an end to the Old Covenant, the system of sacrifices was active to restore people back to right standing with God, so long as they were not mixed with pagan ritual. The Jews at the time of Jesus and after were very strict with Old Covenant details.

As strict as they may have been with such rituals, the Old Covenant was over. Rejecting the Son of God was sin, and paradoxically such rejection was ultimately part of the permanent solution to sin and ultimate reconciliation between mankind and his creator.

They continued to sacrifice till they ran out of animals during the war with the Romans. Such sacrifices were useless in covering their rejection of Jesus as they were no longer under a covenant with God. Even if some might argue they were still the "people" of God, it was not going to change the fate Jesus had warned them of before they killed him.

For Believers Too?

There is an important qualification needing to be made. I did say earlier these apparent unpardonable sin verses in Hebrews could also be addressed to Hebrews in the church.

Was the author of the Epistle also stating if a Hebrew Christian in Judea was to fall away from their faith, they could not count on supernatural protection during the destruction of Jerusalem?

The city of Jerusalem was destroyed by fire. Many thousands were killed in the siege and eventual capture and destruction wholesale of the city. I have to assume God had some means of protection in mind for his people who remained in Judea at the time.

Some traditions state God told the church to leave Jerusalem before the Romans cut off the city. We can even argue Jesus had already laid out the game plan in Matthew chapter 24:

> *"So when you see standing in the holy place 'the abomination that causes desolation,' spoken of through the prophet Daniel—let the reader understand— then let those who are in Judea flee to the mountains. Let no one on the housetop go down to take anything out of the house. Let no one in the field go back to get their cloak. How dreadful it will be in those days for pregnant women and nursing mothers! Pray that your flight will not take place in winter or on the Sabbath.* **Matthew 24:15-20** (NIV)

Here we have Jesus telling his followers there would be a time to flee Jerusalem and seek shelter in the mountains. If my memory of Church history serves me correctly, this is indeed what the church in Jerusalem eventually did before the city was destroyed.

I can't help but think it was not a good time to have abandoned the Christian faith, and find oneself remaining in Jerusalem, with the Roman armies of General Titus looming large on the horizon.

The Epistle to the Hebrews had this partly in mind when it gave its warnings about turning from enlightenment. What was due to come upon those who had killed Jesus and persecuted his followers would also fall on anyone in Judea who had abandoned their Christian faith.

I expect some did fall away from the church. It is part of the reality of walking with God in this hostile world. Some of us waver under pressure. I dare say at least some who had fallen away would have realised what was going on, and also could see they had no way out. It would have been a harsh awakening.

Crucify Again.

I've just discussed how I do think these verses in Hebrews 6 and 10 do present a warning to those Hebrews who might give up on their Christian walk. It doesn't change the fact I also think they refer to the unbelieving Hebrews too who were never in the Church.

There is another point to make and so conclude this aspect of the discussion. It focuses on a key statement in Hebrews 6:4-6:

It is impossible for those who have once been enlightened, who have tasted the heavenly gift, who have shared in the Holy Spirit, who have tasted the goodness of the word of God and the powers of the coming age and who have fallen away, to be brought back to repentance. To their loss they are crucifying the Son of God all over again and subjecting him to public disgrace. **Hebrews 6:4-6** (NIV)

Somehow, the people who have fallen away, as referred to above, are crucifying Jesus all over again. They are also subjecting him to public disgrace.

I can understand the latter point. If someone falls away from their faith, they are making a statement, even if not a verbal statement. To walk away from what Jesus has done for us does create a focus for mockery in the minds of those who have never believed. Still, how do we make sense of crucifying Jesus all over again?

It is not hard to view this "crucify again" statement as figurative. We use figurative terms all the time in our standard every day parlance. It would even make sense to refer to the public disgrace, and not even make a comment of crucifying Jesus again. Still, the statement is there. Regardless of what I think, they are, or were, nearly 2000 years ago, crucifying Jesus again, even if only figuratively.

To understand this, do we need to revisit what the death of Jesus represented for mankind?

It basically paid the price for all the sins of mankind, past, present, and future. The death of Jesus made the way for mankind to be restored to his maker. Would this restoration be necessary again, for those who gave up on their Christian walk before the destruction of Jerusalem?

If God really is keen for all to be saved, including "all Israel" as mentioned earlier, it does make sense a future restoration back to their faith in Jesus would be necessary for those who are saved in this lifetime, yet turn from their faith before they die.

I seriously doubt Jesus would have to die again. What I don't doubt is the price Jesus paid would have to be applied one more time for their ultimate redemption. This is what it means figuratively to my mind. Having to reapply the death of Jesus to cover again the sins of one who once fell away from their faith is figuratively like Jesus dying again.

What I find so interesting is the mention of Jesus being crucified again affirms my view of how there is a future hope of redemption for these individuals who could not stomach the persecution.

Yes, it does say "to their loss", which might seem like a direct contradiction of what I have just said. I don't think it is a contradiction. The "loss" is how they miss out on the first resurrection at the return of Jesus. They only get to be a part of the Great White Throne resurrection spoken of in Revelation 20. The "loss" is also how they receive no protection from the destruction of Jerusalem.

Both of these losses for falling away from the faith are serious enough. There was good reason why the writer to the Hebrews gave this warning.

To summarise, the statement of crucifying Jesus again is not saying giving up on the faith has no allowance for a revisit of redemption. It is really saying it will force such an allowance. It gives room to consider the normal salvation process which takes place in this present life, before the first death, is repeatable, but it will involve loss.

Crucifying Jesus again does not mean salvation is impossible through the later process taking place in the context of the White Throne Judgment and following lake of fire. It really means this is the opportunity waiting for those who could not stomach the pressure of persecution against Christians.

Once again, does this sound like good news?

Was That It Then?

So many have always viewed these verses in Hebrews chapters 6 and 10 as proof for a belief in unpardonable sin. If we change who we think those verses are referring to from only Christians, to also include Jews who rejected Jesus and persecuted the Church, do we still think there is no possible redemption in this context?

With the suffering experienced in the destruction of Jerusalem, would these same people who rejected Jesus have no future hope of salvation?

Before I leap to the worst of possible conclusions, perhaps I should ask further questions?

Further questions would seem to be a good place to begin, lest I start constructing thoughts presenting major contradictions with the rest of scripture, the nature of God, and how he has already revealed himself to me.

Here's a good question - what is this point of no return in Hebrews 6:4-6?

> *It is impossible for those who have once been enlightened, who have tasted the heavenly gift, who have shared in the Holy Spirit, who have tasted the goodness of the word of God and the powers of the coming age and who have fallen away, to be brought back to repentance. To their loss they are crucifying the Son of God all over again and subjecting him to public disgrace.* **Hebrews 6:4-6** (NIV).

If there really is a point at which there is no turning back (to repentance), how do we know what it looks like? Just how bad must we be to disqualify?

I did refer earlier tongue-in-cheek to people who have left and then come back to their faith in Jesus. I questioned whether they only thought they were saved, but really were no longer saved, and never could be simply because they had earlier abandoned their faith, and then returned.

I really don't think these people I know ever did cross a line from which they could never return. The fruit in their lives is testimony to this. I also can't imagine the God I know so well as being so callous towards human failing.

I have to wonder if the impossibility of repentance mentioned in Hebrews 6 was only impossible in the context of the time in history surrounding the fall of Jerusalem.

I understand it is the kindness of God which leads people to repentance:

> *"Or do you show contempt for the riches of his kindness, forbearance and patience, not realizing that God's kindness is intended to lead you to repentance?"*
> **Romans 2:4** (NIV)

Perhaps the point of no return looks like the city of Jerusalem finally surrounded by the Roman army under General Titus? By this time the Christians in the city have fled to the mountains as per Jesus' instructions in Matthew 24. By then it would be impossible to experience a repentance which would allow escape.

In this historical context, with the fate of the city sealed by the besieging Roman army, God was no longer going to show any kindness to those still in the city. With no apparent kindness, how can there be repentance?

Will such people meet his kindness in the future resurrection of the dead?

This current life and its salvation context do not have the refining power of a lake of fire. Neither does it have the advantage of a face-to-face with God, like the one which the White Throne Judgment represents.

Just maybe there is ultimate redemption for these individuals. It may come through the future lake of fire. Or were the fires of Jerusalem sufficient to render the future lake of fire in Revelation 19 needless for many of these Jews? If not, perhaps a simple meeting with God at the White Throne Judgment will suffice? Would they then have experienced all the fire they needed?

I cannot say this would not be the case. The language employed in Hebrews 6 would allow for this. I say this in particular with the reference in verse 8. The mention of land being burned is particularly interesting:

> But land that produces thorns and thistles is worthless and is in danger of being cursed. In the end it will be burned. **Hebrews 6:8** (NIV).

The end result of a land subject to burning is the land remains, but the weeds and "defilement" are removed. Is the warning here more about avoiding the temporary fires God has in mind for those remaining in Jerusalem in AD70?

I do have to wonder. They may not be fires with an eternal consequence, but they would be a horrific experience worth avoiding.

We should also remember Paul stated clearly in Romans 11 all Israel would be saved. He didn't say when they would be saved. It was clear in Romans 11 he had a time in the future in mind.

If we believe some sins really can't be forgiven, do we end up with another "infinite exception" which speaks of a sin which was somehow bigger than the death of Jesus? Not even Jesus' death could atone for this sin? Is this what we have?

We have a choice. Do we decide there is sin bigger in magnitude than the atoning power of the death of Jesus, or do we decide Jesus' death is more powerful?

I personally lean towards the power of God. I also lean towards the love of God. What does the parable of the prodigal son (see Luke 15) tell us of God's love towards a departed son? He didn't only love the son when he came back. He loved the wayward son without ceasing till he returned.

Concluding this section on the Epistle to the Hebrews, and unpardonable sin, I didn't start reading Hebrews with the primary context of Jerusalem's destruction in mind. After I began to see it, the Jerusalem context did sit well with me. It provided a logical and sound way of understanding sin seemingly unpardonable, yet actually quite pardonable at the White Throne Judgment in the future. It is clear to me, and anyone reading this can make up their own mind.

We will never have 100% certainty. High probability conjecture is the best we can do. I'm fine with that.

It Takes Ages.

I think I've covered the verses in Hebrews enough. I'm now going to examine the references Jesus made to unpardonable sins. To be safe and conservative, let's continue to assume these words on unpardonable sins are directed at Christians who might fall away.

At this point I will refer back to the statement of Jesus in Matthew 12 and Luke 12 on this subject. If we return back to the Matthew 12 statement, we see in verse 32 Jesus gives a specific timing to the idea of the sin against the Holy Spirit not receiving forgiveness:

> *And so I tell you, every kind of sin and slander can be forgiven, but blasphemy against the Spirit will not be forgiven. Anyone who speaks a word against the Son of Man will be forgiven, but anyone who speaks against the Holy Spirit will not be forgiven, either in this age or in the age to come.* **Matthew 12:31-32** (NIV)

Jesus said this particular sin would not be forgiven "in this age, or in the age to come". One could speculate on what age was what. When did "this age" end? When would "the age to come" end?

We could ignore such questions and say they are irrelevant. To do so may be an error of judgement. I cannot say for sure. All I know is when I ask questions, I do find some interesting answers.

One argument maintains "this age" is the age in which Jesus and his disciples lived. It was the Old Covenant age. That age ended by some reckoning at the death of Jesus around 31 AD.

Some would say Jesus died in 33 AD. I don't care at this point to debate the matter as it is not relevant to the current discussion.

Another argument holds "this age" ended at the destruction of Jerusalem in 70 AD.

I really don't know what year and specific event Jesus was referring to as the end for "this age". I'm happy for 31 AD, 33 AD, or 70 AD. I'm prepared to say it had to be around this timing as the Old Covenant needed to end, and it historically did.

This leaves us with "the age to come". We are possibly in this age now. If so, it means those who sinned against the Holy Spirit only have to wait till after this current age we live in for those sins to be forgiven.

Could this event tie in with the White Throne Judgment?

It does make sense this event is in an entirely new age from the one we are in now. I don't have to be dogmatic. I only know it could be so. It does make sense, and it is logical.

Salvation in this present age has a great deal to do with a reward system where a position of authority in God's Kingdom is the prize. This likely does not exist for salvation during a later age. Matthew chapter 25 gives some insight on this subject.

This might explain why God seems to call so few in this current age. He does not want too many chiefs in the age to come.

Old Testament Encounters.

So far we have only considered New Testament references to unpardonable sins. Is there any mention of this in the Old Testament?

In 2 Kings chapter 24, it would seem there is:

Surely these things happened to Judah according to the Lord's command, in order to remove them from his presence because of the sins of Manasseh and all he had done, including the shedding of innocent blood. For he had filled Jerusalem with innocent blood, and the Lord was not willing to forgive. **2 Kings 24:3-4** (NIV)

It is clear here Manasseh the king of Judah did all manner of evil to the point God would no longer tolerate it. Things were so bad; God was finally at a point where he was not willing to forgive these sins. That's heavy!

Manasseh did turn from his evil ways well before he died, as shown in 2 Chronicles chapter 33. However, his repentance was not enough to bring God to forgive those sins, and how they impacted on Judah as a people.

It is important to note here God's forgiveness in the Old Testament was demonstrated by how he displayed his favour and disfavour towards his people. It was not necessarily given in the context of salvation Jesus was to reveal later.

Would these sins of Manasseh never be forgiven? Does the language used allow for the possibility of the sins to eventually be forgiven, but not at that specific time?

If the impact of Jesus' eventual death on the cross is anything to go by, then the answer has got to be "yes" to this question.

One could even argue the sins of Manasseh were forgiven well before the death of Jesus. We see above Judah suffered for the sins of Manasseh. Judah was going into captivity. They came back from captivity too, which fits with how God demonstrated forgiveness in the Old Testament. The forgiveness of God was demonstrated by his allowing Judah to return from the Babylonian captivity.

Judah did return from captivity. This return does imply the sins of Manasseh were finally forgiven by the time Judah returned from captivity. It was an example of forgiveness in the context of the Old Covenant, for the nation of Israel.

Manasseh himself would probably have to wait for the White Throne Judgment before his sins personally would be absolved. It depends on the depth of his repentance before he died. This too would depend on whether God moved and made it possible for him to repent sufficient for him to be resurrected before the White Throne Judgment.

Once again, time will tell.

If we really want to insist so-called unpardonable sins will never be pardoned, how could Paul refer to the eventual salvation of all Israel?

This was referred to in the previous chapter, and is drawn from Romans 11:25-27:

> *I do not want you to be ignorant of this mystery, brothers and sisters, so that you may not be conceited: Israel has experienced a hardening in part until the full number of the Gentiles has come in, and in this way all Israel will be saved. As it is written:*
> *"The deliverer will come from Zion;he will turn godlessness away from Jacob.And this is my covenant with themwhen I take away their sins."* **Romans 11:25-27** (NIV)

Do we have a contradiction in scripture here?

Is Paul saying all Israel will be saved, when the author of the Epistle to the Hebrews is saying some will never ever be forgiven?

I don't think so and understand this with a sound examination of context. There is no need to consider any part of scripture contradicts. There is scope to consider a number of different interpretations. How we do will be determined by our view of God himself.

By now it should be evident in some cases, if not all; an unpardonable sin may only be unpardonable for a specific duration of time.

Is there room for this forgiveness in a good news context?

Discipline.

There was another point to arise in my big-picture reading of Hebrews. Just as there were two groups of people referred to (the Old and New Covenant people of God), there were two ways of God dealing with his peoples when they went astray.

One way of God dealing with his people was hard judgement. This is already referred to in Hebrews chapters 6 and 10. This is the judgment which can be thought of as reserved for those who have no personal relationship with God.

The second way of God dealing with his people was discipline as a father disciplines a child. It was clear to me this discipline was reserved for those in the church, and not the unbelieving Hebrews still living with the church in Judea.

Discipline is for those who have a personal relationship with God. Obviously it is only reserved for those moments of serious wayward need. Discipline is not the signature of our relationship with God. Rather, love is the signature, and discipline can at times be expressed out of such love.

We should ask if Jesus' statements about the unpardonable sins in Matthew 12 and Luke 22 were the same issue spoken of in Hebrews. I think this is a fair question.

I like questions. They help a great deal in making sense of scripture. I don't like it when questions are left unanswered. I do apologise if someone has more once I'm done here. I hope we can engage with those later, perhaps via my website.

Continuing, I cannot be 100% certain Jesus' references to unpardonable sin in Matthew 12 and Luke 12 are the same type of sin as those spoken of in Hebrews chapters 6 and 10. We do see in Hebrews 6:4 and in Hebrews 10:29 references to the Holy Spirit, making a link, perhaps, to Jesus' statements.

I see reason to think the sin type is the same. If it isn't, then the message to the Hebrews still may be a specific warning to the Church about how God would deal with the problem of falling away from the faith in the region of Judea, given the pending doom of Jerusalem.

If it is the same type of sin, then the original recipients of the Epistle to the Hebrews knew the references to severe judgment in Hebrews chapters 6 and 10 applied to the Hebrews who were not Christians.

In a way, it was similar to saying though the Hebrew Christians may have suffered under the hands of unbelieving Hebrews who rejected the Gospel, there would be a reckoning. God would eventually deal with those who abused his people. He certainly did come AD70 with the destruction of Jerusalem.

Falling away from the faith would not have been a sound decision given how Jerusalem was going to be destroyed and the country surrounding ravaged by war.

History tells us the Christians were saved from that awful fate. The warning they received to leave would not have been heard by those fallen away and cynical of Christianity. Neither would it be heard by those who were not yet called by God to follow Jesus. Many of these were those who participated in the death of Jesus, and persecution of the church, which followed.

Now the destruction of Jerusalem is well and truly behind us, does my perspective of unpardonable sin mean falling away from the faith has no consequence now?

What does the writer to the Hebrews say about this?

> And have you completely forgotten this word of encouragement that addresses you as a father addresses his son? It says,
> "My son, do not make light of the Lord's discipline, and do not lose heart when he rebukes you, because the Lord disciplines the one he loves, and he chastens everyone he accepts as his son."
> Endure hardship as discipline; God is treating you as his children. For what children are not disciplined by their father? If you are not disciplined--and everyone undergoes discipline--then you are not legitimate, not true sons and

daughters at all. Moreover, we have all had human fathers who disciplined us and we respected them for it. How much more should we submit to the Father of spirits and live! They disciplined us for a little while as they thought best; but God disciplines us for our good, in order that we may share in his holiness. No discipline seems pleasant at the time, but painful. Later on, however, it produces a harvest of righteousness and peace for those who have been trained by it. **Hebrews 12:5-11** (NIV)

How effective is God with the discipline of his children?

Does God know exactly what we need in discipline to produce the outcome of holiness referred to above in verse 10?

I personally would not be surprised if God is effective with discipline, and knows how to tailor it for each of his children. Let's say that's just my hunch.

Still, I can't deny there does appear in scripture sufficient reference to fire as God's final necessary measure for some people, for their redemption. Nevertheless, it may be such fire is only reserved for the Old Covenant people of God – the Hebrews still in Judea at the time of Jerusalem's destruction, who were not in the church.

Some view the entire book of Revelation was fulfilled with the fall of Jerusalem. This perspective is called "Preterism".

I can see how much in the book of Revelation was fulfilled in this event surrounding the AD70 destruction of Jerusalem, but not the whole book of Revelation. So much of Revelation 20 and after still seems to be ahead of us. Once again, time will tell.

I will answer my most recent question now. It is possible to be weak or messed up enough to fall away from our faith in Jesus, or buckle under the pressure of persecution. If so, I've no doubt my God who so loves us as a father will simply discipline us in the manner he knows is necessary. By this means we can all eventually share in his holiness.

Is it too much to think God knows exactly how to discipline his children who are born again, so they don't require the type of fire reserved for Jerusalem so long ago?

I don't think it is, but don't discount God could have also used this specific event for his disciplinary purposes with certain wayward children.

It could well be those who needed such discipline also missed out on the rewards which would come with the first resurrection referred to by Paul in 1 Corinthians 15, and John in Revelation 20:4-6. The writer of Hebrews refers to this resurrection as a "better" resurrection:

> *Women received back their dead, raised to life again. There were others who were tortured, refusing to be released so that they might gain an even better resurrection.* **Hebrews 11:35** (NIV)

The rewards of the first resurrection were described by Jesus in certain parables, if my understanding is correct. The parable of the talents in Matthew 25 does seem to indicate Jesus had in mind positions of authority as a reward for service for those in the church in this current age.

It would make sense the same degree of reward was not available for those who would receive salvation at the later time of the Great White Throne Judgement. Hence we have a reference to a "better" resurrection above.

If there is a better resurrection still available for those who respond to the Gospel message today, I can't help but think of this as good news.

The Nature Of Fire

At this point, it is worth giving some thought to the nature of "fire".

There is no immediate reference to fire in Jesus' statements about so-called unpardonable sin in chapter 12 of both Matthew and Luke. The references in Hebrews 6 and 10 do refer to fire in the context of perceived unpardonable sin. Certain questions come to mind about fire:

- Does it have to be real literal fire?
- Could it be figurative fire?
- Could it be both literal and figurative fire?

I suspect there is a case for the references to fire to be both literal and figurative in nature.

Consider the references of Jesus to Gehenna hell fire. They found fulfilment in the destruction of Jerusalem. Many died by fire in punishment on the city. Others died by other means.

Some did not die in the destruction of Jerusalem. They were taken into Roman slavery to experience a form of living hell. Both literal and figurative forms of "fire" as punishment would serve the same purpose.

Remember the references made earlier to refining silver in a furnace. They related directly to God's dealing with Israel in the Old Testament. Once again, the use of fire to achieve God's purposes with Israel was both literal and figurative.

Many cities of Judah and Israel were destroyed by fire in the Old Testament. Similar to Jerusalem in AD 70, many of the people died in those destructions, and a remnant, the survivors, went into slavery to experience a living hell over perhaps a much longer span of time.

I then have to wonder about the nature of the lake of fire mentioned at the end of the Book of Revelation:

- Is it literal?
- Is it figurative?
- Could it be both?

My personal perspective on such a question is simple. The wisest answer to such a question is simply "I don't know".

I could only wish for everyone thinking of such a topic to be able to think and say the same. I really doubt any person knows at this present time. At best we only think we know. God certainly does and I'm happy to speculate as my only option.

Reference is made to Satan being tossed into a fire in which he will be tormented. Can a spirit being feel fire?

I expect not. I could be wrong. If the fire was representative of something else, then I could expect it would torment a spirit being. We will all know one day. I'm looking forward to it. I am curious to know.

It does make sense to me harsh life experience, often leading to death, was the equivalent of a fiery furnace for Israel. A lake of fire just might be a figurative way of describing more harsh life experience as the final necessary redemptive measure after the White Throne Judgment.

I really don't know. All I do know is God loves everyone, and he wants to save everyone. If anyone knows how to achieve such an end, he does.

I understand a large number of theologians think he can't achieve such an end. Perhaps they know God better than me? I'm sure many probably do.

Another Word on Judgment.

This only came to me quite recently from a conversation with a friend at my church.

He was saying how we needed to be saying more about judgment in our presentation of the Gospel message.

It didn't sit too well with me but I know the Bible has plenty to say about judgment. I just didn't know how to explain my unease with what he was saying.

People naturally have a sense of justice. Right and wrong is in the thinking of most people. If someone wrongs us, we want justice. We want them punished. They have to pay a price for what they did to wrong us.

I think I'm correct in thinking most people understand everyone has done something wrong in life. The religions of the world are structured around this understanding. We offend our deity and have to do something to fix it, or right the wrong.

The 10 Commandments do this well for us. They show us we have done wrong at some point in life. They show us we have sinned or missed the mark or standard we would want from our behaviour. If we are really honest we realise we are probably pretty good at missing the mark. Sin is a natural part of life without God.

This realisation is really where the Gospel begins. We realise things are not perfect with our lives. We are under judgment. The Gospel sets us free from being under judgment.

I guess if we say more about judgment so it is clear we have a need for a Gospel message, then I guess judgment does have a place in the Gospel message. It serves as a good place to begin. It certainly isn't the end of the message.

My unease with the concept of judgment came from thinking we need more messages on judgment and justice without knowing their proper place in the Gospel. My friend has always had a great deal to say about judgment. I'd never been too sure if he had any understanding of how much good news there really was.

When things are not right between us and God, we do need to know. If a solution or "good news" is never given, how complete is that message?

The subject of unpardonable sin has centred on the judgment which came on Jerusalem in AD 70. For many Christians, the view is those who died there are eternally lost. For me, to understand redemption is still possible for so many considered eternally lost, is good news indeed.

The Back of the Book

I do find something to be really strange. It is strange after all this consideration of whether God will destroy the wicked or redeem them. We have this picture right at the very end of the story, as described in Revelation 22:

> *Look, I am coming soon! My reward is with me, and I will give to each person according to what they have done. I am the Alpha and the Omega, the First and the Last, the Beginning and the End.*
>
> *Blessed are those who wash their robes, that they may have the right to the tree of life and may go through the gates into the city. Outside are the dogs, those who practice magic arts, the sexually immoral, the murderers, the idolaters and everyone who loves and practices falsehood.* **Revelation 22:12-15** (NIV)

The setting here, as best as I can understand it, is we finally have a new Heaven and new Earth, with a heavenly city now established on Earth. God is finally living with man.

Still, after all this has happened, and perhaps even after the so-called "second death" as a direct function of the lake of burning sulphur (see Revelation 21:6), we still have those who continue to live in sin.

They live in sin outside the city.

Perhaps this life of sin "outside" is a figurative lake of fire?

Perhaps it is achieving some final sorting of messed up thinking?

What does the future really look like?

We understand there will be a new Heaven, and new Earth, with God finally living with man in a new Jerusalem on Earth. Is there still room and time for redemptive work on those outside this heavenly city?

My best speculation has the answers to all these questions must somehow look like good news.

I see room for all manner of conclusions on this subject in scripture. Whichever conclusion we lean to, it will all depend on how we read and understand the Bible and the dogmas we have received over the span of our lives.

How then we read and understand our dogmas will by necessity depend on how we know God as our personal father. That to me is the final word.

The news Jesus brought has got to be good. "How good?" is up to how we are able to receive it.

I hope by presenting a number of different perspectives I've at least broadened the horizons of our thinking to consider ideas we may have held for many years just may be best left behind for perhaps a clearer more positive perspective on the subject.

19: Putting It All Together.

For some, my view of the good news in the Gospel would be quite radical. A radical perspective can then conjure up all manner of questions:

- Did I somehow force scripture to come up with this view?
- Am I just trying to find a way to escape the plain teaching of scripture in the Bible?

These are fair and just questions. I'm really glad someone asked. I knew someone would eventually, if I didn't ask first.

Obviously, my answer in the face of such questions is "no". The village idiot could have told anyone this. But let's examine what is really going on here.

Fooling With Scripture

Over 40 odd years of Christian journey, I've been witness to all manner of doctrines. I've also been witness to the fruit of such doctrines.

Jesus was not necessarily thinking of me specifically when he said we would be able to identify truth from error by the resulting fruit. Still, I've certainly had a lot to think about over 40 plus years.

No good tree bears bad fruit, nor does a bad tree bear good fruit. **Luke 6:43** (NIV)

"Watch out for false prophets. They come to you in sheep's clothing, but inwardly they are ferocious wolves. By their fruit you will recognize them. Do people pick grapes from thornbushes, or figs from thistles? Likewise, every good tree bears good fruit, but a bad tree bears bad fruit. A good tree cannot bear bad fruit, and a bad tree cannot bear good fruit. **Matthew 7:15-18** (NIV)

Some doctrines I won't name specifically have had people I know terrified when they were children for extended periods in their youth. I'd never lived under such a doctrine myself. I can see all their pain was needless if only they'd had clearer teaching.

I have friends who were witness to husbands beating their wives as a form of discipline. Their warped personal perspectives on scripture seemed to justify such violence in their marriages.

Good fruit?

I even have some friends who grew up in a particular Australian cult not widely heard of. They were witness to some members being physically beaten with iron fire pokers ("rod of God's wrath?") for apparent misdemeanours.

I've no doubt the persons performing such violence would claim a divine right for such actions.

They would even probably claim they did it all in love too, no doubt.

Really good fruit?

When I think of the unpardonable sin teaching I have been under for many years myself, I'm always reminded of a former close friend who studied with me during my formal Theology studies.

Somehow he got focused on unpardonable sin. He then decided it referred to him. He had in no way fallen away from the faith when he drew this conclusion. His faith was something he took very seriously.

He became a recluse, holding to a faith holding no hope for him, in his own twisted, tragic thinking. He then died a tragic premature death, and I can only wonder what forms of torment he held in his mind before he finally woke up to discover the real good news.

I cannot say his behaviour was the defining statement on any doctrine concerning unpardonable sin. I will say he does illustrate at least some of the confusion surrounding the subject, given how subjective it really is. I will also say his example gives reason to consider the question of fruit once more.

All the questions I have asked surrounding this subject and the related scriptures are sound within the bounds of possible contexts. They are not put forward to create confusion for anyone reading this.

If confusion is an outcome, such confusion is founded on a foundation which has nothing to do with what I'm saying here. Whatever foundations one has when they read this book; they were already in place before one ever read this.

My filter of choice for understanding this topic is God desires to save everyone, and this desire is driven by a big love for everyone - not just some.

It does not take any leap of imagination to recognise the filters I depend on are positive and constructive in my understanding of God. Obviously I understand this too will be disputed by some.

I suspect there are only two verses in the whole Bible specifically saying God wants to save everyone (1 Timothy 2:4, and 2 Peter 3:8-9). Nevertheless, I see the bulk of scripture is saying the same when I step back and look at it in its entirety. This is my big-picture view of scripture.

Call it my gut feeling if you like, with two core specific scriptures to support it, and the rest of the Bible with the bigger picture it presents. More subjectively, add to this all which comes to me from walking with God, getting to know him, for over 40 years now.

Another filter of choice states God is more than capable of knowing how to achieve what he wants. We can believe in a lesser God if we really want to. Many do. I don't. What more can I say?

I'm well aware some will propose some kind of great nobility on the part of God for loving us so much he gives us "free choice" to resist his will and refuse salvation.

It takes a great deal of philosophical thought to come up with this process, and then explain it with all the questions it raises.

I will also propose it demands all manner of ideas unable to withstand serious scrutiny and questioning.

Few in church will ever ask such questions. We can tend to be too trusting in church with the messages we receive from the pulpit. I've noticed this over many years.

I've briefly touched on these issues in this book and understand a book dedicated to unpacking the problems of this thinking and the inevitable bad fruit following is needed. I'll do my best to respond to this need in a later book, all things being equal.

If I accept once again the simple view of unpardonable sins, which states some sins will never ever be forgiven, then I'm left with apparent contradictions in my Christian worldview.

When faced with possible contradictions, I'm forced to dig deeper.

I'm forced to ask questions about what assumptions I'm carrying into my understanding of certain scriptures. These assumptions can be effective at hiding the real meaning from me and others.

Knowing or uncovering truth is for me a process with the end in mind of freedom:

Then you will know the truth, and the truth will set you free. **John 8:32** (NIV)

I write with this end in mind.

An Outline Of Salvation

At this stage, I should put together a basic outline of what I think God is doing to see people saved.

In the initial life into which we are all born, very few are offered salvation. Before Jesus came, we can understand salvation was given to people like Abraham, Moses, Samuel, and King David.

I won't list them all. They were in essence saved before their time, as Jesus had not yet died for their sins. Given God lives outside of time, I doubt this was a problem for God. It might be for some of us.

We can only speculate on the state of the dead, once they have departed this current earthly life. I'm sure plenty think they really do know. Personally I only think they do because they do not realise how subjectively the issue is covered in scripture.

Those saved before Jesus came could have gone to Heaven, or they could have been "asleep" in the grave waiting for their resurrection at a future point in time. This is how the return of Jesus is depicted in Paul's first letter to the Corinthians, in chapter 15:

> I declare to you, brothers and sisters, that flesh and blood cannot inherit the kingdom of God, nor does the perishable inherit the imperishable. Listen, I tell you a mystery: We will not all sleep, but we will all be changed— in a flash, in the twinkling of an eye, at the last trumpet. For the trumpet will sound, the dead will be raised imperishable, and we will be changed. **1 Corinthians 15:50-52** (NIV)

Those unsaved, being the vast majority, could also be asleep in their graves, waiting for the White Throne Judgment, but unconscious. Sleep is a picture of unconsciousness after all.

I have never come across the use of the term "sleep" for a state of consciousness outside the Bible. It is only in the Bible where some choose to understand the term in such a way. I'm not sure why, but think it is driven by tradition and dogma more than logic.

It would make sense the dead are unconscious, waiting for this future event called the White Throne Judgment. It would be incredibly boring waiting in a hole in the ground, or in the sea.

The sea gave up the dead that were in it, and death and Hades gave up the dead that were in them, and each person was judged according to what they had done. **Revelation 20:13** (NIV)

Revelation 20 speaks of them coming from their graves (Hades) and the sea. I expect this is where ever their bodies ended up when they died, prior to decomposition and the ultimate disappearance of the mortal frame.

I assume an unconscious wait for resurrection, rather than assuming they were in some place like purgatory or a place like Hades modelled after Greek mythology. I see neither as Biblically sound, but I could be wrong.

I find it interesting so many who have died on an operating table and then come back speak of being totally unconscious during that time. This fits well with the idea one is unconscious while waiting for a resurrection.

It seems only a small number who die in this manner and then return have a conscious experience. Neither type of after-death experience really proves anything, but they are interesting nevertheless.

It doesn't really matter. I doubt God will miss anyone when it comes to bringing them back. They could be waiting on the moon for all I care. I'm sure God won't miss them.

In fairness to those who want to believe in a place where people are consciously waiting for their resurrection, the language of "death and Hades" used above, has sufficient poetic license to allow for all manner of theories on where and how the dead are waiting for their resurrection.

At the same time, it would demand one explain the frequent use of the term "sleep" in the same discussion. The use of such a term presents an apparent contradiction. At least it does to me.

Once Jesus came, died for our sins, and began the Church, salvation began to open up for far more people. Just as Pentecost was a celebration of the first smaller harvest in Judea, we can see the "harvest" of souls now happening with the Church in action is still small in scale.

As I've pointed out earlier, it should be obvious those unsaved far outnumber those who are saved and part of the Church. It makes sense God is well aware of this and knows what he is doing in the face of it.

In this present New Covenant age of the Church, when someone dies, they can go straight to heaven, or as some theorise, they too wait unconscious in the grave, waiting for a future coming of Jesus.

This future return of Jesus is called "Premillennialism". It is one of a number of theories out there on the return of Jesus and what his millennial reign will look like.

I don't really want to get bogged down in prophetic speculations and details here. I'd rather give a more general picture and perhaps follow up with a future book looking at possible details surrounding the various theories out there.

What I will say is I grew up under Premillennial dogma, with no idea there were other valid perspectives. When I learnt more about the broader topic of the theories on the return of Jesus (Eschatology), my eyes were really opened.

For those curious, I found both Amillennial and Preterist views were worthy of some consideration.

After the age of the Church we do have a new age depicted by the White Throne Judgment. I view this as the time when those who never had a chance to respond to the Gospel message of salvation finally have their opportunity.

For those holding to a Premillennial view, we would have a future millennial reign of Jesus as a new age too, before the age of the White Throne Judgment.

After this judgment, we will then see a salvation harvest on a scale never seen before. There will still be a smaller group, who I'd assume to be very few, who won't find it so easy to accept salvation like the majority would. They will still need some sorting of their head space. With this need, there is a figurative or literal refining fire to help them get ready for an eternity with God.

If I'm wrong about this final few, they will probably be snuffed out in that final lake of fire. I'd rather be wrong on the side of considering the scale of God's love, than the other side of considering the scale of God's punishment.

It is all speculation, and we all need to keep this in mind, lest we get too aggressive with the defence of one viewpoint over another.

The end of the story - the good news story, is all or very nearly all are reconciled with their creator God. The life before them will be a good life, stretching before them into eternity. Such is in stark contrast with the life of the majority today. I couldn't think of better good news than this.

This is a Gospel message unable to leave me feeling embarrassed or intellectually challenged by others who will attempt to find flaws in it.

I don't need to make excuses for God, and neither do I shy away from robust intellectual debate. I welcome sound debate with open minded people. It is sometimes the best road to truth.

I don't fear being wrong in a debate as the outcome is truth. How can I lose with an outcome of more truth and understanding?

As far as I understand to date, there is no better message out there from any of the religions of the world I'm aware of. I'm more than happy to be proven wrong.

Death By One, So Life By One.

One could consider ending the story after the outline I've just given. There are still some technical matters I want to address. They lend further support to the perspective I have of a God with a plan to save 99.99%, if not all of humanity.

The first topic I want to unpack is what I refer to as the "ledger" of salvation. Ledger is an accounting term referring to a collection of financial accounts. Accounts are balanced in a ledger format to ensure nothing is missed and to highlight errors if they exist. This is through what is referred to as "double entry".

Sorry if I'm sounding too technical here. It is only an analogy, and no analogy is perfect. I apply it to the following verses:

> Therefore, just as sin entered the world through one man, and death through sin, and in this way death came to all people, because all sinned. To be sure, sin was in the world before the law was given, but sin is not charged against anyone's account where there is no law. Nevertheless, death reigned from the time of Adam to the time of Moses, even over those who did not sin by breaking a command, as did Adam, who is a pattern of the one to come.
>
> But the gift is not like the trespass. For if the many died by the trespass of the one man, how much more did God's grace and the gift that came by the grace of the one man, Jesus Christ, overflow to the many! Nor can the gift of God be compared with the result of one man's sin. The judgment followed one sin and brought condemnation, but the gift followed many trespasses and brought justification. For if, by the trespass of the one man, death reigned through that one man, how much more will those who

receive God's abundant provision of grace and of the gift of righteousness reign in life through the one man, Jesus Christ!

Consequently, just as one trespass resulted in condemnation for all people, so also one righteous act resulted in justification and life for all people. For just as through the disobedience of the one man the many were made sinners, so also through the obedience of the one man the many will be made righteous. **Romans 5:12-19** (NIV)

In its simplest terms, the above verses from Paul's Epistle to the Romans are saying through the action of one man, Adam, death came on all humanity.

Conversely, through the action of one man, Jesus, everyone is saved.

This is where I see the ledger analogy. On the debit side of the ledger we have death. On the credit side of the ledger we have life.

Do the books balance?

Are there any obvious errors highlighted in the double entry format?

This depends on your salvation theology.

By my understanding of Calvinistic and Arminian salvation theology, very few are saved. Both salvation theories understand by Adam death came on all people, with no exception except Jesus who was not a normal human given his father was God.

The debit side is 100% death. It doesn't look too good. The credit side also doesn't look too good. Not many are saved. I'd be surprised if the credit side had even 10% saved.

The books don't balance.

The obvious point to be made by those with a Calvinist or Arminian leaning is my accounting analogy fails. It doesn't suit an application involving salvation. I understand this argument.

Look at it this way. On one side we have the work of Adam. It brings death on everyone born of a man and woman, whether they like it or not. No one disputes this.

On the other side we have the work of Jesus - what he accomplished on the cross. His work achieves the salvation of way less than those on the debit side of the ledger.

We can argue it achieves the salvation for everyone if they just choose to receive it. This argument in itself does not balance the ledger.

On Adams side we have no choice in the matter; on Jesus' side we have choice. It still doesn't balance.

The death side of Adam is way larger than the life side of Jesus. I know this is hypothetical, but serious questions are raised here.

If the accounts don't balance on the credit and debit sides, are we not saying the work of Adam is greater than the work of Jesus?

Adam achieved 100% death results. Jesus gets far less. Who was greater in terms of impact on humanity?

Surely Jesus should at least get a result somewhat akin to a near perfect score. If some have to find their end in a lake of fire, their number can at least be statistically insignificant. Can't it?

Verse 15 above says the gift from Jesus' death is not like the original trespass of Adam. The term is used: "how much more". This indicates there really is no room to view the impact of Jesus work on the cross as being somehow less in impact compared to Adam's impact.

Surely the impact of Jesus – God himself(!) has to be greater than the first man Adam. Surely!

It just doesn't make sense to me Adam's impact on mankind can be so much bigger than Jesus' impact on mankind.

Yes, if anything, the books should be out of balance on the credit side. But we can't have more saved than those already condemned to die, so they at least have to balance out and be equal.

If the work of Jesus is really so much more superior to that of Adam, and I really do think it is, then all will be saved. This makes sense to me.

I may be wrong. There is always more to learn – something I've missed. If so, then fair enough if not all are saved.

Maybe God is happy if a tiny minority end up unsaved. He may not be a perfectionist, even if I currently think he is.

This lesser outcome still makes far more sense than the absurd theologies impacting on my youth and so many of my friends to this day.

Sorry to be so heavy in my use of terms like "absurd" to describe those theologies. I know many who have a great deal invested in such theologies. It can be offensive to tell someone their money is in a dodgy bank.

Still, given the weight of logical evidence and obvious contradictions, can we not at least consider there might be a more secure bank someplace else?

Is it not worth giving some serious thought to what I'm saying?

If Jesus really has achieved justification and life for all people, as it says in verse 18 above, does it not make sense all will be saved?

Yes, we can argue Jesus gives life to everyone, but we can still throw it away. A man convinced against his will is indeed of the same opinion still. Paul confronted this in Romans chapter 8.

Nothing Can Separate

Nothing can separate us from the love of God. This is my view anyway. I'm happy to take ownership of such a perspective. Many probably agree. One would think this message is quite clear in the Bible. Take a look at what the Apostle Paul had to say on the subject:

> *For I am convinced that neither death nor life, neither angels nor demons, neither the present nor the future, nor any powers, neither height nor depth, nor anything else in all creation, will be able to separate us from the love of God that is in Christ Jesus our Lord.*
> **Romans 8:38-39** (NIV)

I might be misunderstanding things here, but it really does look like Paul is saying the same - nothing really can separate us from the love of God! Surely this is clear?

Sorry, it ain't!

I'll never forget some years ago leading communion in my church. I'd heard enough communion messages where the speaker gets everyone to contemplate their navels, and how evil they are.

It would almost have been fitting to expect blades to be handed out for a mandatory slashing of wrists. The call was always to not dare take communion without first making sure everything was right between us and God.

I wanted a break from self-flagellation. Just maybe communion could be positive for once?

I do understand why so many get negative with communion. Paul's words to examine ourselves were given in a context of drunkenness and gluttony. We can read about this context in 1 Corinthians 11:17-34.

There was never any reason to think such a context existed in my particular congregation. To be perfectly honest, I've never come across any congregation where drunkenness and gluttony was on display. It may be possible, but it is indeed rare.

So back to my Communion message – it was time for something positive. This is what I thought anyway.

With this in mind I figured the best place to start was from the same chapter of Romans, but at the beginning:

Therefore, there is now no condemnation for those who are in Christ Jesus, because through Christ Jesus the law of the Spirit who gives life has set you free from the law of sin and death. **Romans 8:1-2** (NIV)

I love those verses. As imperfect as we may be, we are not under condemnation. It almost sounds like good news. One would think so anyway....

If it was good news I was preaching, it was not going to be received as such.

I like to be fairly interactive when I speak in church. Getting the listeners involved is far more effective a method of teaching.

They certainly interacted with me then!

It was not everyone, fortunately, but a significant number did not agree there really was no more condemnation on us.

They weren't harbouring dark secrets, as best as I can know. They were sincere dedicated followers of Jesus.

Still, they seriously believed there was condemnation on them for a fair chunk of their Christ-centred lives. This was no doubt because they knew they were not yet perfect.

I'm no perfect father. My wife Jane knows this, and so do my kids. Nevertheless, no matter how badly my kids might step out of line, I've never disowned them, and never intend to, no matter what they do.

The God who I believe in and worship is much the same - only a much better parent than me.

Some of my friends in the congregation didn't know this! They lived their lives thinking they were falling in and out of favour with God.

Talk about religion. Yuk!

What is the end of such thinking?

From my understanding, if we follow through such thinking to its logical conclusion, we end up with nothing more than salvation (or favour from God) by works.

If we really choose to think this way, the end of such thinking is deciding we have to work it out and make things right with God.

How exhausting could this be?

We can put all Jesus accomplished to one side, and work it all out ourselves!

These friends also had a problem with the end of the story and chapter as well. By their thinking, as much as Paul really tried to labour the point there was nothing conceivable that really could separate us from God's love; they knew clearly Paul was wrong.

Paul's perspective is as follows:

> *For I am convinced that neither death nor life, neither angels nor demons, neither the present nor the future, nor any powers, neither height nor depth, nor anything else in all creation, will be able to separate us from the love of God that is in Christ Jesus our Lord.* **Romans 8:38-39** (NIV)

Some may think Paul covered all bases in making his point above. However, Paul had forgotten something, in the thinking of these particular friends of mine.

What Paul failed to understand was how there really was something able to separate us from the love of God. This is weird I know, but guess what some in my congregation were thinking about?

Themselves!

They'd had many years of peering into the darkest recesses of their navels from exhortations in communion messages. All they could see in the end was human failing, and guess who owned this failing?

Not only were they thinking of themselves, they had a really inflated view of their capabilities.

They were greater than "angels", and greater than "demons". They were even greater than "any powers", and "anything in all creation".

What is even scarier is in all these years of knowing these people, I never had a clue that I was in the presence of so much greatness!

If this isn't religion at its worst, I don't know what is. At the core of it was a dogma I know too well – Arminianism. It taught them they have so much free choice, they can even exhaust God of all his love for them. How clever are we?

With Arminianism, we have to either start re-writing scripture, or come up with more of those annoying "infinite exceptions". Will there ever be an end to this?

I don't think so, if we insist on clutching tightly to identities wrapped up in dogma like Arminianism.

We'll fall flat on our faces 1000 times, but religion will stop us seeing our dogmas give us contradictions which cannot be reconciled. The best thing we can do is throw them out and start again.

Is there a bottom line to all this?

Definitely! Paul is correct in thinking in chapter 8 of the Epistle to the Romans nothing at all can separate us from the love of God. Not even we can! This my current view, for better or for worse.

After all these verses on salvation, I have to wonder if we really should be asking how anyone could not be saved at the end of time, rather than trying so hard to defend dogmas indicating so many will end up unsaved, with no further hope of redemption.

What are we really thinking here?

Is the Christian message good news, or bad news?

Speaking for myself, the evidence is strong enough for me to go out on a limb and put all my money on good news.

20: The Beginning.

God on Paper

If anyone is left reading this who really does believe nothing can separate us from the love of God, I'm elated.

Can we take this perspective now to our understanding of God's plan of salvation, and the depth of its reach?

Can we take this understanding to the core of our belief in the Gospel message, and for whom it is intended?

How good is the good news of a God and his love for us which is way bigger than our dysfunctional thinking and negative conditioning?

I really hope anyone reading this far knows we can't fix ourselves. My friend stuck with his imaginary unpardonable sin knew this too.

Please, if any of us still think we only need to try just a little bit harder to do better at being good enough for God, please try harder! Let's keep trying till it finally dawns on us how we are all unable to fix ourselves.

I've had 40 plus years of trying. Maybe I need just one more year to get there? I hate being dogmatic with theology, but I'm sorely tempted with this topic.

Knowing a God, Jesus, who can fix us, is good news.

Knowing a God who knows how to save the unsaved and seemingly irredeemable is good news.

Knowing a God who is way bigger than our small-minded theologies is great news too.

Please by all means take everything I've said with a grain of salt. I could be totally wrong. I've been wrong before. It won't be the last time. Nevertheless, please do put some solid thinking into the points I've raised.

The following makes sense to me. I've seen it first-hand too often: how dangerous is a teacher who really doesn't grasp how wrong he or she can be? Show me a cult without a leader like this!

We need to ask ourselves who really has formed and shaped our opinions on what God is really trying to achieve here on earth. Is their view positive or negative about God?

Are there nagging questions behind it all, like those I've presented in this book?

As hard as it may be, we need to really try to get a handle on what we think God is really like. I'd even suggest writing it down. Writing can be an excellent way of putting our thoughts in order. Make it bullet points. For some reason they are easier to read.

Our list might look something like this:

"My God...

- Loves me.
- Cares about me.
- Is very personal.
- Has a love that is bigger than I can imagine.
- Thinks I matter to him.
- Thinks others matter to him too.
- Is really smart.
- Has a solution for everyone's problems.
- Is much bigger than any problem of anyone.
- Reveals himself through the pages of the Bible.
- Reveals himself by means other than the Bible too.
- Is very much misunderstood.
- Is a God worth getting to know better."

I didn't want to encourage too much negative thinking with the above list. I could well imagine many with points like:

'My God is really tough on me when I get it wrong'.

Let's be really honest in our list if we think God is harsh like this. We can try to line those thoughts up with the positive scriptures I've referred to in this book. We can also ask him to show us what he is really like. He might surprise us.

We can also try to find Christian friends who we can share our journey with on discovering how loving God really is. Many really do understand how hard it is to fathom the love of God. Many don't too, but please let's not let that discourage us.

The Great Unknown

Wouldn't it be amazing if when we all finally meet God, we find he is far more likeable than we ever thought possible?

The longer I've been getting to know my God, Jesus, particularly over the past 15 years or so, the better I've come to grasp how good the Gospel is. He keeps blowing my mind. The more I've been learning, the more I've been waking up to just how good this Gospel is.

I don't think I've arrived. I know there is still much I probably still misunderstand. My God makes up for my failings. This is a huge burden I don't have to carry.

I may have got my thinking muddled on some of the points I've raised, but not necessarily all of them. There is so much room for uncertainty, and I do hope I've been honest with such as I've tried to look at things with a fresh perspective. Please pardon my enthusiasm when I've been more dogmatic than the available facts warranted.

If most readers are left realising the good news is better than what they thought it was, even if the idea of God saving everyone is at this point beyond reach, then my time has been well spent here.

I can't be 100% certain God will eventually save everyone. It makes sense he can; it makes sense he wants to. It also makes sense he is God, and I'm not. There is so much I just won't grasp until I see him face to face, and even then, probably, the learning won't all come at once.

In so many ways I really feel like I'm starting all over again. I've been stumbling around under the weight of religion for decades, and slowly I'm shaking it off. The more I've learnt, the more I realise there is still yet more to learn.

My wish for you and everyone else who might read this book is to understand the same.

Appendix 1: The Survey Responses

Survey Responses to "What Is The Gospel?"

The gospel is: The truth about Jesus and God's plan of salvation which culminates in the reign of God on earth. **Friend from the USA.**

The gospel is the testimony of Christ. **Friend from Queensland.**

Freedom to choose life. **Friend from NSW.**

The Gospel means good and good is God in HIS purity and Holiness. Christ Jesus is Truth, God is good and Holy in us, so when it says, Go into ALL the world and preach the Gospel it is meant to speak of the Good and Truth of HIS purity and Spirit in us, and flows through us. Jesus spoke of the Kingdom of God, that was near, at hand! At hand (From G1451; to make near, that is, (reflexively) approach: - approach, be at hand, come (draw) near, be (come, draw) nigh.) If we are in the Spirit of God, HE flows through our Spirit of our new creation in HIM...therefore we are speaking good, truth and purity through God in us. This is Spirit led and the Gospel of the Kingdom of God. Mar 1:15 and G2532 saying,G3004 theG3588 time G2540 is fulfilled, G4137 and G2532 the G3588 kingdom G932 of God G2316 is at hand: G1448 **Friend from Queensland**.

My understanding is that it's from the German "Gotspiel", or "God speaks", (i.e., the Word of God). Yes, we also hold that the other books of the Bible were inspired by God, but Jesus was The Word made incarnate, therefore the Gospels have a central place. **Friend from Queensland**.

Without thinking about it too much, threefold reply. 1. Good news about the kingdom of God. To be established first within/among us to eventually be established as the Government model for the planet. 2. Good news of Salvation from sin through Jesus Christ. 3. Good news that we can be like Jesus and receive eternal life. **Friend from NSW.**

The good news of the kingdom of Jesus as Lord, and all that entails. **Friend from Queensland.**

Father God manifested through his son Jesus redemptive power, in love and freedom given from above with strength and power, magnified. **Friend from Queensland.**

The Gospel is the good news of the Kingdom and how God will bring it about through Jesus. **Friend from the USA.**

"Brief as possible: an adumbration." **Friend from Indiana**.

The good news that Jesus came to take away sin and give life, establishing an eternal kingdom of peace and joy. Restoring the communion with God that was lost at the fall. **Friend from Western Australia**.

The gospel is the Good News of God's direct intervention/plan for humanity to reverse all the evil that has ever been done in people's lives, remove God's judgement of death on mankind, give eternal life and establish God's will on earth (as it is in heaven). Through Christ we are no longer enemies of God but under God's grace for an eternal and bright future. **Friend from British Columbia**.

The gospel is the good news that Jesus came, died for us and the HS now lives in us to help us attain the life God has planned for us from the beginning. **Friend from Colorado**.

The gospel for me is the first several books of the New Testament... It is the final truth, the new covenant... The gospel! **Friend from Queensland**.

"Good News" of Jesus! It is the news of the coming of the Kingdom of God (Mark 1:14-15), and of Jesus' death on the cross and resurrection to restore people's relationship with God. It also includes the descent of the Holy Spirit upon believers and the second coming of Jesus. In a nut shell, it relates to the saving acts of God due to the work of Jesus on the cross and Jesus' resurrection from the dead which brings reconciliation ("atonement") between people and God. **Friend from the USA.**

Briefest –hope.

More detail - We are an immortal soul with an earthly body. There is an uber-powerful force that exists outside of time and space that has made cities fall, lightning incinerate, rivers stop, food appear and miracles happen upon request. For over 4000 years, It communed with us and knew us to be disobedient, frustrating and occasionally hopeless. It manifested in human form, experienced our experiences, taught us to love without ceasing, and we killed Him for it. It resurrected Its body to prove power over death, offers a piece of itself to help us to do Its Will, and, when we die, to allow our soul to survive in Its presence. We are not hope-less anymore. **Friend from British Columbia.**

The roots of the word "gospel" are before 950; Middle English go (d) spell, Old English gōdspell (see good, spell2); translation of Greek euangélion good news. So since you are asking Christians, I assume you are asking what is the gospel of Christ? Given this definition I think the gospel of Christ is the good news he brought us and the good spell (or blessings) He cast on us. The primary ones that come to mind are: John 3:16 - He gave his life for ALL of us John 10:10 - He came that we would have life and have it more abundantly Mark 12:30-31 - His commandments are not burdensome - they are that we love God and we love our neighbor and ourselves Personally I think that the example He set of including women, and the sick and the slave and the outcast in His community was also tremendously good news even though perhaps not explicitly stated. I think there are many other elements of the good news that He brought but these are 3 that came to mind immediately. **Friend from Minnesota.**

The gospel, to me obviously, is that God loves us. Jesus came to demonstrate that idea in no uncertain terms. Jesus came to reconcile us to God (himself). This act is accomplished, and there is nothing we can do, or not do, to separate us from God's love. The simplest is the old children's song: Jesus loves me this I know... **Friend from Texas.**

Jesus. **Friend from Queensland.**

It is my belief that the gospel is the good news and hope found in Jesus Christ. His existence and legacy provides comfort, atonement, purpose for this life and promise of life beyond the current.

It's a huge subject, but I've tried to be brief, as you requested. As you know, in WCG it was really simplified to: Gospel = Good News.

I feel now that the Good News part needs a little more fleshing out, but essentially, there is hope for today and hope for a future... that is pretty good news, in my opinion. **Friend from Ontario.**

Ephesians 2:8 For by grace you have been saved through faith. <u>And this is not your own doing</u>; it is the gift of God. **Friend from New Jersey.**

God, the Creator who made us in love, for love, and to love, has literally loved us to death in Jesus Christ and through him invites us and enables us to forsake our past with its mix of good and evil and love Him and each other with the same self-sacrificial love in order to partake of His divine life for an eternity of happiness. The negative implication of the gospel is that those who do not take this offer of love will not partake of His divine life. **Friend from New York.**

God became flesh and dwelt among us. He died, and rose again, saving us from God's wrath and reconciling us with God by his grace, not through our good works, but unto works. **Friend from Queensland**.

I chewed on it for a few days. I don't use "the Gospel" a lot because outside of my church circles, not a lot of people have any idea what it stands for. What is the Gospel? Shortest form: No matter how messed up we think we are, no matter how imperfect we know we are, we are loved by God. Slightly longer, add this bit: It is the wonderful knowledge that we are loved by the God who created us, regardless of every good or bad thing that we have done in our lives, regardless of the imperfections we struggle with. To explain my response, I'd like to make the comment that we live in a world that appears to have no understanding of the concept of "sin". To say that "Christ died for your sins" to most people is to say something that is incomprehensible and meaningless to most. Until you have a divine revelation of your sin, to know that your sin is forgiven has no meaning. When you do have that revelation, it does blow your mind. People understand that they're not perfect, and they know that they've done stuff that's messed up It is the most amazing thing in the world when you know and you understand that you are loved and that nothing in the world can take away that love - you are loved for who you are, and nothing you can do will change that. And in a lonely, messed up world, it's the most incredible thing in the world. It's divine. **Friend from NSW.**

The Gospel is the good news that Christ has given his life to reconcile man to God. **Friend from Western Australia**.

The gospel is the good news that salvation is available as a free gift by believing in Jesus Christ as our Lord and Savior. It is the message of how our sins are redeemed / forgiven by the blood of Jesus Christ shed on the cross. **Friend from Tennessee**.

The Gospel is very simple. It is the good news of a Messiah (Jesus Christ) who gave up his life so that our sins might be forgiven and we might have life with God for all eternity. It is the sweetest thing I know. **Friend from Tennessee.**

The Gospel is Good News to set the captives free through what Jesus did on the cross (he paid a ransom with his life to buy back those in Satans grip) and to help people live this life loved. So we can experience the fullness of God's love which enables one to love themselves and others in ever increasing ways (from glory to glory). Aka we love because he first loved us... and as our love for God grows it liberates us in ever increasing areas in our lives on this earth helping us to be the best version of ourselves.. **Friend from Queensland.**

It is a really hard question to answer for me. First thing coming to my mind when thinking about the Gospel is the 'good news'. I think that's how it's called in English. German: Frohe Botschaft I think the Gospel has the main contents of the Christian religion. Especially about Jesus dying for our sins. This is a really short answer. **Friend from Germany.**

TRUTH **Friend from Queensland**.

The good news is that God has this solution to all of humanity's problems--Jesus Christ is the answer to all the questions! **Friend from Nova Scotia**.

My first response is that the Bible is the gospel since it's God's word, and it's all good news.

My next response would be that it's the gospel Jesus preached in Mark 1:14 -- the gospel of the kingdom of God. But for those of us who grew up hearing that over and over, there is "baggage" in that statement. However, after your question, I can see that as the gospel.

Reading through Paul's writings, it may seem to some that he is preaching a "different gospel," however, to me it seems he may be emphasizing different things about the gospel due to the different backgrounds of the various congregations. For example, emphasizing that the Messiah did come and His crucifixion and resurrection are important (since some, like him, didn't at first believe Jesus' and His disciples' claims about Him). **Friend from South Carolina**.

The gospel for me is "good news" that Jesus Christ died to pay for our sins so that we might become children of God through faith in Christ. **Friend from Victoria**.

The Gospel is the good news of grace that through Christ we can come before God. **Friend from Queensland**.

The Gospel is Christ. **Friend from Uganda**.

Survey Responses to "To whom is the Gospel intended, and what is the end for anyone who rejects it?"

Hi Roger. My take is that the gospel is intended for man (not the Angels). Christ was a kinsman redeemer so only Mankind can benefit from his sacrifice. And the end for those who reject it is eternal separation from god. Hell was created for the Angels who rejected God. I know scripture indicates this is also the end destination for some (definitely the beast and the false prophet). Would prefer to believe in annihilationism over eternal torment. But I just don't know. **Friend from British Columbia.**

Hi Rog. Yep... I think it's for all of mankind. Those who died before Christ died in anticipation of his coming. I am not sure how God determines that all have a chance for salvation for those groups who existed prior to or external to the chosen people of Israel, however I have to trust that somehow they had a chance to hear the gospel. **Friend from Queensland.**

Roger - I left biblical scholarship alone many years ago mate, not sure my opinion will be the most useful.

I believe the gospel was for all mankind, when and if it crosses their path.

I have no idea if the theories of a 2nd and 3rd resurrection are valid (including the way mankind is managed, herded, evaluated and finally promoted or dispatched).

I believe God is more secure in the face of billions of "unconverted" than most Christians think. I also believe he is more love than the lake of fire theory implies.

Good luck in your quest my friend. Looking forward to what you come up with. **Friend from Western Australia.**

I'll answer from the gut on this, and see how I go. The Gospel is for everyone. "Jerusalem, Judea and to the ends of the earth" seems fairly open-ended. Jesus' willingness to talk to the Samaritans - and examples of almost every other kind of outcast, social, religious, political or otherwise (examples as needed) - and to tell them the Gospel sets up a strong example of inclusion.

Anyone that rejects it... it's a hard one, because I'm not God. I have to base it on my understanding of God's character, which continues to evolve as I experience life. (I don't know that I would have given the same answer 10 years ago, for example).

I think that rejection of the Gospel is only final at the point of death. Until that point, there is always a chance to accept it.

So I would say that the end (after death) of anyone who rejects the Gospel is that God will honour their choice, and that they will spend eternity without God and his goodness. Rejection is not final until death, but a life without a living, vibrant relationship with God is always going to be missing something. **Friend from NSW.**

First to the Jews, then the Gentiles. A source I unfortunately cannot determine.

If you don't accept the party invitation, there will be no hors d'ouvres when you arrive. **Friend from British Columbia.**

The Gospel is for EVERYONE. I'm certain it was God's plan for ALL to hear the Gospel (that's part of our responsibilities as Christians to spread and walk in the gospel) and I am certain He hopes all who receive it follow it! However those that don't hmmmmm well I guess they won't have eternal life with Him. John 3:16. **Friend from Queensland.**

The Gospel is for the entire world. I feel that those who hear about Jesus and reject him in this life will have another chance prior to an eternal death. I don't believe in a suffering hell. After the angels rebelled, I don't think that God would create man in a state of eternal suffering like the demons experience. **Friend from Colorado.**

The point of the Gospel is to reap the harvest--to "go into all the world" and preach the good news unto everyone. So it is really meant for everyone, but will only be heard by certain ones... at least at this time. I believe all will have a chance.

It seems to me that there will be some who reject the Gospel in the final analysis, and "there will be weeping and gnashing of teeth" as in the parable of guests invited to the wedding feast.

I leave it up to the Lord to sort out and pray I will be among those counted worthy...as "let he who thinks he stands take heed lest he fall"...The Bible does seem to point to the principle of holding fast and not giving it up, as many stories and examples give of those who were doing what God wanted and then went and undid it all... what does it mean for the saved follower of Christ. I believe we have choices to make all throughout and it is possible to reject the Gospel even if we once accepted it. **Friend from Nova Scotia.**

I believe the Gospel is intended for all created beings. As for anyone who rejects it? I am not certain on that one aka the verdict is still out on that one for me. **Friend from Queensland.**

To whom is the Gospel intended: everyone. What is the end for anyone who rejects it? I suppose someone could reject God's love, but since my definition of the gospel involves what God has done, rejection isn't an option. I could reject my wife's love, but I can't reject the fact that she loves me. I think C.S. Lewis had a good analogy in The Last Battle. The dwarves were in Narnia, grand and glorious Narnia, but they believed that they were in a barn, so they couldn't enjoy it. So I guess that the end result of rejection is an inability to enjoy the same heaven that everyone inhabits.

In my case the concept of hell is incompatible with a loving God, at least in the case of the eternal conscious torment idea. The WCG idea of hell was always more palatable in that the individual simply ceases to exist; that has the tone of at least "putting someone out of their misery".

In terms of salvation, in my mind, we are all saved by the gospel, so that isn't even a question. Any other idea seems, to me, to require explanations of the infinite exceptions: people who have not heard, what about little children, what about extenuating circumstances of life experience.

So, again, I go to the scene in The Last Battle. Everyone is in heaven at the end...well, with the exception of those who didn't enter the tent.

C. Baxter Kruger wrote a book called The Great Dance which influenced me greatly. We are all present at the party, but we aren't all dancing. This image holds much meaning for me with the experience at AC dances.

In terms of rejection, how do you react when your children reject you? I know that I grow frustrated, but my child never ceases to be my child.

And children have no choice in adoption, so if God chooses to adopt us how can we reject that? We can run away, perhaps. But he is always on the porch waiting for us to come home. **Friend from Texas.**

Well, pretty much from the top of my head, without really delving into the Bible to research it, here is how I see it. The Gospel is intended to be shared with every person on earth. The ultimate end for anyone who rejects it is to be destroyed in a Lake of Fire. It's death. The question of whether a person who rejects it in this life still has a chance in the next life to accept it is controversial in Christianity. I believe people have a chance in the next life to accept Jesus. But there is a lot to be learned on this topic! **Friend from New Jersey.**

John 3:16-18 For God so loved the world, that he gave his only begotten Son, that whosoever believeth in him should not perish, but have everlasting life.

For God sent not his Son into the world to condemn the world; but that the world through him might be saved.

He that believeth on him is not condemned: but he that believeth not is condemned already, because he hath not believed in the name of the only begotten Son of God.

Gospel is for ALL men and women to be saved. Those who reject the gospel message will receive the punishment for their sins - death / hell. **Friend from Tennessee.**

The gospel is intended for all of mankind. The end for anyone who rejects God is eternal death. I doubt that the end result of what this literally looks like can truly be envisioned by us. The God I know will not tolerate disobedience and the rejection of Himself as the great I Am but in his grace and inclusiveness I believe that he will use every opportunity to bring an individual to Him, perhaps even working outside the time frame that we think we understand. I also believe that eternal death is more likely a permanent death instead of burning forever in hell fire. **Friend from Tennessee.**

Hi Roger. My answer is that the Gospels are intended for all mankind ("Go forth to all nations..."). And so I assume that anybody who knows and UNDERSTANDS the Gospels (and that's probably a topic that needs parsing) is rejecting salvation, and therefore Heaven in not a destination that one would expect for such people. **Friend from Queensland.**

Hi, Roger. I think there is no question that the gospel is intended for all. The old covenant seemed to be a very human covenant (you do this for me and I'll do that for you) and an isolating covenant. The new covenant has no horse trading; Jer 31 only says what God is giving to us no strings attached and it is an inclusive covenant, a catholic covenant - a term used as early as Ignatius of Antioch writing in 110 AD.

Sadly, human propagation of the gospel has often had more of a flavor of conquest than invitation but from the beginning it has been an invitation to be accepted or rejected. Those who accept it and are transformed into the divine nature of love, always sacrificing self for other as demonstrated on the Cross, inherit Heaven. Those who reject it, who wish to do what they want to do rather than subject themselves to the needs of others, choose Hell.

That wording is important. Although there is an undeniable punitive element to what the scriptures say about Hell, we often do a Satan act and turn around to blame it on God - as if He has cast us there because we broke His arbitrary rules. I believe it was in a dialog with Saint Faustina that God said He never sends anyone to Hell; all who go there choose it. The best description I have for Hell is the place where everyone does what they want to do. God offers Heaven to those who are willing to live its lifestyle of sacrificial love. Those who choose not to, go to the place which is not Heaven, the place where people do not self-sacrifice but do what they want. That separation from God is the second death and the place is Hell.

The thought is frightening. A place where everyone does what they want. They can inflict any pain, any sexual desire, take anything, say anything, do anything. Power to the powerful who destroy their own selves by their oppression and in a place where humans are no longer the top of the food chain - where demons can do what they want as they destroy their own selves, too. And in this horror, death cannot be an escape because we are already dead and there is no hope of it ever getting better as it is an eternal judgment. What a horrifying thought!

So God offers Heaven to all through the Gospel even if only at hour of death. All are free to accept that gospel and choose a life of love in the abode of Heaven or they can reject it and go to the place where everyone does what they want.

I'll try to find some time to reply to your earlier query as well. Thanks for the invitation! Peace **Friend from New York.**

As to your questions, the gospel is for everyone. As to the fate of those who reject the Gospel I think the most complete work on this subject was done by Edward Fudge in "The Fire that Consumes". It is a scholarly, exhaustive work on the "fate of the wicked". I think Fudge has a very strong case and I agree with his reasoning. In addition, I personally believe God has a plan for everybody but it is hard to make a case for that directly from the scriptures so I don't push it. So, Fudge shows the fate of the wicked is death, and I agree, and I also believe ultimately there will be no wicked. **Friend from Western Australia.**

Jesus Christ's instruction is that all mankind is to be saved, those who embrace it, receive eternal life with him, those who reject, lose life to live no more. There's only one place to live life and that's with Jesus. On saying this, during the great white throne judgement those not found in the book of life are in the book of death and they will have to enter the court room of God to face judgement. All things will be brought up; even the hidden things of the heart. It will then be Jesus' decision to give the judgement depending on what he decides. They are not first fruits; just as all those who did not hear of God, or babies, and children. All children will be saved according to the Gospel of John as those who have not yet received, will believe. **Friend from Queensland.**

Sorry Rog haven't really had the time to think on this too much other than what I already know.....I've been busy with other things God is putting on my heart.....but what I will say is the gospel is to those God is ready to move in their hearts and if it is Spirit-led it won't be rejected for long outside of in HIS timing.... **Friend from Queensland.**

Maybe it not only is for all humans but maybe it is not rejectable in the end. I'm open to expanding the gospel's intent to others such as Cro-Magnon man or Neanderthals. I don't see how our puny brain could resist and reject the power of the Holy Spirit, Jesus the Christ, and God the Father - once they are fully revealed and once the brain is fully healed from faulty ungodly reasonings. **Friend from Indiana.**

For whom is the Gospel intended? For mankind.

The end for any who reject it is eternal death; complete ceasing of existence. Life without God is not possible according to Genesis 1.

God will offer salvation to all mankind, not all will accept. So it is for all but the end result will be fewer.

Not sure if they are embarrassed or just that something inside them tells them that idea does not square with scripture. **Friend from Washington.**

The Gospel is for everyone. Eternal separation from God is the fate of those who reject the Gospel. **Friend from Queensland.**

The Gospel is for mankind – all of us. They miss out on eternal life (separation from God). **Friend from Uganda.**

The Gospel is for all mankind. For those who reject the Gospel, they will be eternally separated from God. **Friend from Queensland.**

Appendix 2: Scriptures on Free Choice.

As I've pointed out in this book, the subject of "free choice" or "free will" is full of controversy.

Most of us exist in a world where free will does play a part in so much of our daily lives. For many there is less free choice than we can often care to acknowledge. This is also true with the subject of Christian salvation.

The following scriptures provide insights which I hope will help us form a healthy world-view on the subject:

Deuteronomy 5:15 You shall remember that you were a slave in the land of Egypt, and the LORD your God brought you out from there with a mighty hand and an outstretched arm. (ESV)

Deuteronomy 5:29 Oh that they had such a heart as this always, to fear me and to keep all my commandments, that it might go well with them and with their descendants forever! (ESV)

Deuteronomy 29:2-4 And Moses summoned all Israel and said to them: "You have seen all that the LORD did before your eyes in the land of Egypt, to Pharaoh and to all his servants and to all his land, the great trials that your eyes saw, the signs, and those great wonders. But to this day the LORD has not given you a heart to understand or eyes to see or ears to hear. (ESV)

Isaiah 6:9-10 And he said, "Go, and say to this people: "'Keep on hearing, but do not understand; keep on seeing, but do not perceive.'

Make the heart of this people dull, and their ears heavy, and blind their eyes; lest they see with their eyes, and hear with their ears, and understand with their hearts, and turn and be healed." (ESV)

John 6:44 No one can come to me unless the Father who sent me draws him. And I will raise him up on the last day. (ESV)

John 6:65 Then Jesus said, "You cannot come to me, unless the Father makes you want to come. That is why I have told these things to all of you." (CEV)

John 10:24-29 So the Jews gathered around him and said to him, "How long will you keep us in suspense? If you are the Christ, tell us plainly."

Jesus answered them, "I told you, and you do not believe. The works that I do in my Father's name bear witness about me, but you do not believe because you are not among my sheep. My sheep hear my voice, and

I know them, and they follow me. I give them eternal life, and they will never perish, and no one will snatch them out of my hand. My Father, who has given them to me, is greater than all, and no one is able to snatch them out of the Father's hand. (ESV)

John 12:39-40 Therefore they could not believe. For again Isaiah said,

"He has blinded their eyes and hardened their heart, lest they see with their eyes, and understand with their heart, and turn, and I would heal them." (ESV)

John 17:6 "I have manifested your name to the people whom you gave me out of the world. Yours they were, and you gave them to me, and they have kept your word. (ESV)

Acts 2:47 ...And the Lord added to their number day by day those who were being saved. (ESV)

Acts 13:48 And when the Gentiles heard this, they began rejoicing and glorifying the word of the Lord, and as many as were appointed to eternal life believed. (ESV)

Acts 16:14 One who heard us was a woman named Lydia, from the city of Thyatira, a seller of purple goods, who was a worshiper of God. The Lord opened her heart to pay attention to what was said by Paul. (ESV)

Romans 6:17-18   But thanks be to God, that you who were once slaves of sin have become obedient from the heart to the standard of teaching to which you were committed, and, having been set free from sin, have become slaves of righteousness.   (ESV)

Romans 8:7   because the mind of the flesh is enmity against God; for it is not subject to the law of God, neither indeed can it be: (ASV)

Romans 10:20   Then Isaiah is so bold as to say, "I have been found by those who did not seek me; I have shown myself to those who did not ask for me." (ESV)

Romans 11:5-8   So too at the present time there is a remnant, chosen by grace.

But if it is by grace, it is no longer on the basis of works; otherwise grace would no longer be grace.

What then? Israel failed to obtain what it was seeking. The elect obtained it, but the rest were hardened,

as it is written, "God gave them a spirit of stupor, eyes that would not see and ears that would not hear, down to this very day." (ESV)

Romans 11:25-26   Lest you be wise in your own sight, I do not want you to be unaware of this mystery, brothers: a partial hardening has come upon Israel, until the fullness of the Gentiles has come in.

And in this way all Israel will be saved, as it is written, "The Deliverer will come from Zion, he will banish ungodliness from Jacob"; (ESV)

Romans 11:32   For God has consigned all to disobedience, that he may have mercy on all.   (ESV)

2 Corinthians 4:3-4   And even if our gospel is veiled, it is veiled to those who are perishing.

In their case the god of this world has blinded the minds of the unbelievers, to keep them from seeing the light of the gospel of the glory of Christ, who is the image of God.   (ESV)

Galations 4:7-8   So you are no longer a slave, but a son, and if a son, then an heir through God.

Formerly, when you did not know God, you were enslaved to those that by nature are not gods.   (ESV)

Ephesians 2:8-10   For by grace you have been saved through faith. And this is not your own doing; it is the gift of God, not a result of works, so that no one may boast.

For we are his workmanship, created in Christ Jesus for good works, which God prepared beforehand, that we should walk in them.   (ESV)

Philippians 1:6   And I am sure of this, that he who began a good work in you will bring it to completion at the day of Jesus Christ.   (ESV)

1 John 5:19-20   We know that we are from God, and the whole world lies in the power of the evil one.   And we know that the Son of God has come and has given us understanding, so that we may know him who is true; and we are in him who is true, in his Son Jesus Christ. He is the true God and eternal life. (ESV)

Appendix 3: Scriptures on God's View of Salvation

Genesis 18:14   Is anything too hard for the LORD? (ESV)

Isaiah 14:24   The LORD of hosts has sworn: "As I have planned, so shall it be, and as I have purposed, so shall it stand, (ESV)

Matthew 18:14   So it is not the will of my Father who is in heaven that one of these little ones should perish. (ESV)

John 3:16-17   "For God so loved the world, that he gave his only Son, that whoever believes in him should not perish but have eternal life. For God did not send his Son into the world to condemn the world, but in order that the world might be saved through him. (ESV)

Romans 5:18-19   Therefore, as one trespass led to condemnation for all men, so one act of righteousness leads to justification and life for all men. For as by the one man's disobedience the many were made sinners, so by the one man's obedience the many will be made righteous. (ESV)

1 Timothy 2:3-4 This is good, and it is pleasing in the sight of God our Savior, who desires all people to be saved and to come to the knowledge of the truth. (ESV)

2 Peter 3:8-9 But do not forget this one thing, dear friends: With the Lord a day is like a thousand years, and a thousand years are like a day. The Lord is not slow in keeping his promise, as some understand slowness. Instead he is patient with you, not wanting anyone to perish, but everyone to come to repentance. (NIV)

Appendix 4: What the Critics Say.

Just as I alluded in the closing line of the Forward to this book, challenging long held dogmas leaves one open to all manner of criticism. Teaching in the body of Christ is a dangerous occupation. With this in mind, I thought I may as well get the jump on everyone by sharing a few beauties here:

"You are unteachable!"

Feedback from senior admin when I sought an evaluation during my Theology Degree studies.

"You are too intelligent to stay in the Church, and you will never be used in the ministry."

A comment received from one of the faculty during my Theology degree studies.

"If you disagree with me, then you have to be a false prophet."

Comment over a coffee with a leader of a well-known para-church organisation, who considered himself to be "as Paul".

"Will you submit to us no matter what we decide!?"

A rather shrill question posed to me from an Elder at a Church meeting after my first church plant.

"He is a false prophet. Read this book at your peril!"

Comment from a good friend of mine from North Queensland after the Brisbane Broncos lost to the North Queensland Cowboys.

TO BE CONTINUED....

The Next Step...

Thank you so much for taking the time to read this far. If you have, it hopefully means you did enjoy it. Assuming you did, please do tell your friends, and also post a short review on Amazon. If you know of anywhere else to post a review, that would be great too! :)

Reviews and word of mouth are the best friend of any author. Many thanks again! :)

I do intend for this to be the first book in a "Project" series. My next I hope will be on the thorny issue of Free Will. The story is by no means over, and I certainly won't claim to have the final word on any topic. In so many ways I could claim this journey if deeper understanding has only just begun.

If you would like to be added to our mailing list, I will give you notice of when the next book is out. I promise not to share your email with anyone else. I'll only contact you when a new book is out.

You can email me at roger@thegospelprojects.com, and I will add you to the mailing list by that means.

If you have found any of the ideas in this book resonate particularly well with you, please consider joining our Facebook community at:

https://www.facebook.com/groups/TheGospelProjects/

Bibliography.

Dirty Harry. Dir. Don Siegel. Perf. Clint Eastwood. 1971. Film.

Farley, Andrew. *God Without Religion.* Grand Rapids: Baker Books, 2011. Book.

Fonck, Leopold. *"Epistle to the Hebrews" The Catholic Encyclopedia.* Vol. 7. New York: Robert Appleton Company, 1910. Encyclopedia.

Josephus. *The Works of Josephus.* Trans. William Whiston. Lynn: Hendrickson Publishers, 1984. Book.

Liefeld, Walter L. *The Expositors Bible Commentary.* Ed. Frank E. Gaebelein. Vol. 8. Grand Rapids: Zondervan Publishing House, 1984. 12 vols. Book.

Lucado, Max. *God Came Near.* Portland: Multnomah Press, 1987. Book.

Mangalwadi, Vishnal. *The Book That Made Your World.* Nashville: Thomas Nelson, 2011. Book.

Meyers, Rick. *e-Sword.* Version 10.0.5. 2000-2012. Computer Software. <www.e-sword.net>.

Muir, Clive. *One Digger's Diary.* Ed. Roger Hooper. Brisbane, 2019.

Peterson, Jordan B. *https://jordanpetersonquotes.com/order-able-think-risk-offensive/*. 16 January 2018. 29 June 2018.

Peterson, R.A. and M.D. Williams. *Why I Am Not An Arminian*. Downers Grove: Intervarsity Press, 2004. Book.

Prince, Joseph. *Unmerited Favor*. Singapore: Charisma House, 2009.

Strong, James. *The New Strong's Exhaustive Concordance Of The Bible*. Nashville: Thomas Nelson Publishers, 1984.

Tattersall, Barry. *What Is Hell?* August 2010. <barrysgracespace.blogspot.com.au>.

Tennyson, Alfred Lord. *www.poetryfoundation.org*. n.d. 16 April 2018.

Thayer, Joseph Henry. *The New Thayers Greek-English Lexicon Of The New Testament*. Lafayette: Book Publisher's Press Inc., 1981. Book.

Vine, W.E. *Vine's Expository Dictionary Of New Testament Words*. Unabridged Edition. Iowa Falls: Riverside Book And Bible House, n.d. Book.

Walls, J.L. and J.R. Dongell. *Why I Am Not A Calvinist*. Downers Grove: Intervarsity Press, 2004. Book.

Yancey, Philip. *What's So Amazing About Grace?* Grand Rapids: Zondervan Publishing House, 1997. Book.

www.ingramcontent.com/pod-product-compliance
Lightning Source LLC
Chambersburg PA
CBHW031229090426
42742CB00007B/126